THE SEXUALITY
OF **JESUS**

✦

William E. Phipps

D0063039

THE PILGRIM PRESS

Cleveland, Ohio

The Pilgrim Press, Cleveland, Ohio 44115
© 1996 by William E. Phipps

Quotations from the Bible are usually the author's own translation,
but quotations from a variety of versions can be found.

All rights reserved. Published 1996

Printed in the United States of America on acid-free paper

01 00 99 98 97 96   5 4 3 2 1

Library of Congress Cataloging-in-Publication Data
Phipps, William E., 1930–
    The sexuality of Jesus / William E. Phipps.
      p. cm.
    Includes bibliographical references and indexes.
    ISBN 0–8298–1144–3 (alk. paper)
     1. Jesus Christ—Sexual behavior. I. Title.
  BT303.P47 1996
  232.9—dc20   96–30147
                                 CIP

To my sons-in-law,
Charles Anderson Engh III and Jeffrey Robert Chapman.
Their relationships well exemplify Jesus' commandment,
"Love one another."

CONTENTS

ONE

Introduction

Initial Responses

✦ Throughout most of church history, Christians have not raised questions about the sexuality of Jesus. They have accepted the prevailing tradition from the church fathers that Jesus, like his mother, was a lifelong virgin. A carefully researched survey of a large American denomination, conducted a generation ago, revealed that only one out of every five Lutherans believed that Jesus had sexual desire.[1] Probably an even lower percentage of contemporary Lutherans believe that he engaged in sexual intercourse, in spite of Martin Luther's counter position.[2]

Many Christians not only hold the unquestioned notion that Jesus renounced marriage, but also believe that celibacy must therefore be a holier way of life—at least for some people. As Benedictine monk Ignatius Hunt notes: "The life of Jesus has been one of the great factors in presenting to Christians, and especially to priests, the ideal of celibacy."[3]

Current assumptions about Jesus' sexuality are amply illustrated by letters I received in response to my first publication on the topic in a theological quarterly.[4] When I suggested that Jesus was probably married, I was amazed to find how much it irritated a broad spectrum of people. After my controversial hypothesis was publicized internationally by print and broadcast journalists, a voluminous and overwhelmingly negative response came from the general public. As a result of that unexpected great interest in the question of Jesus' marital status, I devoted a sabbatical year as a Visiting Fellow at Princeton Seminary to investigate the subject more thoroughly. Working like a detective with the historical issue foremost in mind, I pieced together what biblical and nonbiblical sources say about the sociology of marriage in ancient Palestinian culture. By freshly exegeting passages in the New Testament appealed to by those defending the single status of Jesus, and by combining this with data from ancient scrolls discovered this century at Qumran and at Nag-Hammadi, I defended at length my thesis that Jesus probably had a wife sometime during his adult years.

Much more controversy followed after Harper & Row's 1970 publication *Was Jesus Married? The Distortion of Sexuality in the Christian Tradition.* I found that religion becomes explosive when mixed with sex, for the responses were related less to the historical than to the hysterical. Those who opposed my opinions sometimes included personal threats, which made me grateful to live in a remote mountain region! There were also some leading biblical scholars and theologians who claimed that I made a convincing case that Jesus probably married.[5] In addition, Spanish writer Manuel Vino was stimulated by my position and went beyond it to assert in his book titled *Maria Magdalena* that "Jesus was married to Magdalena and the fruit of their love was John Mark."

To give a sample of what contemporary people think of my thesis that Jesus probably married, a potpourri of letter excerpts follow. Some respondents regard marriage as a hindrance to noble achievements. A married woman asserted: "Jesus was absolutely celibate throughout life. He was the artist type whose media was his life. The crucifixion was the culminating focus of his life force. Marriage drains off necessary creative energy." A medical professional stated: "Jesus sublimated his urge for sexual indulgence into channels more beneficial to society." One letter writer argued that Jesus was unmarried because he carried only one cross: "If Jesus Christ were married he wouldn't have had to go through Calvary to redeem mankind. Most marriages are hell on earth." A male Bible teacher wrote: "Jesus' purpose was to ransom lost humanity, so he did not have time to waste satisfying the sexual desires of a woman." A married woman likewise judged marriage to be a vocational distraction: "Jesus said, 'I must be about my Father's business,' but when we are married we are about each other's business."

Some thought that Jesus could not have been married both to a wife and to the church: "If Jesus had married, the Scriptures would not speak of his bride the church, but of his bride Mrs. Jesus bar Joseph." "In his letter to the Ephesians, Paul describes the bride of Christ as without spot, wrinkle, or blemish. All human women have such defects, so his spouse could only have been the church."

The frequent responses received from Jehovah's Witnesses indicate that a historically unmarried Jesus is part of their scheme of salvation. On the basis of the apocalyptic imagery in the last book of the Christian Bible,[6] they believe that Jesus has been betrothed to his church for nearly two millennia. His virginity will remain intact until his midair "rapture" in the near future with his bride, the 144,000 redeemed from the earth. That spectacular wedding will be followed by a honeymoon lasting for a millennium.

A number of Christian laypersons presumed that the human sex drive is an evil inherited from disobedient persons described in Genesis, so the holy Jesus could not have had it. A sampling follows: "Jesus, like Adam in his state of original righteousness, was without sexual desire. Urges below the belt were introduced when Adam and Eve sinned, and were part of their punishment." "Just as Adam was without navel, Jesus was without sex." "Jesus was not conceived in iniquity as the rest of mortal men. Therefore man's perverted sexual appetite was not transmitted to him and he had no desire to marry." "If Christ had had a wife he would not have been a spotless lamb sufficient to bear our sins. He would have been in the same shoes as Adam." "The wickedness that caused the flood at the time of Noah was 'Sons of God' copulating with human women and starting a super race. Jesus, the righteous Son of God, would not have taken a fair daughter of man and produced giants."

Some assume that the erotic desire is intrinsically evil, but did not explicitly trace it to our alleged first parents. One respondent urged me "to love Christ as the Supreme and Holy Being who is all good, and certainly incapable of love affairs and other shameful things." Another asked, "Does not the word Jesus mean passionless and sexless?" And another declared: "Marriage is a lust of the flesh. Jesus was a perfect person so he could not have indulged in such sin." Again: "God prefers virginity, so [God] had the mother of [God's] Son and her offspring to remain virgins. Jesus taught that only those who remain as little children, who are innocent of sexual thought or action, will enter heaven."

Also included in the responses were those that took for granted a deep rift between Judaism and Christianity. Some claimed that Jesus repudiated Jewish tradition as worthless and felt no constraints to follow the "corrupt" marital standards of Judaism. One wrote: "The assumption that Jesus married tends to make Christ lower than the angels and more like us. If he was completely a man then our Christian religion is no more pure than Judaism." Another letter stated: "Jesus could not have been part of Jewish culture. If Jesus were a Jew, then God His father would have to be a Jew. But God is a Christian."

For some, the incarnation doctrine of Christianity is not taken seriously. A physician wrote: "The Lord was not born from the flesh; he was born from the Spirit. Being God himself, how could he possibly react like a common man. . . . Any speculation on the subject of Jesus' marriage is an abomination." Another letter stated: "The Lord could never have married one of his own mortal creations." A Mocjogan "prophet" wrote: "Jesus said, 'My father and I are one,' so to say that Jesus married is the same as saying that God also married. Now, what need would the Almighty God have of a wife?" A Catholic priest dismissed my inquiry with this dichotomy: "Christ was divine, not married." An Australian Mormon, evidently not realizing her church's historic position on Jesus' plural marriages, argued that he could not have engaged in sex since he was essentially a neuter spirit.

Some persons appealed to occult teachings to inform me about Jesus' intimacies. A member of the Unarium Brotherhood sent me a book by Alexander Smyth containing revelations that the California-based sect accepts as authoritative. Smyth claimed that Jesus physically expressed his love for Mary of Bethany who had earlier been his childhood companion in Nazareth.[7]

Several responders referred me to "The Gospel of the Holy Twelve," which was allegedly written in Aramaic by Jesus' disciples. It claims that Jesus married a Jewish girl named Miriam when he was eighteen, and that she died seven years later. A Buddhist priest took this Gospel to Tibet, where it remained in a monastery until an Englishman discovered it in the nineteenth century and had it translated. In another Buddhist country there is different lore regarding Jesus. Shingo, a Japanese town, claims that Jesus settled there after narrowly escaping crucifixion. He then married a woman named Miyuko, and they produced three daughters. (This legend helps to explain why the Japanese translation of *Was Jesus Married?* has remained in publication for decades.)

The Rosicrucians have published books about Jesus, affirming that he married after his crucifixion and had children. They claim that one of their founders was descended from a child that Jesus fathered by Magdalene. One Rosicrucian shared with me her reincarnation conviction. She reported from her previous ancient enfleshment that the women with Jesus were consumed with jealousy: "Magdalene was, of course, Jesus' woman, but not officially. He handled the situation as Queen Elizabeth I did; he kept the opposite sex satisfied by not marrying any of them."

Considerable international attention has resulted from the revival of medieval folklore about the children of Jesus popularized by the best-selling *Holy Blood, Holy Grail*. Authors Michael Baigent, Richard Leigh, and Henry Lincoln, encouraged in part by my treatments of Jesus, hypothesize that ancient French and much of subsequent European royalty may be descendants of Jesus and Magdalene. They think that the latter may have brought to Gaul at least one child of her marriage and the chalice from which her husband drank at his Last Supper.[8] That offspring conveyed Jesus' holy genes, and some of his DNA characteristics have been biologically transmitted to the present day.

Margaret Starbird also claims that the bloodline of some noble families of southern France can be traced to the progeny of the daughter of Jesus and Magdalene named Sarah, and that widow Magdalene was buried in Provence, France. Starbird thinks Catholic orthodoxy established shrines for Mary of Nazareth to channel veneration from Jesus' wife to his mother. Starbird writes: "In raising the mother of Jesus to be Queen of Heaven in the celestial paradigm, at least one beautiful image of the eternal feminine principle was preserved, although the flesh-and-blood wife of Jesus was deliberately denied."[9]

Other responses share no common theme: (1) "Jesus could not have been a husband for the simple reason that he was not a historical person. He is no more real than Hamlet or Don Quixote. In the Hebrew Bible he is not mentioned." (That writer bet me a large sum of money that I could not prove that Jesus ever existed, but he would not agree to my insistence that the wager be placed in the hands of a neutral judge.) (2) "Jesus was single because he stayed with his mother, and when he left this earth he did not turn her over to his wife, but to John." (3) "At the wedding party in Cana, Jesus' mother tried to boss her son. Had he been married, his wife would have been telling him to replenish the refreshments." (4) "Jesus' disciples were amazed that he spoke privately to a woman at a well. This shows that Jesus had never before been alone with any woman except his mother." (5) "Jesus once said: 'Foxes have holes and birds have nests, but the Son of Man has no place to lay his head;' only a cad would have invited a woman to share his bed." (6) "If by any chance Jesus was married, God would have let it be known since he told us by the prophets everything else about his life." (7) "Jesus speaks of himself as unmarried in 1 Corinthians 7:8. He never owned a wife for his only earthly possessions were the clothes upon his back." (8) "Jesus did not marry because his love for all the world was not at all like the love that a man has for his wife." (9) "In marriage the two become one. If the divine Jesus married, this would have made his wife divine also. But we know that there has been only one divine human." (10) "Jesus was a mule-like hybrid, which explains why it was said, 'Never man spake like this man.' Since his parentage was not confined to the human species, Jesus was asexual and specially equipped to bear the yoke for which he was destined."

Just the thought of inquiring into Jesus' marital status alarms many Christians. One wrote: "Even if Jesus was married, why bring up this smear now?" Sharing that sentiment, another letter contained this rebuke: "You feel it is your duty to damage the image most of us have. Why break a beautiful bubble? . . . After all, sex may be necessary to propagate the world but it has also done more damage than good." More than one letter called my conjecture that Jesus was sexually alive a greater sacrilege than the declaration by some theologians that God is dead. Another wrote that to raise the question that Jesus might have married is a sign of our "sex-mad culture."

Some published responses to *Was Jesus Married?* were telling. Kenneth Wilson, the editor of a Protestant journal, confessed:

> The biggest hurdle for me was getting past the title question. . . . One's immediate and automatic rejection of the question reveals an attitude toward sex. To say, immediately, "Of course not!" (with no recourse to the biblical record one way or the other) is to say that marriage is less holy than nonmarriage—a view that has been fostered, and is still being fostered, overtly in the Roman Catholic Church and covertly among many Protestants.[10]

When Stephen Sapp followed my lead and ventured to comment on how Jesus might have expressed himself sexually, he recognized that he was entering a forbidden realm. He assessed the situation and its consequences in this way:

This has probably been the most taboo topic in Christian thought for two thousand years, with devastating effects not only upon the Church's ability to think constructively about sexuality in general but also upon the credibility of its pronouncements to a secular world.[11]

A year after *Was Jesus Married?* was published, George Gallup conducted a mail survey of 2,517 clergy in the United States. Only four percent of the Catholic priests thought that Jesus might have married. Significantly, a majority of the priests questioned thought they should be permitted to marry, and ninety percent admitted they had considered leaving the priesthood. Seventy-nine percent of the Protestant ministers and eleven percent of the Jewish rabbis thought Jesus was not married.[12]

Writing in the last decade of the second Christian millennium, Episcopal Bishop John Spong has this searching question for fellow participants in church tradition: "Why is there still a continuing sense, ranging from dis-ease to revulsion, that arises in us when we hear the suggestion that Jesus might have been married?" Spong thinks that the presumed sinfulness of passion or indignity of the sex act is not the basic reason. Rather, he thinks Christians have generally rejected the notion of Jesus having a wife because women have been viewed as corrupters of otherwise righteous men. Spong suggests that "far more than any of us realize we are subconsciously victimized by the historic negativity toward women that has been a major gift of the Christian church to the world."[13]

Reason for Further Inquiry

The predominantly negative responses to my historical probe into Jesus' marital status reveal more important general considerations that need thorough exploration. There appears to be much confusion over the whole scope of Jesus' sexuality, from womb to tomb. Several years after my first book, I wrote a sequel, *The Sexu-*

ality of Jesus: Theological and Literary Perspectives. It attempted to ascertain what can reasonably be deduced about Jesus' sexuality from information contained in Jewish and Christian documents pertaining to the era in which he lived. Also examined critically were the variety of ways in which his sexuality has been treated by some theologians and literary artists. An extensive probe was made of what William Blake, D. H. Lawrence, and Nikos Kazantzakis imagined Jesus' sexuality to be.

My second study was more basic than the first, which mainly questioned whether Jesus was or was not married. A person's sexuality is an essential part of one's self-definition, not an added accretion that one may or may not elect to have. Genetics has demonstrated that sexuality is an intrinsic quality of developed organisms. Psychology has shown that it is neither an occasional type of behavior nor a mere organic activity. Sexuality is related to the entire gamut of desiring and achieving communication among embodied selves. By way of distinguishing it from genital activity, Catholic Bishop Francis Mugavero states:

> It is an aspect of personality which lets us enter other persons' lives as friends and encourages them to enter our lives. The dimension of sexuality must be developed . . . if we are to follow Jesus' command to become "lovers." It is a relational power which includes the qualities of sensitivity, understanding, warmth, openness to persons, compassion and mutual support.[14]

Catholic priest Donald Goergen, in a book defending celibacy, is aware that sexuality is a prominent component of Jesus' personality. He states: "It is not possible to accept Jesus' humanity without accepting his sexuality. . . . Compassion is a supreme sign of a well-integrated sexual life. The Gospels portray Jesus as a compassionate, gentle, loving, tender, and warm person."[15]

That sexuality is a fundamental part of human nature—physiologically and psychologically—is displayed in a simple but profound way by the older Genesis creation account. Although made from moist dust like the rest of the animals, the androgynous human is discontinuous with other species because none of them satisfy Adam's desire for a partner. The Hebrew account then tells of a surgical procedure that divides the human into two parts—not a "rib" extraction as inaccurate translations render it.[16] Only after the severance of the androgyne into sexual parts is satisfaction found. The male sees his other half and cries out in delight, "This is it!" Whereupon they cling together and "become one flesh" (Gen. 2:23–24). Lactantius, an early Christian, expresses well the outlook of that ancient storyteller: "When God invented the plan of the two sexes, he placed in them the desire of each other and joy in union . . . so that they might rush most avidly into these emotions."[17]

Understanding and appreciating the emotions of Jesus has been especially difficult for Christians. The first "scandalous" matter the earliest Christians were asked to explain was the horrendous suffering of God's Messiah. Theologians from apostolic times onward have given considerable attention to explaining why their righteous Son of God could be punished like a criminal, and have converted into an asset what early critics of Christianity denounced.[18] Unfortunately, little effort has been made to interpret some other facets of Jesus' emotional life. For example, Pier Pasolini's acclaimed film *The Gospel According to Saint Matthew* shows Jesus touching the lives of others while not being affected by them. The "passion of Jesus" has come to mean exclusively his agony during the "Passion Week" that climaxed in his crucifixion. Yet the Jesus revealed in the Gospels was a passionate person in other ways as well.

Jesus occasionally exploded with anger when encountering adversaries. To some Pharisees who were scornful of his Sabbath healings, he is reported as having reacted in this manner: "He looked around at them with anger, distressed by their callousness" (Mark 3:5). When he frequently exclaimed, "Damn you, scribes and Pharisees, hypocrites!" and when he "drove out all who sold and bought in the Temple," he was certainly emotional (Matt. 23:13, 23, 25, 27, 29; 21:12). Yet the church has tended to caricature Jesus as the "meek and mild" lamb whose full viewpoint is expressed in these words of the Sermon on the Mount: "Whoever is angry with his brother shall be liable to judgment" (Matt. 5:22). Jesus' indignation has been muted in the Christian tradition principally because some of the church fathers glorified passionlessness, an ideal imported from pagan philosophy.

Sexuality is another area fraught with human passion, which has been even less related to Jesus than anger. Jesus vis-à-vis sexuality is often anxiously dismissed with a comment from the Sermon on the Mount that demonstrates, at least to the person supplying the proof-text, that he was against it. There, according to the customary translation, Jesus proclaims: "I say to you that every one who looks at a woman lustfully has already committed adultery with her in his heart" (Matt. 5:28). Thus, if Jesus was perfect, he must not have had human sexual yearning.

A number of things have stimulated me to rethink some of my interpretations since I wrote about Jesus' sexuality a generation ago. Rosemary Ruether's insightful hypothesis that Mary Magdalene was denigrated in the Christian tradition in order to elevate Jesus' mother has caused me to back away from accepting the traditional identification of Magdalene with a prostitute described in the Gospels. Also, as a result of the more open discussion of homosexuality in recent years, my homophobia has diminished. My more extensive study of Islam and ancient religions of the Mediterranean has caused me to modify some views on comparative sexuality in varied cultures.[19] In addition, fresh insights obtained from numerous recent publications on gender roles in history have enabled me to alter some positions. Lastly, the information now being made public on the dysfunctionality of mandatory celibacy for current priests has enabled me to strengthen some of my earlier judgments.

In this inquiry an attempt will be made to release the pivotal personality of the Bible from dehumanizing treatments in much of

Christian tradition. For example, there is only a comma separating Jesus' birth from his death in the so-called Apostles' Creed, which is recited by millions of churchgoers every week. As the Jesus Seminar scholars have pointed out, that doctrinal statement tended to "smother" the sage of Nazareth, except for affirming his suffering under Pontius Pilate.[20] Written more than a century after the era of the apostles, the Apostles' Creed refers to several days after Jesus' death but disregards several decades before his death. Yet it was the quality of his life that gave significance to his manner of dying. Jesus was among thousands who were crucified in Palestine by the Romans during the time when he lived.

Consider what various scholars have said about the relationship between the humanity and sexuality of Jesus. Catholic Joseph Blenkinsopp, in the context of discussing Jesus' sexuality, states: "Christian theology has never, despite enormous efforts, found a satisfactory way of presenting the humanity of Jesus."[21] Protestant theologian Tom Driver wrestles with the dilemma in this way:

> Christianity has never entertained the image of a Christ who shared the sexual experience of most of the human race. Hence that experience is rendered suspect, to say the least. If we now try to see sex as a good gift of God, as something properly writ into our pre-fallen constitutions, the image of the celibate Jesus looms up to haunt us. If God meant us to fall in love with each other and to lie down together in marriage beds—which is, after all, a rather fundamental matter—why in heaven does his incarnation, not to speak of his Son's conception, have nothing to do with this?[22]

During the past generation some Anglicans have honestly faced the common failure of the traditional interpretations of historical Jesus to relate to our understanding of the humanizing qualities of sexual interaction. Bishop John Robinson has discerned: "The real difficulty for many is to admit that Jesus had any sexuality—and was therefore a normal human being."[23] Christologist Norman Pittenger writes:

> It is of first importance to stress that to speak of Jesus as being truly human is also to speak of him as a sexual being. Whatever ways he may have chosen to express or to re-channel his sexuality . . . it is clear that when his sinlessness is mentioned we do not, or should not, take this to imply a-sexuality. Alas, however, much Christian thinking has done just this; in consequence we have the anaemic, lifeless, almost effeminate Christ of the Victorian stained-glass windows and of some popular portraits.[24]

Most of the artistic images of Jesus hinder our picturing him as an ancient Palestinian Jew. This is true of the early representations as well as of the later blond, blue-eyed portraits. The early paintings of Jesus, dating more than two centuries after his death, usually depict a haloed person in a white toga. Such an image would have been more appropriate for a figure in the culture of the ancient Greeks and Romans, for their art often portrayed circles of light about the heads of heroes and gods. More particularly, an ancient biographer of Pythagoras states that "his robe was white and spotless."[25]

Artists pay little attention to the feature of Jesus' clothing that gives him cultural identity. Every devout Jew wore a distinctive fringe on his clothing as prescribed by the Torah.[26] Yet few paintings of Jesus show the tassels attached to the edges of his outer garment to which references are made in the Gospels.[27] Jewish painter Marc Chagall provides an unusual depiction of Jesus wearing the tallith.

The perennial distortions of the probable external appearance of Jesus are symptomatic of a more serious malady. Culturally conditioned mental images of Jesus' role have been projected onto the screen of the Christian's imagination. In the medieval era he was thought of as an ascetic monk; scholars in the Age of Enlightenment viewed him as a rationalist; others have conceived of him as an idealized Rousseauan romanticist, or as a Marxian socialist, or as a Kierkegaardian existentialist, or as a superman from outer space.

Recognizing human foibles, it may be unavoidable that our internal creations of a historical model of morality display little more than a clustering of the admirable characteristics of a current hero. But the one-sided representation of Jesus in every century since his death has also been due to a lack of genuine information about his social environment. The early church leaders who lived after the destruction of the Jewish state had few opportunities to talk with Jewish scholars or Palestinian natives. With one or two notable exceptions, the church fathers could not even read Hebrew. Later, in medieval times, it was a rare scholastic who had access to rabbinic literature even if he desired to learn about the Jewish culture.

In view of the ready availability nowadays of a variety of extrabiblical writings by participants in the ancient Palestinian culture, coupled with a heightened awareness of the importance of cultural milieu in understanding an individual, there is now less excuse for fanciful projections onto the figure of Jesus of later conceptions of ideal lifestyles. The findings of archaeologists in this century, together with the results of textual and historical criticism of ancient documents, put serious students today in a better position to know more accurately about the era in which Jesus lived than scholars in any other century since his death. The first step in comprehending the historical Jesus is the full realization that he was raised by faithful Jews and that his Jewishness persisted throughout life, in spite of his rigorous criticism of conventional Judaism. Accordingly, the gospel testimony will be dovetailed with comments culled from ancient Jewish sources in the discussion that follows.

Some explanation for the organization of the chapters ahead may be helpful. Attention will first be given to Jesus' genetics and childhood environment. The physiology of sex begins with conception, so it is relevant to our inquiry to relate the sexuality of

Jesus to that of his mother. If an ovum of Mary was not fertilized by a human, then Jesus' nature could have been qualitatively different from human nature as universally experienced. Some influential Latin church fathers derived from the accepted virginal conception doctrine that Jesus did not have normal sexual impulses. Bishop Hilary claimed that Jesus had a special physical constitution void of sexual desire because of his miraculous generation.[28] Bishop Augustine endorsed Hilary's position, and consequently it became widely accepted. He wrote: "Christ had no strife of flesh and spirit, which came upon human nature from the transgression of the first man, inasmuch as he was born of the Spirit and the Virgin, not through fleshly desire."[29] That prevailing doctrine of Gentile Christians will be contrasted with the perspective of the source material used in the Christmas stories of the Gospels.

After trying to comprehend the stories of Jesus' conception, his process of maturation will be surveyed. This crucial question will be investigated: to what extent was Jesus a product of his Jewish culture and to what extent was he independent of Judaism—especially with regard to his sexuality? Leander Keck has observed that "far more needs to be done to rehabilitate the Jewishness of Jesus, not simply because good Jewish-Christian relations commend it but because the integrity of our picture require it."[30] The meager information in the Gospels about Jesus' private life in Nazareth and public life as a rabbi will be supplemented by a substantial amount of extrabiblical documentary material pertaining to the coming of age of an ancient student of the Torah.

The inquiry into the impact upon the maturing Jesus of his culture's customs leads into an examination of the sexuality of the adult Jesus. An exhaustive study will be made of the pro and con arguments pertaining to Jesus' celibacy. Probing the adult Jesus will also involve looking at him as the women of the Gospels saw him, because any person's behavior toward the opposite sex discloses much about that person's own sexuality.

The matrix for early Christian sexual morality was the Jewish ethos, but as the church gravitated westward it was infiltrated by sharply different standards. Robert Gordis describes that Hellenizing process thus: "As Gentile Christianity all but submerged the original Jewish-Christian nucleus, the Greek element triumphed over the Hebrew. . . . The most palpable illustration of this thesis lies in the area of sex and family life."[31] This shift in Christian sexual morality is prominently displayed by those scholarly churchmen who were much affected by the prevailing currents of Greco-Roman philosophical ethics. Hence, this study will examine those Christian interpreters of sexuality from non-Jewish cultures who presented Jesus and his mother as ones who were dedicated to sensual renunciation.

Our study will conclude with some theological musings: In what ways should Christians attempt to imitate Jesus? He accentuated those distinctive human qualities of freedom, worship, and compassion. Should he also be admired as one who brought sexuality to full flowering? The relevance of Jesus as a model of humanity will be pondered.

Because of Jesus' unique impact, anyone—whether religious or nonreligious—who is interested in our culture's understanding of sexuality should join me in this probe of his male-female relationships. Historian Jaroslav Pelikan begins his important book on the place of Jesus in European culture with this significant fact: "Regardless of what anyone may personally think or believe about him, Jesus of Nazareth has been the dominant figure in the history of Western culture for almost twenty centuries."[32] An even broader statement has been made by Claude Montefiore, a distinguished Jewish scholar. He writes that Jesus was "the most important Jew who ever lived, one who exercised a greater influence upon mankind and civilization than any other person, whether within the Jewish race or without it."[33] Evidence of current respect for Jesus is indicated by a survey conducted by a secular American magazine. When asked to write down a ranking of their ideal men, Jesus was far ahead of the second person listed by either gender.[34]

Beginnings and Maturation

Dual Parenthood

✦ Understanding Jesus' sexuality involves probing both his genetic inheritance and his postnatal environment. Few matters related to the Bible have provoked more rancorous disputes over the past century than the question of how the earthly existence of Jesus began. Many Christians first become aware of scholars' literary-historical interpretation of the New Testament—often called "higher criticism"—as they examine arguments pertaining to Jesus' alleged virginal conception, commonly but less precisely called his "virgin birth." Early Christians assumed that the actual birth or delivery of Mary's infant was normal.

The traditional assumptions about Jesus' conception were first intensely investigated by biblical scholars a century ago. That discussion has subsided during the past generation, but unfortunately not because Christians have arrived at a general consensus on the issue. One sociological survey shows that approximately half of the Protestants and three-quarters of the Roman Catholics in the United States accept as completely true the statement, "Jesus was born of a virgin."[1] Memories of harsh fundamentalism-modernism fights and a proneness to let a sleeping dogma lie are more operative in this lack of discussion than general agreement. The battle lines can still be distinguished. The supernaturalists hold that Jesus was not conceived as other humans by the biological union of a male sperm with a female ovum. This outlook is opposed by those who maintain that human reproduction occurs only when a male supplies half of the chromosomes, and that therefore Jesus was born by ordinary generation. Naturalists tend to explain away the traditional birth stories as little more than pious fairy tales. They posit that Jesus must have been sired either by Joseph or by some other man, or else he was not a historical and human person.

An examination of the treatises written on the "virgin birth" show that most polemicists do little more than marshal tired arguments to justify either their supernaturalist or their naturalist stance. Little progress has been made toward achieving a common understanding, since no thoroughgoing attempt has been made to understand an outlook on conception that permeated the ancient eastern Mediterranean. For instance, Catholic exegete Raymond Brown and the German theologian Hans von Campenhausen, who have written scholarly studies on Jesus' virginal conception, do not give serious consideration to a most germane ancient point of view, which might be called "dual parenthood."[2] In their more mystical moods, some ancient Israelites and Gentiles thought of a procreative trinity composed of deity, husband, and wife.

The instrumental presence of God in both ordinary and extraordinary human conception may be found in Hebrew Scriptures. An illustration of the former is found in the story of Ruth: "Boaz took Ruth and she became his wife. When he had intercourse with her, Yahweh caused her to conceive and she bore a son" (4:13). The divine presence was considered even more significant when a wife conceived who had been thought barren. The most prominent example of such is found in the story of Sarah: "Yahweh visited Sarah as Yahweh had said, and did to her as Yahweh had promised. She conceived and bore Abraham a son in his old age" (Gen. 21:1–2). This dual parenthood is described by John Otwell:

> The new life given the people of God came into being because the Lord worked in the woman's womb, bringing to fruition the sexual relations of husband and wife. Thus the woman was uniquely the locus of the basic manifestation of the benign pres-

ence of God in the midst of the people, for without new life the people would soon cease to exist.[3]

In some other Hebrew birth accounts, the human father is implicitly assumed but not explicitly mentioned. As a way of expressing piety, it is said of Rachel, and again of Leah, that God "opened her womb" (Gen. 29:31; 30:22). A psalmist likewise thought of God as the prime cause of his conception. Without intending to deny the role of his human father, that poet addressed God in this way: "You formed my inward parts./ You knit me together in my mother's womb" (139:13). Jewish scholar Geza Vermes points out that "such divine intervention was never interpreted as divine impregnation."[4]

The interaction between divine and human agents in the Hebrew culture was a product of both poetic expression and theological conviction. Living as they did in prescientific culture, the Hebrews were not awed by physical causation. Although they did at times show a naive awareness of such, they considered it relatively insignificant by comparison with divine causation. In the Exodus prose account of the crossing of the Sea of Reeds, for example, there is mention of "a strong east wind" that blew all night and separated the shallow waters. But that explanation was not as important to them as the poetic affirmation of God's action: "At the blast of your nostrils the waters piled up" (14:21; 15:8). Although that anthropomorphic figure was not intended to be literally interpreted, it expressed omnipotence in an awesome manner.

As part of their belief in a continuously creative God, the Hebrews held that organic life could not be adequately explained in a physiological manner. Acting as a life force was one function of God's Spirit (*ruach*).[5] The Spirit produced land fertility and animal reproduction as well as human offspring.[6] Job affirmed: "The Spirit of God has made me" (33:4). Accordingly, humans were sometimes dignified as "children of the living God" (Hos. 1:10; Deut. 14:1; Isa. 43:6). By means of Nathan's oracle, God endorsed dual paternity in addressing David regarding Solomon: "I will raise up your son. . . . I will be his father and he shall be my son" (2 Sam. 7:12, 14). The etymology of "procreation" suggests the ancient theology of generation. A procreator was viewed as one who acts on behalf of the Creator, just as a pronoun is a word that represents a noun.

Ancient Jewish tradition made more explicit the theory of dual parenthood suggested by Hebrew Scriptures. In the Talmud there is an interpretation of the first conception account of Genesis in which Eve exclaims, "I have brought a boy into being with the help of Yahweh" (4:1). From that text comes this rabbinic deduction: "There are three partners in the production of any human being: the Holy One, . . . the father, and the mother."[7] According to Jewish scholar Israel Abrahams, "the rabbinic theory of marital intercourse is summed up" in the belief that God participates as a third parent in every act of procreation.[8] A Genesis midrash declares:

> In the past Adam was created from the dust of the ground and Eve was created from Adam. Henceforth it is to be "in our image and after our likeness"—meaning, man will not be able to come into existence without woman, nor woman without man, nor both without the Shekinah.[9]

"Shekinah," literally "One-who-dwells-within," is a postbiblical circumlocution for Yahweh and is often used interchangeably with "Holy Spirit" (*ruach hakodesh*).[10] Those immanent expressions of God are feminine words in Hebrew. Juxtaposing them with the masculine imagery for deity in Hebrew displays that ultimately God is sexually undifferentiated. The transcendent deity can be called androgynous or psychically bisexual.[11] The Spirit or the Shekinah is present when the devout assemble to worship[12] and among marital partners: "When husband and wife are worthy, the Shekinah is with them."[13]

Motherly images for God are occasionally found in the Hebrew

Bible.[14] Such occurs in a negative way when agitated Moses denies that he created the Israelites: "Did I conceive all these people and give birth to them? Why should you (God) ask me to carry and suckle them like babies?" (Num. 11:12) More positively, Isaiah represents God as saying: "I cry out like a woman in labor, gasping and panting" (42:14). Hebrew specialist James Muilenburg explains that the biblical God, who does not belong to a pantheon in which there are both goddesses and gods to represent the genders, is no more father than mother and that "the feminine attributes as well as the masculine are absorbed into his holy being."[15]

The Hebrews coupled the notion of dual parenthood with that of dual matchmaking. Motherly Naomi laid most of the plans that resulted in Ruth becoming married to Boaz.[16] Abraham's servant followed orders in selecting a mate whom Isaac had never seen before.[17] Concomitant with this family custom, rabbinical Jews added that "marriages are made in heaven."[18] The providential claim was based on an assertion made while Isaac's marriage was being arranged: "The thing proceeds from Yahweh" (Gen. 24:50). That Hebrew marital idealism is expressed in this teaching of Jesus: "What God has joined, let no one separate" (Mark 10:9).

The idea of dual paternity was found in a variety of ancient pagan Mediterranean cultures. The earliest example is from Egyptian mythology. A story from the royal family of Thutmosis I thirty-five centuries ago expresses an outlook that began dynasties earlier and was to continue later. At the Deir el-Bahri temple at Karnak there is a relief in praise of its builder, Queen Hatshepsut. Her mother, Ahmes, is seated on a couch with the god Amon, and the deity announces: "Hatshepsut shall be the name of this my daughter whom I have placed in thy body. She shall exercise excellent sovereignty in this whole land."[19] King Thutmosis was commonly recognized as Hatshepsut's human father, for it was through him that she was able to claim to the throne. In her struggle for power with other family members, this religious propaganda of divine as well as human paternity was of great help. Akhenaton, another

Egyptian king, did not view human and divine paternity as mutually exclusive when he sang to god Aton: "Creator of seed in women, / Thou who makest fluid into man, / Who maintainest the son in the womb of his mother."[20]

The notion of double paternity was expressed in the Greek culture as early as the Homeric epic. For example, Odysseus is acknowledged as both the son of King Laertes of Ithaca and the son of Zeus.[21] Cyrus Gordon finds here a comparison to the story of Jesus' conception in the New Testament: "While Jesus and Odysseus have each two fathers, one divine and the other human, their claim to kingship is based on the ancestry of their mother's human husband."[22] The two genealogies of Jesus show many variations but they agree that he was descended from King David through Joseph, the husband of Mary.[23]

Other great persons of the Greek culture were said to have had two fathers. Speusippos told an Athenian story of how his uncle, the eminent philosopher Plato, was conceived. Ariston, who became his father, had no success in impregnating Perictione, who became his mother. Apollo, the god of wisdom, then appeared to Ariston and assisted the couple in producing a child. Plato's genealogy went back to Solon, the first prominent Athenian patriarch.[24] Consequently, the philosopher's sublime wisdom could be attributed to Apollo while his family pedigree could be attributed to his human ancestry.

In the first century of the Christian era, Plutarch related a birth legend of Alexander the Great. He stated that Philip was his father, but he claimed that a god, in the form of a snake, impregnated Olympias, who became Alexander's mother.[25] Suetonius maintained that the only subsequent conception like this was when Apollo, appearing as a snake, copulated with Atia, who became Emperor Augustus' mother. The Senate had declared Augustus to be divine after his death, and Suetonius, a century later, assisted in glorifying one of the most worthy of the Caesars. Suetonius also calls Augustus the son of Octavius, Atia's husband.[26]

Philo of Alexandria shared with the Mediterranean tradition the belief that procreation resulted from divine-human cooperation.[27] For example, he stated that Isaac was a son of Abraham and Sarah, yet also a "son of God" because he was begotten by God.[28] In one treatise, Philo drew allegorical significance from the fact that there is no overt mention of the Hebrew patriarch engaging in marital intercourse. Figuratively that meant their children were sired by God.[29]

Although this review of dual parenthood ideas has been focused on the Mediterranean area, cultures in other regions independently accepted the same viewpoint. For example, Ku-liang Chaun, a classic commentator on Confucius' teachings, said: "The female alone cannot procreate; the male alone cannot procreate; and Heaven alone cannot produce a child. The three collaborating, a person is born. Hence, anyone may be called the son of his mother and the son of Heaven."[30] Also, the Bantu of Africa have this saying: "We should not boast, 'I have begotten'; for it is God who begets."[31] Since pregnancy occurs in only a small percentage of the instances of human intercourse, a pious explanation for productive inseminations has been heterosexual intercourse plus God's will.

What does the New Testament say about dual parenthood and Jesus' parents in particular? Paul, who provides the earliest historical reference to Jesus' mother, does not claim that he was conceived of a virgin, but states merely that he was "born of a woman" (Gal. 4:4). The apostle refers to seminally generated Christians as "children of God"; they are privileged to call God Abba (Rom. 8:14–15), the Aramaic designation that Jesus favored. Also, Paul makes the theological comment that Isaac was "born according to the Spirit" (Gal. 4:29). The apostle was not declaring that the Spirit physically caused the pregnancy; the affirmation was not intended to exclude recognizing that Isaac was biologically the son of Abraham and Sarah. Paul brought divine and human parentage together when he referred to Jesus as the "Son of God" who was born "of David's sperm according to the flesh" (Rom. 1:3–4). Since it was through Joseph that the early Christians traced Jesus' descent from King David, it would have been nonsense for Paul to make that claim if Jesus was not a physical son of Joseph. No New Testament writer asserts that Joseph was only Jesus' legal or foster father.

There is nothing about virginal conception in the earliest and the latest Gospels. "Son of God" is used to designate Jesus in the Gospel of Mark, but also his Nazareth family of brothers and sisters are mentioned (6:3; 14:61–62; 15:39). The prologue of John's Gospel affirms that the life of Christians originates from more than the desire of human parents. "Children of God" are not conceived as a result of the human desire to have sex, but are "offspring of God" (1:12–13). According to the Fourth Gospel, the complete life includes being born of the Spirit in addition to natural fleshly conception (3:6–7). Jesus is there called both "Joseph's son from Nazareth" (1:45) and "God's only son" (1:18; 3:16). Some Jews asserted: "Is not this Jesus, Joseph's son? We know his father and mother" (6:42). Subsequently Jesus declares to some Jews: "You certainly know me and where I come from" (7:28).

The only New Testament books that appear to state that Jesus was virginally conceived are Matthew and Luke, which were written nearly a century after the event supposedly happened. After the Gospel of Matthew begins by tracing Jesus' genealogy through Joseph to Abraham, it associates Jesus with a prophecy of Isaiah about a young woman (*alma* in the Hebrew text, *parthenos* in its Greek translation) conceiving one who would be called Emmanuel, meaning "God is with us" (Isa. 7:14; 1:22–23). In the annunciation stories of both Matthew and Luke it is unfortunate that *parthenos* has usually been translated "virgin," a word that refers to a woman who has not had sexual intercourse. The word is best defined, in both biblical and in ancient nonbiblical usage, as a girl who has reached marriageable age.[32]

Due to the fact that a young woman was customarily married at the age of puberty, and that social sanctions protected unwed Hebrew daughters from seduction, a *parthenos* would usually not be sexually experienced prior to betrothal. Even so, *parthenos* does sometimes refer to a woman who had had sexual intercourse. In the Greek Bible, commonly called the Septuagint, *parthenos* is used to describe a girl who had been raped, and another time to describe a wife.[33] Moreover, in classical Greek, the term could refer to a nonvirginal young woman; in a nonliterary papyrus, the word could refer to a mother; and in Jewish sepulchre inscriptions during the early Christian era, it could connote someone who had married.[34] After a careful examination of the terms translated as "virgin" in ancient Jewish and Christian literature, Josephine Ford concludes:

> The term "virgin" is not necessarily confined to one who has not experienced coitus, but, on the one hand, may be used of a minor who has married and been widowed, and, on the other, of people who have only taken one spouse during their lifetime.[35]

Joseph and Mary were probably married not long after puberty. There were several reasons for matching boys with girls as soon as procreation was possible. Graveyards of that era show that the average life span was about twenty-five years.[36] By fifteen, sixty percent of those born alive would have died. Probably only ten percent of the population survived their forty-fifth birthday. In light of such high mortality, it was imperative to reproduce early and frequently in order to maintain the human species. Another reason for what seems to modern culture to be early marriage is the importance of the unruptured hymen in the Hebrew culture. A girl who could no longer show physical evidence of being a virgin was regarded as damaged goods and would bring little or no dowry to her guardians. According to the law of Moses, a bride who lacked evidence of virginity could be stoned to death.[37] Also, parents no doubt realized that children were more docile before they attained adulthood and would accept with less resistance the spouses that the parents had procured.

Betrothal in the Hebrew culture legally constituted a marital relationship.[38] It was sealed by a transaction in which the boy's guardian paid an agreed sum to the girl's guardian. Breaking a betrothal was so serious that it involved obtaining a bill of divorce.[39] Not long after the betrothal was contracted, the groom had the privilege and responsibility of cohabitating with his bride. Tobias, a devout ancient Jew, slept with Sarah in her home on the night following their betrothal. People would not have been greatly surprised had she become pregnant before the wedding feast, which was held later.[40] The Mishnah, the prime codification of Jewish legal traditions, indicates that marital consummation occasionally occurred while the betrothed girl was still residing in her parent's home, and that any child conceived as a result who was accepted by the husband was not stigmatized as illegitimate.[41] Joseph initially doubted that he was responsible for the pregnancy, since his betrothed had not come to live in his home, but he later accepts Mary even if she had been raped.[42]

In Judaism, nonconjugal marriage was a contradiction in terms. According to the Torah, it was the husband's sacred duty to give his wife her marital rights.[43] Regarding this, Marcus Cohn has stated: "The most important common obligation of the married couple is the performance of the marital act."[44] Paul introduced that Jewish custom into Christianity when he insisted that having sexual relations is the right and duty of all married couples.[45]

Matthew refers to Mary's pregnancy as being "from the Holy Spirit" (1:18, 20). The pre-Matthean tradition probably did not intend to claim that divine activity was substituted for the act of a human progenitor. Borrowing the Hebrew outlook on conceptions, the account affirmed that Mary's child was ultimately caused by God. Charles Davis has shown that the earliest tradition, which has been obscured by the later redaction contained in the New Testament, probably contained no instruction to Joseph to abstain from sexual relations with his wife.[46]

If the opening chapter of Matthew is taken literally, the genealogy in the first part contradicts the last part, which presumes that Jesus had no paternal family tree. Vermes reasons:

If Joseph had nothing to do with Mary's pregnancy, the intention prompting the reproduction of the (genealogical) table is nullified, since Joseph's royal Davidic blood would not have been passed on to Jesus. . . . The logic of the genealogies demands that Joseph was the father of Jesus.[47]

John Robinson comments on the New Testament treatments of Jesus' conception in this way:

Clearly the men of the first century did not intend the genealogies to be set against the assertion of Jesus' heavenly conception, or vice versa. They were affirming both in the closest juxtaposition, just as the early formula had conjoined the statements that "on the human level he was born of David's stock, but on the level of the spirit—the Holy Spirit—he was . . . Son of God." In other words, each is true—at its own level. The purpose of the nativity story is not to deny something at the level of flesh asserted in the genealogy, but to affirm something at the level of spirit—namely, the initiative of God in and through it all. The significance of Jesus is not to be understood solely from the point of view of heredity and environment. Yet these solidarities are not abrogated—any more than they are for Christians who, as children of God, insists John in his parallel prologue, are "not born of any human stock, or by the fleshly desire of a human father but (are) the offspring of God himself." But this is not, of course, to deny that at the level of nature they are so born. The one truth does not contradict the other.[48]

Rosemary Ruether, with her usual perspicacity, shares Robinson's outlook:

It is possible that in the earliest Christian traditions the idea that God specially intervened in Jesus' birth also did not exclude the fatherhood of Joseph. The young Mary might have been thought of as a girl who is betrothed at too early an age to be fertile (a not uncommon practice at this time) and who conceives before menstruation gives the first evidence of her fertility. Rabbinic writings refer to such births as "virgin births." So God's miraculous intervention does not need to exclude Joseph's biological role. At least some of the traditions that shaped the New Testament clearly believed Joseph to be Jesus' biological father. Otherwise there would be no point in the genealogy recorded by Matthew that traces Jesus' Davidic ancestry through Joseph. We know that some groups of Jewish Christians in the early centuries of the church, such as the Ebionites, continued to regard Jesus as the divinely chosen, but natural, son of Joseph.[49]

Luke's Gospel begins with the story of Elizabeth conceiving a child after the normal years of childbearing had passed. God's role in the divine-human triangle is emphasized without denying the impregnating role of her husband Zechariah. "His wife Elizabeth conceived," according to Luke; and she said, "This is what the Lord has done to me in the days when the Lord looked on me and took away the disgrace I have endured among people" (1:24–25). The angel Gabriel then announces to a young woman who is "espoused" to Joseph that she would bear a son who will be named Jesus. Luke uses the verb "espoused" (*mnesteuo*) to refer to Joseph's relation to Mary at the time of Jesus' birth as well as at the time of his conception (1:27, 2:5). *Parthenos* in reference to Mary stands in contrast to Elizabeth, who conceives as an older woman.[50]

After Gabriel's annunciation, Mary is represented as inquiring, "How can this be since I know not a man?" (Luke 1:34) Perhaps she was puzzled over receiving before her wedding celebration this forecast of becoming pregnant. The angel then reiterates that the conception is a future matter: "The Holy Spirit will come upon you,/ And the power of the Most High will overshadow you" (Luke 1:35). Characteristic of Luke's theology is that the Spirit works through the interaction of human agents, although the process by which this occurs is not fully expressed.[51] To interpret this bit of poetry about the Spirit's union with Mary in a literal manner would do violence to the biblical outlook. G. B. Caird perceptively comments: "It would never have occurred to a Jew to consider the overshadowing of Mary by the Holy Spirit as a substitute for normal parenthood."[52] Jewish mythology did not tell of God copulating with goddesses or with human women. Consequently, Luke's account of divine parenthood should be understood as a metaphor picturing God's activity in bringing Jesus into the world. After the generation is symbolically accomplished by the Creator and biologically by the husband, the fetus in Mary's uterus had a normal gestation period before being born.

After reviewing the opening chapters of Matthew and Luke, Edward Barrett wisely suggests that the virginal conception stories are poetic expressions, to be interpreted seriously but not literally. Similar to the conception stories of Sarah and Abraham, Hannah and Elkanah, Ruth and Boaz, and Elizabeth and Zechariah, the story of Mary and Joseph highlights the role of God in the biological process.[53]

Apart from the annunciation stories, the rest of the writings of Matthew and Luke unambiguously support a theory of dual parenthood. In Matthew, Jesus is referred to as "the carpenter's son" (13:55). He instructs his disciples to call no earthly man father because God is Father for the new surrogate family.[54] In a Temple episode of Luke, Jesus' mother is represented as saying during his boyhood: "Your father and I have been searching for you anxiously" (2:48). To this Jesus responds by claiming that he was in his "Father's house" (2:49). Luke does not suggest here that Joseph stood *in loco parentis*. About two decades after that happening in Jerusalem, Luke has citizens of Jesus' hometown question, "Is not this Joseph's son?" (4:22) Along with assertions in the Gospels pertaining to Jesus' natural family are frequent references to him as son of the divine Father.

Jesus' frequent references to God as father were to stress the closeness of the divine-human bond, not to declare God's essential maleness. Mary Baker Eddy aptly opens her paraphrase of the "Lord's Prayer" with the phrase "Our Father-Mother God."[55]

Since Jesus believed that both genders are created in the divine likeness,[56] God can be no more male than female. The God of Jesus is more like a nurturing parent than a stern judge or a remote monarch, sharing a psalmist's and a prophet's image: "As a father has compassion for his children, so Yahweh has compassion for those who revere God" (Ps. 103:13); "As a mother comforts her child, so I [God] will comfort you" (Isa. 66:13). Jesus would have perceived, as ancient rabbi Shemuel did, that those verses depict God as acting as a caring parent of either gender.[57] In parables that Luke joined together, God is compared to a searching woman and to a forgiving father.[58]

Jesus seemed to presume that he and John the Baptizer were inspired by Sophia, a feminine personification of divine wisdom. After pointing out that differing prophetic voices have their place in God's scheme, he concluded, "Sophia is proved right by all her children."[59] Sophia is the Greek rendering of Hokmah (Wisdom Woman) who is featured in the Hebrew Book of Proverbs. She is there described as having been begotten before the earth and heavens existed and as assisting God in executing the work of creation.[60]

That companion of the Creator probably figures prominently in the thinking of the writer of the prologue to John's Gospel, who claims that the "word" (*logos*) was with God from the beginning and was God.[61] The Fourth Gospel then parallels the reference in Proverbs to Wisdom Woman as lifegiver by associating the *Logos* with bringing life into the world. The prologue concludes by declaring that Jesus is the enfleshment of that divine reason (1:14–18).

Since the creative activity of God is personified in both feminine and masculine ways in the Bible, the gender inclusive dual parenthood is more adequate for interpreting the origin of Jesus than dual paternity. The latter is appropriate in discussing cultures such as the ancient Egyptian and Greek where goddesses could be introduced into myths if divine maternity were desired in stories of heroic births. Goddesses were not sanctioned by the biblical monotheists, so biblical writers who were able to rise above patriarchal biases incorporated into the Godhead qualities associated with both human genders. Thus, the motherhood of God metaphor belongs alongside the more common fatherhood of God metaphor in understanding Jesus' conception.

Elizabeth Cady Stanton was among the first modern writers to be aware that gender inclusiveness can be found in the Bible. On the image of God passage of the opening chapter of Genesis, she commented: "It is evident from the language that there was consultation in the Godhead, and that the masculine and feminine elements were equally represented."[62] Accordingly, as Stanton reflected on the virgin conception doctrine in Christianity, she raised this criticism: "If a Heavenly Father was necessary, why not a Heavenly Mother? If an earthly mother was admirable, why not an earthly father?"[63] She realized that the doctrine slighted maternity on the deity level and paternity on the human level.

The Gospels do not indicate that Jesus ever referred to his birth. Had the "son of man" spoken of his biological beginning, he might have expressed himself in a manner similar to the earthy testimony of a Jewish contemporary:

Like everyone else, I am mortal, a descendant of the first earthling. I was molded into flesh in a mother's womb, where, for ten moons I was compacted in blood, the result of male semen and sexual pleasure. When I was born, I breathed the common air and was laid on the earth that bears us all. My first sound was a scream, like everyone else; I was wrapped in swaddling cloths and nursed with care. No king begins life differently; for there is only one way into life and one way out.[64]

Ignatius, a second-century bishop of Syrian Antioch, was the first "church father" to write about Jesus' birth. To combat the current docetic denial of Jesus' full humanity, Ignatius stressed that Jesus was physically like other humans from his conception onward. In one letter he advised Christians: "Be deaf to any talk that ignores Jesus Christ, of David's lineage, of Mary; who was really born, ate, and drank."[65] In another letter, Ignatius affirms dual parenthood: "Our God, Jesus the Christ, was conceived by Mary in accordance with God's plan—being sprung both of the sperm of David and from the Holy Spirit."[66] Sometimes Ignatius refers to mother Mary as a *parthenos*,[67] which probably means "woman of marriagable age" rather than "virgin." Virginity is actually excluded from the meaning of the word when he writes of "*parthenoi* who are called widows."[68] It would have gone against Ignatius' desire to show Jesus' genuine humanity to claim that his conception was only half human and thereby unlike other mortals.

The notion of dual parenthood for Jesus was lost after Christian doctrine jelled in the latter part of the second century, and the idea of Jesus' virginal conception became a part of the basic dogma. The last trace of dual parenthood for Jesus in early Christian literature is found in the Gospel of Philip, which was written in the third century. It was lost soon afterwards in the sand of Egypt and was rediscovered in 1945. Jesus is declared to be the son of Joseph, yet "the Father of everything united with the virgin" to produce Jesus.[69] The Gospel claims that Jesus would not have referred to "My Father in heaven" unless he were distinguishing God from his earthly father.[70]

Origen explained that the pagan Greeks invented myths of gods having a special role with human women in order to enhance the wisdom and power of the offspring they conceived, but he was unwilling to accept that there could have been a similar motivation by those who told Christian nativity stories.[71] Tertullian, another third-century theologian, claimed that Mary was Jesus' only human parent: "Otherwise he had two fathers, a divine and a human one, the thought of which is ridiculous, like the stories of Castor and Hercules."[72] The view of those church fathers prevailed in subsequent centuries, for Christians came to believe that in the unique case of Jesus, male-female parentage and divine-human parentage were mutually exclusive.

A Jew from Nazareth

Even though Jesus spent approximately ninety percent of his life
as a private Jewish citizen out of the public eye, little attention has
been given to the environmental setting for those formative years.
Many Christians would like to forget that Jesus and his family
were devout Jews, immersed in the milieu to which they belonged.
Leonard Swidler describes the persistent mind-set:

> Both Christians and Jews automatically think of Jesus as the
> name of someone other than a Jew. This simple fact tends to cut
> Christians off from the taproot of their religion, the Hebrew-
> Jewish tradition. On the other side it also tends to cut Jews off
> from a very important son of their tradition, one who has be-
> come the most influential Jew of all history.[73]

Some attempts to picture Jesus as a Gentile Christian rather
than as a Palestinian Jew seem to be a deliberate effort to be invidious. Since one device for making a portrait stand out is to set
a luminous face in bold relief, Jesus has been exalted by darken-
ing his Jewish background. A notable example of this approach is
found in the influential writings of Alfred Edersheim, a Jew of the
past century who converted to Christianity. He engaged in a vast
investigation of Jewish tradition for the purpose of showing "the
infinite distance between Christ and the teaching of the synagogue."[74] Edersheim's voluminous *Life and Times of Jesus the
Messiah* is devoted to proving that the substance and spirit of
Jesus' teaching were absolutely contrary to Judaism, even though
they were cast in Jewish form.[75] To expose the absurdity of this
evaluation, at least on one basic point, one need do no more than
realize that Akiba, a leading rabbi in the century when Jesus lived,
pointed to "Love your neighbor as yourself" as the comprehen-
sive law of the Torah.[76]

When Christians who share Edersheim's outlook write about
the postexilic centuries of Jewish history, they imply that earlier

religious vitality was exhausted and that little was left at the beginning of the Christian era beyond a calcified casuistry. Yet during that period many psalms were written that profoundly influenced Jesus. That was also the time when the synagogue became established as the hub of Jewish life. A perusal of the Mishnah, the rabbinic record of the era in which Jesus lived, displays that delight in studying the Torah—not lethargic ritualism—was the pervading spirit in the sector of Palestinian Judaism that had the greatest impact on Jesus.

A realization that Jesus was not a Christian has become prominent in the latter part of the twentieth century. Frederick Grant, an eminent New Testament interpreter, wrote a generation ago: "The thorough Jewishness of Jesus is assumed by all present-day scholars competent to judge."[77] Jewish, Roman Catholic, and Protestant scholars are now giving even more focus to that assumption.[78]

George Moore, in his definitive Judaism in the First Centuries of the Christian Era, has pointed out that early Judaism specified five principal responsibilities for a father toward his son.[79] The duties were later recorded in the Talmud in this sequential way: "He must circumcise him, redeem him, teach him Torah, teach him a trade, and find him a wife."[80]

Circumcision, the first duty, was a mark of identification with the offspring of Abraham, but it had a sexual purpose as well. It originated as a puberty rite and was associated with making a young man fit for marriage.[81] Philo explains that it was performed for the physical purpose of facilitating sexual intercourse.[82] Early in Hebrew history, infant circumcision was substituted for the more severe operation that had been performed when a boy came of age.[83] Akiba pointed out that the mark of circumcision was a symbolic reminder of having consecrated the body to God.[84] Martin Buber comments in a similar way: "Sex is hallowed by the sacrament of the circumcision covenant which survives in its original purity and not only confirms the act of begetting but converts it into a holy vocation."[85]

Sociologist David Mace explains why the penis is singled out for special honor:

> Every Hebrew man carried on his body the mark of his identity as a member of God's chosen race. And it was no accident that he carried this mark on his sex organ. Far from being disreputable, this was the most sacred part of his whole body; therefore it was appropriate that it should be specially dedicated to God as the symbol that his whole body, his whole person was dedicated to God. For it was with this organ that he became, in a special sense, a co-worker with God.[86]

Luke portrays the parents of Jesus as fulfilling the traditional rite of passage for their son. Joshua, the baby whom the Greek writers of the New Testament called Jesus, was circumcised and shortly thereafter was dedicated to God at the Jerusalem temple. At the latter ceremony, an animal sacrifice was presented to "redeem" the firstborn son in remembrance of God's liberation of the Israelites from Egypt.[87] This scrupulous observance of the Mosaic law by Jesus' parents is one of the several indications that they should not be classified by the technical term *amme-ha-aretz* (people of the land). Herbert Danby has accurately defined this phrase as pertaining to Jews who were ignorant of the Torah and who failed to observe purification regulations.[88]

Of all parental duties, teaching children about their religious heritage was given top priority. Josephus speaks for fellow Jews when he writes: "Our principal concern is to educate our children and we think it to be the most important business of our whole life."[89] In reciting the Shema, the Jewish affirmation of faith, fathers obligated themselves to communicate the Mosaic commandments to their offspring in the ongoing day-to-day living.[90] In all likelihood Jesus began to learn from early childhood the basic scriptural traditions from Joseph and Mary. Included in his instruction would surely be the duty to marry and "multiply" (Gen. 1:28), in fulfillment of the first law of the Torah.

Philo, a contemporary of Jesus, states that Jews "from their very swaddling clothes are taught by parents, teachers, and those who bring them up, even before instruction in the sacred laws and unwritten customs, to believe in one God, the Father and Creator of the world."[91] The focus on God as father would have been especially meaningful to a child. That metaphor was taken from Jewish Scriptures and was frequently expressed by the Aramaic term *abba* in the era when Jesus lived.[92] It is significant that *Abba*, one of the first words in Jewish children's vocabulary, was sanctioned for use in speaking both to their human father and to their heavenly Father. Two petitions of the daily prayer were: "Cause us to turn, O our Father, to Thy law," and "Forgive us, our Father, for we have sinned."[93] In accord with that filial mode of speaking, a faithful Jew considered himself a son of God.[94]

As regards formal schooling, the Mishnah states: "At five years old one is fit for the Scripture, at ten for the Mishnah, at thirteen for the fulfilling of the commandments, at fifteen for the Talmud."[95] During the era in which Jesus lived there had probably been established in local communities an elementary school called the House of the Book (*Bet-ha-Sefer*).[96] It was appropriately named, since the Torah was its sole textbook. The school was conducted by the synagogue superintendent (*hazzan*), who instructed boys in reading and writing by means of recitations from the Hebrew Torah. The intermediate school, called the House of Study (*Bet-ha-Midrash*)[97] was also administered by the community synagogue. Popular instruction was given in the oral tradition as well as in the written Scriptures.[98] This school was conducted on Sabbath afternoons, so that those who participated in this study could also engage in daily work.

Jesus probably received at least elementary instruction at the Nazareth synagogue and learned to read the Hebrew Bible.[99] Then, at the age of puberty, he "fulfilled the commandments" and acquired the status of an adult[100]—a rite of passage subsequently called Bar-Mitzvah. At that time he was expected to have an adequate knowledge of his culture's spiritual and social heritage.

Josephus, for instance, claimed in his autobiography that he had acquired an accurate knowledge of the Torah by the age of four-teen.[101] He asserted that a righteous Jewish child had had the laws of his culture so engraved on him that he could recall them even more readily than his own name![102]

Sex education was an important part of Jesus' nurture. From the Genesis accounts of creation he would have learned that sex, like the rest of the natural order, is an essential part of the divine design. In both accounts the marital union climaxes God's bless-ings, indicating that human sexuality is endowed with more grandeur than other aspects of the natural world. Sex is provided for human happiness and is judged by God to be "very good." *Tov*, the Hebrew term used in both accounts, means "beautiful" as well as "good." By contrast, single life without an intimate com-panion is the first thing that God judges to be not *tov*. Frederick Bruner muses on the implications of the creation doctrine:

> If God had supremely intended solitary life, God would have created humans one by one; if God had intended polygamous life, God would have created one man and several women; if God had intended homosexual life God would have made two men or two women; but that God intended monogamous het-erosexual life was shown by God's creation of one man and one woman.[103]

Mace shows how this biblical outlook on sex affected the an-cient Jews: "The Hebrews so ordered their community life that no one was likely to be left in the condition of prolonged sexual frus-tration. Sex was a gift of God, and it was given to be used."[104] Mace quotes a famous Jewish saying to express the characteristic outlook: "A man will have to give account on the judgment day of every good thing which he refused to enjoy when he might have done so."[105] In the years immediately before the coming of Jesus the leading schools of Hillel and Shammai, while differing on many points, agreed that no one may abstain from carrying out

God's first command, which was to marry for the purpose of pro-creating.[106] Israel Abrahams, an authority on Jewish marital ethics, writes: "The act of sexual intercourse was consciously elevated . . . from an animal function to a fulfillment of the divine plan announced at the Creation."[107] Appropriately, the ordinary Jewish term for marriage, *kiddushin*, comes from a root meaning "holy." Since holiness is related to wholeness in Jewish theology, the union of husband and wife sanctifies life.

Genesis states: "When God created man, he made him in the likeness of God. Male and female he created them, and he blessed them and named them man" (Gen. 5:1–2). This passage was also interpreted in classical Judaism as showing the psychological and physical commingling in marriage. It was observed that "man is not even called man until united with woman."[108] The adult Jesus appealed to the authority of the creation story of his scriptures about two becoming "one flesh." Believing that the marital state afforded a fuller self-realization, he advocated a splicing that provides a union of genital organs as well as a bonding of personalities.[109]

Luke is the only New Testament writer who provides any information about Jesus' boyhood. This has suggested to some critics that he was troubled by the earliest Gospel having no treatment of Jesus' life prior to his public ministry, and accordingly filled in the biographical void by a fictitious story. But Luke displays the marks of a serious historian in the prologue to his Gospel, for he there gives value to accuracy and firsthand observation. Although the "many" whom Luke acknowledged as having undertaken to compile a narrative of the Jesus movement before him may well have recorded some legendary accretions, it was Luke's stated purpose to provide authentic knowledge about the beginnings of Christianity. Robert Grant cogently demonstrates that Luke's methodology is similar to that of ancient Greek historians such as Aelius Theon.[110] The burden of the proof rests on those who claim that Luke's record of the early years of Jesus' life is essentially unreliable.

According to Luke, Jesus sought out some Jerusalem teachers in order to learn about current theological issues when he visited the traditional capital of his country at the age of twelve. As a serious student, he combined active inquiry with absorbing what the Torah authorities had to say. Hillel and/or Shammai, the most prominent Jewish debaters at the time of Jesus' birth, or their disciples, were teaching in Jerusalem when the boy Jesus visited there.

Jesus' study of his Bible by way of formal education, or by his own independent probing, provided him with a profound comprehension of that literature. Rabbi Klausner claims regarding Jesus: "He is as expert in the Scriptures as the best of the Pharisees, and he is quite at home with the Pharisee's expository devices. He is saturated with the great ideas of the Prophets and the Psalms."[111] David Flusser, a New Testament specialist at Hebrew University in Jerusalem, has maintained that Jesus had the finest Jewish education available: "He was perfectly at home both in holy scripture, and in oral tradition, and knew how to apply his scholarly heritage."[112]

Concomitant with Torah study was training in a craft. It was incumbent upon all fathers to provide vocational instruction for their male offspring, for, as a Jewish saying put it, "He who does not teach his son a trade, teaches him to steal."[113] Another saying points to the moral necessity of balancing religious pursuits with physically demanding work: "It is excellent to combine study of the Torah with a secular occupation, for toil in them both puts sin out of mind."[114] Jesus probably became skilled at interpreting Scripture during the period of his life when he was apprenticed to his carpenter father.[115] Even those whose primary calling was to interpret the Jewish religious tradition were expected to gain their livelihood in ways other than charging for their instruction. Hillel warned against teaching for compensation: "He that makes a profit off the Torah removes his life from the world."[116]

The last of the five duties laid down for a Jewish father was that of arranging a marriage for his son. In the patriarchal society in which Jesus lived, children were generally given little voice in deciding who their spouse would be. Around the time when a son became physically mature, his father made a betrothal agreement with the guardian of an eligible girl.[117] Joseph may have frequently had the responsibility for finding spouses for his boys. According to Mark's Gospel, Jesus had four brothers: James, Joses, Judas, and Simon (6:3). Paul states that brothers of Jesus had wives, and historian Hegesippus notes that grandnephews of Jesus were living at the end of the first century.[118]

At what age were marriages arranged? Neufeld replies: "From the general circumstances existing in the East in ancient times it can be assumed that children were married at a very early age— even before the age of puberty—but it seems that marriage was usually entered into soon after puberty."[119] According to the Shulhan Aruk, the standard Jewish law code, every Jewish youth was obligated to have a wife by his eighteenth year, and becoming married between the ages of thirteen and eighteen was laudable. Authorities could compel a single man who was over twenty to get married.[120]

Is there any record of an ancient Jew who did not conform to the marital requirement? Ludwig Kohler calls attention to the fact that the Hebrew Bible has no word for bachelor, so rare was the practice.[121] Even a misogynistic writer[122] advises a husband to "enjoy life with the wife whom you love" (Eccl. 9:9). Some think that Simeon ben Azzai, who lived in the second century of the Christian era, might have been the rare exception. A talmudic story criticized him for not having a wife, when he had taught that the unmarried diminish the image of God. Ben Azzai responded: "My soul is enamored with the Torah; let others preserve the race."[123] But elsewhere the Talmud indicates that he had married the daughter of Rabbi Akiba as a young man but divorced her later.[124] If a marriage had produced children, remarriage was not imperative in ancient Judaism.[125]

Jewish scholars agree that at least one marriage for every man was a divine ordinance. Claude Montefiore states: "Judaism has consistently deprecated and depreciated celibacy; it has required its saints to show their sanctity in the world amid the ties and obligations of family life."[126] Louis Epstein elaborates:

> The flesh and its legitimate pleasure are essentially good. . . . The most important corollary that follows from this teaching is the unequivocal opposition of the rabbis to celibacy. Marriage is a legitimate physical satisfaction; it furthers God's universal purpose in the perpetuation of the human species; it sustains the social unit, the family; it helps us toward our personal salvation in that it keeps us from sin.[127]

It is probable that Jesus married as a young man, even though there is no more mention in the New Testament of his fulfillment of that requirement than there is of his attending school in Nazareth. Even if there were no reference in the Gospels to Jesus' circumcision, it would be wrong to conclude that his father neglected or rejected that duty. The lack of mention of circumcision in the Qur'an also reflects that the rite of passage was taken for granted in the Semitic culture and was practiced in a thoroughgoing manner. Deviations from normative behavior are more likely to be remembered and thus lodged in oral and written traditions, so it makes sense to assume that Jesus and his apostles were circumcised and married.

After a Jewish man became adept at Torah interpretation, skilled at a craft, and successfully married, he was, according to the Sayings of the Fathers, "fit at thirty for authority." If he desired to instruct others, the last qualification was stressed.[128] Luke informs his readers that Jesus "was about thirty years of age" when he began his ministry. At that time Jesus taught in the Galilean synagogues and was regarded by Jews as a religious authority.[129] During Jesus' era, "rabbi" was emerging as the best designation for a teacher of Judaism. According to the Gospels, different people addressed Jesus as "Rabbi" more than a dozen times in the Gospels. This shows the respect given one who was an expert in Jewish tradition and exemplary in its practice. Even though Christians rarely refer to the founder of their religion as Rabbi Jesus, it is one of the more adequate ways of referring to his historical role.[130]

The similarity between the views of Rabbi Jesus and other Jewish teachers can be illustrated by their mutual denunciations of hypocrisy. Jesus frequently exposed the self-righteous who were blind to the gap between what they pretended to be and what they practiced. In a work probably written by a Palestinian contemporary of Jesus, the sham piety of some fellow Jews is likewise castigated: "Their hands and their minds are unclean and their mouths are full of boasting. Yet they say, 'Do not touch me lest you pollute me.'"[131] Another writing of the same general place and period contains this judgment: "Let God remove those that live in hypocrisy in the company of the pious."[132] It is unfortunate that Pharisaism is now regarded as a synonym for hypocrisy, for that vice was condemned as severely by the ancient Pharisees as by Jesus.[133] Seven types of Pharisees are listed in their literature, most of whom are disapproved of because they fall short of what Pharisees profess to be.[134]

Jesus not only had a high regard for fellow Jews, but he evaluated the Pharisees—the party of the rabbis and scribes—as the people with the most adequate understanding of God's will. When a scribe affirmed that the commandments to love God and one's neighbor were more important than ceremonial offerings, Jesus responded, "You are not far from the realm of God" (Mark 12:34). Even in a collection of taunts against the scribes and Pharisees, Jesus advised his disciples to accept their teachings but be wary of the way they act on their own principles.[135] Annulling the Pharisaic interpretations of the Torah was not so much Jesus' aim as going beyond them to a more complete religion. Thus, righteousness should exceed that of the scribes and Pharisees.[136] For example, Jesus regarded their tithing favorably, but faulted them for being overly scrupulous in that practice at the expense of neglecting justice and the love of God.[137]

In defending his rejection of some of the then current Sabbath law casuistry, Jesus appealed to Scriptures like a skilled rabbi. He maintained that the prevailing view that all Sabbath reaping of grain is forbidden is inconsistent with an episode in David's life. When the young warrior and his men were hungry, they set aside ritual law to accommodate human need.[138] To reinforce his interpretation, Jesus quoted Hosea's understanding of God, "I desire mercy, not sacrifice" (Matt. 12:1–7). Thus Jesus did not slavishly follow past interpretations as a mediocre scribe might do. Understandably, the Galilean synagogue-goers "were astonished at his teaching, for he taught them as one who had authority, and not as the scribes" (Mark 1:22).

In a self-descriptive way, Jesus remarked: "Every scribe who has been trained for the realm of heaven is like a homeowner who brings new and old treasures out of his storeroom" (Matt. 13:52). As a scriptural scholar, his values were heavily influenced by Jewish traditions. Like all creative geniuses, he borrowed and assimilated whatever he deemed worthy from the competing authorities of his day. Having a temperament of exceptional receptiveness to what is vital in religion, he was able to discern the pattern of divine providence as it was understood over the centuries by various religious spokespersons. After mastering the best of the past as he grew to maturity, he was able to sprint beyond it. There is an originality in Jesus' teaching and a lifestyle that transcends his predecessors. He expressed that originality by radically selecting from the cultural heritage in which he was immersed. His unique vision of the nature of true religion was possible because he stood on the shoulders of Israel's historians, prophets, psalmists, and scribes.

THREE

The Celibacy Debate

✦ There is considerable agreement among Christians that Jesus was single, but there is no consensus on why he was single. Unlike dogmas regarding Mary of Nazareth's sexuality, church bodies have never established definitive doctrines pertaining to Jesus' virginal or nonvirginal life. An examination of varied pro and con reasons pertaining to his celibacy discloses a great deal about Christian attitudes toward sexuality and marriage. As a method for discussing the issue I will use an informal version of what is found in Thomas Aquinas's *Summa Theologica*. In that highly influential compendium of Christian thought, Aquinas first stated a proposition that is contrary to his own and lucidly summarized all the arguments he could find in its favor. Then he gave counterarguments against the proposition.

Historical Reasons

1. The New Testament states that Jesus encouraged eunuchry.

PRO

The leading current scholarly Bible dictionary states that celibacy in the Bible is "unknown unless alluded to in Matthew 19:12."[1] According to that verse, Jesus taught: "There are eunuchs who have been so from birth, and there are eunuchs who have been castrated by others, and there are eunuchs who have castrated themselves for the sake of . . . heaven. Let anyone accept this who can." A thorough examination of this enigmatic saying is needed in our pursuit of Jesus' sexuality.

Some Russian extremists called *Skoptsys*, meaning "emasculated ones," appealed to this eunuch saying along with another verse from the Gospels to justify their practice of castrating converts with a red-hot iron. Jesus said: "If your right hand causes you to sin, cut it off and throw it away; it is better for you to lose one of your members than for your whole body to go to hell" (Matt. 5:30). ("Hand," in Hebrew Scripture, could be a euphemism for the male genitals.[2]) Szelivanov, the Skoptsy's founder, interpreted those two verses to mean that the amputation of the sin-stimulating genitals was necessary for salvation. Thousands of those sectarians in the nineteenth century imitated Jesus, whom they believed actually made himself a sexual cripple.[3]

Nearly all other Christians have interpreted Jesus' eunuch saying differently from the Skoptsys. Tertullian, the early Latin church leader, asserted: "The Lord himself opened the kingdom of heaven to eunuchs and he himself lived as a virgin."[4] For Tertullian, "eunuchs" could designate not only virgins but couples who had become sexually abstinent after converting to Christianity. He states: "How many there are who, by mutual consent, cancel the debt of their marriage; eunuchs of their own accord through the desire of the kingdom of heaven."[5] Overtones of the eunuch saying can also be found in Jerome's comment on his situation as a desert hermit. In a figurative manner he appropriated a biblical blessing for celibates: "Blessed is the man who dashes his little ones against the rock" (Ps. 137:9). Jerome associated "little ones" with testicles and "the rock" with Christ.[6]

In recent years, New Testament exegete Floyd Filson presumed that Jesus' eunuch saying literally referred only to men with a natural sexual defect and to those who had received the dreadful punishment of emasculation. Underlying the third type, Filson thinks, is Jesus' "deliberate decision to refrain from marriage to be free to devote one's entire time to the cause of the Kingdom."[7] Ian Wilson also attempts to explain Jesus' unmarried state by referring to his eunuch teaching. He comments: "Jesus may well have been defining here a blueprint for human existence and for reaching the kingdom of God, and this would be totally consistent with his philosophy of self-abnegation."[8] Catholic scholar Hans Küng, while suggesting that the eunuch saying comes from a period after Jesus, holds that, if genuine, it would need to be interpreted as "self-justification."[9]

Pope Paul VI appealed to Jesus' eunuch saying as his principal authority for claiming that "Christ remained throughout his whole life in a state of celibacy" and for lauding priests who imitate Jesus' renunciation of genital sexuality.[10] Pope John Paul II has reiterated that earlier papal teaching and encourages anyone who can to follow the example of Jesus and renounce marriage "for the sake of the kingdom of heaven."[11]

Gnosticism scholar Elaine Pagels cites Jesus' teaching on eunuchs to show that he had compassion on the emasculated and others who were unmarried:

> Eunuchs, whom Jesus praised, were despised by rabbinic teachers for their sexual incapacity. Unmarried himself, Jesus praised the very persons most pitied and shunned in Jewish communities for their sexual incompleteness. . . . Jesus endorses—and exemplifies—a new possibility and one he says is even better: rejecting both marriage and procreation in favor of voluntary celibacy, for the sake of following him into the new age.[12]

CON

Exegetes are virtually unanimous that Jesus was not encouraging self-amputation when he spoke favorably about removing body parts. Surgery on diseased limbs can save lives, but Jesus did not intend these words to be taken literally: "If your hand (foot, eye) causes you to stumble, cut it off!" (Mark 9:43–47). Jesus often indulged in humorously absurd exaggerations to make a point.[13] After the hyperbole is removed, the residual meaning is that those accepting the rule of God need stringent self-discipline.

It would be antithetical to the compassionate spirit of Jesus to think that he encouraged his followers to maim their bodies to overcome temptation. The saying was appropriately used in the early church to justify the excommunication of unworthy "members" of the community in order to preserve the health of the rest.[14]

Johann Bengel, an outstanding early biblical exegete, coined the profound epigram: a text without a context is merely a pretext. When Jesus referred to a third type of eunuch he used the term in an unprecedented nonliteral way. His meaning can best be found by relating this eunuch saying to the larger context of Matthew by means of literary and historical exegesis. The saying is embedded in a passage that emphasizes the positive values of marriage and children. Far from advocating a vow of permanent virginity, the context shows Jesus stressing the permanence of marriage.

In light of the main theme of the Matthean passage, would Jesus be likely to give a praiseworthy connotation to a term associated with a horrible mutilation? In his culture, to be a eunuch meant not only the loss of virility but also religious excommunication, because it contradicted God's will in creation. The Mosaic law excluded eunuchs from the priesthood[15] and ostracized "anyone whose testicles are crushed or whose penis is cut off" (Deut. 23:1). Even a castrated animal was deemed unfit for cultic sacrifice.[16] In the Jewish community during Jesus' century, Josephus asserted: "Shun eunuchs and avoid all dealing with those who have deprived themselves of their virility; . . . expel them as though they had committed infanticide."[17] Inflicting such treatment on oneself was so contemptible that Paul hurls at those determined to circumcise Gentile converts this hyperbole: "I wish those who disturb you would castrate themselves!" (Gal. 5:12). Prima facie it is unlikely that Jesus took what was associated with a despicable condition and made it a laudatory term for describing the spiritually self-castrated.

Jesus' response to actual eunuchs may have paralleled his response to lepers. Although the Torah required that lepers as well as eunuchs be segregated from the righteous and treated contemptuously, he did not shun them. Jesus touched such untouchables and treated them with compassion, but he did not advocate that his disciples imitate them and become spiritual lepers.

At the beginning of Jesus' teachings in Matthew 19, some Pharisees set the stage for the dialogue to follow by this question: "Is it lawful for a man to divorce his wife for any cause?" According to the Torah, a husband could write "a divorce certificate" if he found "something obnoxious" (Deut. 24:1, New Jewish Translation) about his wife. At issue in Jesus' era was what types of conduct made a wife obnoxious. Some rabbis argued that grounds for divorce include husband scolding that is loud enough to be heard outside the home, spoiling food under preparation, going out with hair unbound, or the husband finding someone else more beautiful.[18]

Divorce was exclusively a male prerogative in Israelite culture and no hearing was required before a court of justice. A wife could be divorced without her consent but she could not divorce her husband even if he were irresponsible, cruel, lecherous, or otherwise offensive. Before Jesus' ministry began, Herod Antipas divorced a Nabatean princess in order to marry his brother's wife.[19] Jesus found the sanctity of marriage denigrated by a widespread flippant attitude toward divorce, extending from his Galilean ruler to the common people. He must have been chagrined to find that repentance and reconciliation was little considered by the dominating husband for even minor domestic offenses. Marital forgiveness fell short of seven times, not to mention his "seventy times seven" standard (Matt. 18:22).

Over against this, Jesus declared what he held to be the Creator's reason for making two human sexes. Jesus thought that divorce law should be subordinated to the creation principle. He directed his interlocutors to the view of marriage contained in the Garden of Eden story, which stresses sexual companionship. A man's bonding with his wife should replace the close ties he had with his parents.[20] After pointing to the ideal of a permanent splicing, Jesus stated that Moses allowed divorce legislation as a way of dealing with a moral malady. Jesus diagnosed the marriage-destroying disease as cardiosclerosis (Greek, *sklerocardia*), or hardening of the heart. When this condition persists in one or both spouses, legal controls for divorce are needed. Eric Fuchs comments:

> Jesus does not criticize Moses, . . . but he does challenge the turn-about effected by Jewish doctors who raise a contingent law to the status of a norm in God's will. . . . Any repudiation of the wife by the husband is . . . a checkmate to God's plan, will, and promise. . . . Marriage is recognized as the place of man's and woman's apprehending of the promise and grace of God; . . . it can also signify (and more cruelly than in any other realm of human existence) the refusal to believe in the creative and recreative grace of love, a closing-in upon oneself in fear and covetousness—in brief, a refusal of the other.[21]

Jesus acknowledged the Roman practice that permitted either spouse to initiate a divorce. He taught: "Whoever divorces his wife and marries another commits adultery against her; and if she divorces her husband and marries another, she commits adultery" (Mark 10:11–12). "The severity of his pronouncement," Walter Wink comments, "is intended to prevent the wholesale dumping of ex-wives onto the streets."[22] Prostitution was then the usual result of cutting off a wife from the economic security of marriage.

On hearing Jesus' emphasis on permanent commitment, his disciples are astounded by his radical teaching, even as they are by his teaching on the peril of wealth, also recorded in the same chapter of Matthew.[23] They cynically quip that the bond of marriage should be avoided if freeing yourself from it is wrong. To this Jesus first replies that not all can accept his fidelity ideal of no divorce or remarriage.[24] He recognizes that only some have the capacity for the turn-the-other-cheek suffering that he advocates. The issue here is not the indissolubility of marriage but whether one can live when abandoned and not remarry. Jesus then comments on two types of physical eunuchs and a spiritual type of "eunuch." He associates the third type, the celibacy of the de-yoked, with a shattering disability, not with a heroic ideal state.

Jesus' moral imperative of agape, steadfast love when there may be no reciprocation, is exceedingly demanding. Openness to the return of the faithless, not abandonment, is the way of sacrificial love. William Countryman notes that this involves a rejection of patriarchal values: "Jesus demanded that the wife no longer be regarded as disposable (i.e., divorceable) property. Indeed, husband and wife were to be understood as human equals who now constitute one flesh."[25]

The theme of steadfast love in spite of infidelity is at the core of the prophetic theology that Jesus admired. After becoming reconciled with his adulterous spouse, Hosea thought of God as having a similar enduring affection for unfaithful Israel.[26] Likewise, Ezekiel articulated God's brokenheartedness over his precious bride Jerusalem, who brazenly prostituted herself to foreign lovers, and the divine forgiveness awaiting her return to him.[27] Isaiah also used the metaphor of God as the husband of wayward Israel. Her Spouse says: "In sudden anger for a moment I hid my face from you; but with everlasting love I will have compassion on you" (Isa. 54:8). In imitation of God, spouses should attempt to overcome the painful estrangement that follows betrayed trust.

Some of the earliest as well as most recent Gospel interpreters agree that Jesus' eunuch metaphor is unrelated to lifelong virginity. Rather, it reinforces what he had just stated: "What God has joined, let no one separate" (Matt. 19:6). Both Justin and Clement of Alexandria used the eunuch saying to demonstrate that Jesus did not sanction remarriage after divorce.[28] Jesuit Quentin Quesnell concludes his study of Jesus' teaching on marriage in this way: "A man must in marriage take the risk of staking all he has and is on one person, becoming one flesh with her. . . . To continue this loyal and perfect love, even when the love is not returned, is effectively to make oneself a eunuch."[29] William Thompson, another Catholic exegete, agrees with Quesnell that "the 'eunuchs for the Kingdom' are those men who, although estranged from their wives for various reasons, will not remarry but will attempt to reunite with them and in this way remain faithful to their marriage covenant." Thompson argues that Jesus may have personally been in such a situation.[30] Catholic theologian Uta Ranke-Heinemann criticizes those popes who have used Jesus' eunuch saying as their "favorite motto" for defending the vow of virginity. She maintains that the context shows that Jesus was rather defending the "voluntary renunciation of remarriage."[31] Paul Dinter also interprets this passage as referring to celibacy after marital separation.[32]

On examining the eunuch saying vis-à-vis the entire context of Matthew's Gospel, Bruce Malina and Richard Rohrbaugh note that no interest is expressed in celibacy elsewhere. They think that the saying ought to be related to the community that produced Matthew in which divorce in order to remarry was not permitted. A spouse who has been dishonored should strive to forgive the misconduct rather than seek divorce. Jesus commends spouses who patiently and chastely await the return of their prodigal partners. Malina and Rohrbaugh conclude: "Concern for reconciliation here fits in well with the moral teaching of Jesus throughout Matthew."[33]

The first example of Matthew's treatment of Christian love pertains to the presumed sexual misconduct of Mary. "Her husband Joseph, being a just man and unwilling to expose her to public disgrace" decides to accept the child being carried by Mary as his own. In that episode, which is found only in Matthew's Gospel, compassion replaces any impulse of revenge. Joseph's grace in a situation that he initially thinks is disgraceful is the gospel in microcosm. The mutual reconciliation of Joseph and Mary becomes the epiphany of God-with-us, Emmanuel.[34] Consider also the list of Christian virtues contained in the parable of the last judgment, found only in the Gospel from Matthew's point of view. Chastity is not mentioned, but the expression of kindness in various practical ways is emphasized.[35] In the passage immediately prior to Jesus' discussion of marriage and divorce, he teaches that God's forgiveness is withheld from the unforgiving.[36]

Even if Jesus' cryptic aphorism on eunuchs did not originally belong to the context of his marriage and divorce teaching, it is still unlikely that Jesus was acknowledging by means of it that he was a celibate and was encouraging others to take a vow of perpetual virginity. Assistance is given on this point by the Jesus Seminar, composed of dozens of biblical scholars from a variety of religious traditions. They examined carefully over a six-year period each saying in the Gospels that is alleged to have been from Jesus. After cutting out "Let anyone accept this who can," as words that he did not say, the Seminar ranked the saying about three types of eunuchs among the top fifth of those he probably uttered. Seventy-seven percent of the Seminar Fellows judged the saying to have first circulated independently of its later context in Matthew, and suggested this meaning:

> The saying may be understood as an attack on a male-dominated, patriarchal society in which male virility and parenthood were the exclusive norms. The true Israel consisted of priests, Levites, and full-blooded male Judeans, all of whom were capable of fathering children. Eunuchs made so by others and males born without testicles were not complete and so could not be counted among true Israelites and were therefore excluded from temple service. . . . If this saying goes back to Jesus, it is possible that he is undermining the depreciation of yet another marginal group, this time the eunuchs, who were subjected to segregation and devaluation, as were the poor, toll collectors, prostitutes, women generally, and children. . . . In any case, the sayings on castration should not be taken as Jesus' authorization for an ascetic lifestyle; his behavior suggests that he celebrated life by eating, drinking, and fraternizing freely with both women and men.[37]

The interpretation of the Jesus Seminar can be supported by a teaching of Isaiah, a prophet whom Jesus admired. Judean prophets were aware of the cruel practice among their kings, and also among foreign royalty, of castrating palace servants to make them safer for work in their harems.[38] Isaiah announced that the Torah restriction was abolished:

> Thus says Yahweh: "No eunuch should say, 'I am just a barren tree.' The eunuchs who observe my sabbaths, who choose to do my will and cling to my covenant, will receive from me a name better than sons and daughters. I will give them a memorial in my own house and within my walls; I will give them an everlasting name that will not be cut off." (Isa. 56:3–5)

2. The New Testament's silence on Jesus' marital status indicates that he was single.

PRO

Scholars have occasionally interpreted the absence of historical references to Jesus' wife as evidence that he was celibate. Protestant professor Ben Witherington comments: "That Jesus' marital status is a nonissue in the Gospels probably indicates that he was never married."[39] Catholic professors John Meier and Michael Cook find it implausible that Jesus' familial relations and women friends should be explicitly named while no mention is made of his wife.[40] Anglican bishop John Robinson states: "If Jesus, like his brothers, had been known to have been married, it is inconceivable that Paul would not have appealed to the fact."[41] Jesuit Bruno Brinkman accepts Robinson's argument, for he thinks that Paul once tried to list all married leaders who were spreading the gospel.[42]

Jesus probably had children if he married, but there are no allusions to such in historical records. Would not the offspring of a person who was worshiped as a unique manifestation of God gain recognition and have their names recorded for posterity? Jesuit Francis Cleary suggests that Jesus' institution of the Eucharist reflects that he never married and fathered children. Cleary believes that King David's son Absalom had no children and so he set up a commemorative pillar to himself so that his name would not be forgotten in subsequent generations.[43] Likewise, "Jesus was to die without having begotten children; but instead of erecting a monument to perpetuate his name, Jesus instituted a special meal in which he would be truly present sacramentally wherever his followers gathered in obedience to remember him."[44]

CON

The Gospels were largely collections of sermons used by the earliest Christian preachers that only incidentally supply biographical information. For only ten percent of the span of Jesus' life is there New Testament data. For the teen years and the twenties, when humans are generally the most active sexually, there is no historical material about Jesus.

The absence of biblical laws forbidding celibacy cannot be used as an argument that such was sanctioned. Legal prohibitions arise out of pragmatic community needs. They are not directed against what no one does, but against the deviant behavior of some within the group. Had the Torah stated, "Polyandry is prohibited," this would indicate that some Israelite women had multiple husbands. Contrariwise, the Torah law prohibiting the wearing of clothing associated with the opposite sex suggests that there were some Israelite transvestites.[45]

The Gospel writers may not have intended to be silent with respect to the wives of those in Jesus' band. Places in the English translation of the New Testament where "woman" is found, "wife" may be an appropriate translation. In Greek there is one word, *gune*, that means either "woman" or "wife" according to context. Etymologically it is associated with one who gives birth (*gone*), a mother.[46] The New Revised Standard Version provides a more precise contextual translation at places by changing "woman" in the King James Version to "wife" (1 Cor. 11:3) or "married woman" (Rom. 7:2) In Luke's Gospel, *gune* is used in reference to spouses of particular husbands[47] or to women, unmarried or married.[48]

The inability to demonstrate fully that Jesus was married cannot be taken as proof that he was not. The absence of evidence is not the same as evidence of absence. The Gospels do not record that Jesus smiled or laughed, for example, but that silence gives no basis for inferring that he was never cheerful. Also, it is invalid to conclude that Jesus was immune to viruses just because there is no mention of his being sick. Had Jesus never smiled or had he always been in perfect health, those conditions that deviate widely from the norm would more likely have been remembered and recorded. Again, since nothing is recorded about Jesus' physical appearance, it was probably not extraordinary. Unlike Zacchaeus or Saul, who are described as exceptionally short or tall,[49] Jesus was probably of normal stature. Again, unlike John the Baptizer who was clothed with camel's hair,[50] Jesus' clothing was apparently not unusual.

A rather perverse example of the misuse of documentary silence has to do with Jesus' excretory functions. As with the biographies of most historical figures, there is mention in the Gospels of Jesus eating but not of his having bowel movements. Some second-century Christians, who wished to diminish Jesus' participation in animal functions and treat him as a supernatural figure, deduced that "Jesus ate and drank in a peculiar manner without the food passing out of his body."[51]

Theologian Charles Davis turns the silence argument around and uses it as his main reason for a married Jesus:

> If he [Jesus] had insisted upon celibacy it would have created a stir, a reaction which would have left some trace. So, the lack of mention of Jesus' marriage in the Gospels is a strong argument not against but for the hypothesis of marriage, because any practice or advocacy of voluntary celibacy would, in the Jewish

context of the time, have been so unusual as to have attracted much attention and comment.[52]

Ancient writers were less likely to find significant and thus remember women whose behavior was not out of the ordinary. We would not know from the Gospels that Peter was married if his mother-in-law had not once been mentioned.[53] Jean Audet comments:

> If the chance of her having a fever had not happened to bring Jesus to see Peter's mother-in-law, the gospel tradition would in fact have observed total silence on the disciples' marriage. Could we therefore conclude that not one of them was married? No, we could not. All we can say is this: the ideas and the customs of the time and place are enough to make it probable that most of the apostles were married; it is even quite possible that they all were, without exception.[54]

If Jesus were celibate and had taught that the unmarried life is better for Christians, it is surprising that Paul writes to the Corinthians that he had received direction from Jesus on other matters pertaining to marriage but no word regarding celibacy.[55] The apostle acknowledges that his advice on the latter subject is merely his own opinion; he observes that those who marry will have troubles they might have avoided.[56] Joan Timmerman regards Paul's admission that he could not call upon Jesus to justify his celibate lifestyle to be a weighty argument from silence in favor of a married Jesus.[57] In that Corinthian letter, Paul refers to himself as nonmarried (*agamos*), which signifies his de-married situation as a widower or a divorcé; he distinguishes *agamos* from *parthenos*, which refers in that context to a person who has not previously married.[58] Paul admits that he is an exception to the apostles in not having a wife accompany him.[59] A plausible reason why he does not mention Jesus along with his apostles and his brothers who traveled with their wives is that he was discussing a current issue and was appealing to the practice of missionaries who were then itinerating. Another reason might be that Jesus' wife did not travel with her husband during his public ministry.

To read many of the biblical genealogies, one might presume that "begetting" was exclusively a male enterprise! For example, a genealogy in Genesis lists eleven male offspring of Seth over thousands of years, but no women are named.[60] The four mothers included with several dozen fathers in a listing of Jesus' ancestors all stood out because they had been involved in sexually irregular conduct.[61] That listing contains the names of Jesus' paternal grandfather and great-grandfather but not his grandmothers. Historian Vern Bullough has noted:

> Almost everything in the past has been written by men, not by women. Generally male writers have most often pictured women when they departed from the norm, when they became notorious, and only rarely when they fulfilled their expected role of wife and mother or sister.[62]

The absence of overt mention of Jesus' wife does not therefore indicate that he had none. Moreover, since females are not likely to be mentioned, perhaps any children that Jesus might have had were daughters. In spite of a strong sense of duty among Jews to procreate, there were, of course, cases of infertility. So there is the possibility that Jesus was sterile or that his wife was barren. If such had been the case, it might help to explain why there is no reference in the Gospels to the creation account that stresses procreation, and why Jesus referred wholly to the creation story that does not associate procreation with marriage. Also, any children that Jesus might have had could have died before he became an itinerating teacher. The mortality rates of the young in ancient times made the probability of such a tragedy much greater than today.

Further, if Jesus did have children, they did not become prominent in the life of the early church and thus did not become memorable on their own merit. Jesus and his movement belonged to the prophetic stream of Hebrew tradition that did not ascribe significance to individuals merely because of their family status. Even though the prophets married,[63] in most cases no mention is made of their children. Isaiah's children were recorded by his disciples not because they inherited a charismatic mantle, but quite incidentally because their names happened to be titles of their father's sermons.[64] It is probable that Peter, as a married Jew, had children. But even though the early church elevated him to a preeminent standing among the apostles, there is no mention of any son of his in apostolic history. This demonstrates only that the activities of Peter's children were not significant enough to be remembered in the oral tradition and later recorded in scripture. By contrast, Rufus and Alexander are named as sons of Simon of Cyrene, probably because they were notable among second generation Christians.[65]

Another conjecture is that information on children and/or a wife of Jesus may have been removed by those who assembled what would become the New Testament corpus. Editors who completed that canonical process centuries after the time of Jesus probably had attitudes toward sexuality that were little affected by the Jewish culture. Asceticism of Gentile rootage caused Christians from the monastic era onward to be disdainful of marital relations by holy men.

Jesus might have become a widower prior to his public ministry, and he may or may not have remarried later. In the former case, the lack of reference to his first wife would be understandable, for that would have been in the period prior to his becoming known by Christians who would transmit information to subsequent generations. In the latter case, remarriage was not required in Jesus' culture if a man had already begotten children—as has earlier been noted. French priest Jean Barreau, in his biography of Jesus, speculates that he was briefly married before his wife died.[66]

Jerusalem scholar Schalom Ben-Chorin writes: "I am convinced that Jesus of Nazareth, like any rabbi in Israel, was married. His apostles and opponents would have mentioned it, if he had differed from the general custom." Ben-Chorin points out that we know nothing about the wives of Hillel, Shammai, Jesus, and many other notable men of that era and culture, but had they been unmarried, surely their adversaries would have pointed to their violation of sacred duty as a basis for criticism.[67] The fact that Jesus' marital status is a nonissue in the Gospels suggests that he conformed to cultural expectations in regard to marriage.

3. Celibacy was associated with holiness in Palestine during Jesus' era.

PRO

A Jewish religious community called the Essenes was located at Qumran near the Dead Sea during the time of Jesus. A few scholars have argued that their lifestyle influenced the early Christians. According to George Buchanan, Jesus and his disciples shared the Essene belief that the age to come would be only for saintly celibates.[68] Reginald Fuller also presumes that Jesus, like the members of the Qumran community, renounced marriage "to engage in the final battle between the children of light and the children of darkness."[69]

Geza Vermes concludes that Jesus was apparently celibate after his baptism because he, like his contemporary Philo, associated sexual continence with the prophetic calling.[70] That Greek philosopher based this notion on the Torah, which states that Moses asked the Israelites to refrain from sexual intercourse during the days that God's revelation was being given on Mount Sinai.[71] Moses practiced celibacy throughout the period he served as God's spokesperson, according to Philo: "He had disdained (marital intercourse) for many a day, almost from the time when, possessed by the spirit, he entered his work as prophet, since he held it fitting to hold himself always in readiness to receive the oracular messages."[72]

Edward Peters offers this reason for Jesus' celibacy: "It was entirely in accord with Old Law tradition that the Redeemer, as priest and as warrior-king, should remain continent while offering sacrifice and waging war against sin-activites, which fill his entire life."[73] Robert Stern also associates Jesus with the biblical office of priest:

> Jesus, the one Priest of the new dispensation, never married. . . . Celibacy was seen above all else as continence, and continence as an abstention from a necessarily polluting and profoundly worldly desire and behavior. The Hebrew priest, the pagan priest, and pre-eminently the Christian priest, needed to be a man of God, a man apart, a purified man; accordingly he had to renounce or abstain from sexual behavior.[74]

CON

The prevailing view of biblical scholars is that Jesus was not significantly influenced by the Essenes, who are not even mentioned in the New Testament. Although Jesus as well as the Essenes accepted much of the Mosaic legislation, the dissimilarities between the two were greater than the similarities.[75] Moreover, as Linda Elder points out, "no published text from Qumran mandates celibacy."[76] Rather, the discoveries at Qumran and elsewhere of documents written by the Essenes indicate that the sect was composed of married persons who engaged in a cultic continence of limited duration.[77] One scroll refers to members of the community taking wives and fathering children.[78] In addition, female skeletons have been found in several cemeteries at Qumran, showing that women were not excluded. Only the secondary sources of Philo, Josephus, and Pliny—none of whom were members of the Essene community—provide evidence of permanent celibacy being required.[79]

In the biblical culture, marriage was expected in every vocation, including the priesthood.[80] Regarding the requirement for priests in the Book of Leviticus, Judith Wegner comments:

Unlike religions that elevate celibacy above marriage, Israelite religion insisted that even its highest religious functionary take a wife and beget children. Sexuality was an integral part of human life, and marriage and paternity were indispensable aspects of "complete" manhood.[81]

Even among the Nazirites, an Israelite sect noted for its temporary vows of abstinence,[82] refraining from coitus was not expected. A story in the Book of Judges dramatically illustrates that Israelites saw no virtue in remaining virginal throughout life. Jephthah made a rash vow that if he were successful in battle he would sacrifice whatever he encountered on returning to his home. Tragically he found that he had obligated himself to kill his only child, because she came out to greet him. His daughter was not upset so much over knowing that she would be sacrificed as from realizing that she would die without having been married. Accordingly, she requested time to "bewail her virginity" with her companions.[83]

Celibacy was rejected both in theory and in practice in the traditions that influenced Jesus. When Philo wrote of celibacy, he was more influenced by ascetic Greek philosophy than by Hebrew tradition. "In his enthusiasm for the systems of Plato and Pythagoras he surpassed all his contemporaries," noted ancient historian Eusebius.[84] There is no indication that Philo's sexual outlook affected Palestinian Judaism; allusion to his writings is not found in ancient rabbinic or New Testament literature. He distorts the scriptural story of Moses in claiming that continual celibacy was a prerequisite for receiving divine revelation. Only temporary sexual continence for ritual or practical reasons was sanctioned in Jewish tradition. Eating, bathing, and sexual relations were forbidden on the annual Day of Atonement.[85] More extended sexual abstinence was permitted for certain situations: sailors were allowed six months; Torah students and camel drivers, one month. On the other hand, laborers should have marital relations twice a week and the unemployed should perform their sexual duty every day.[86]

Paul allowed a husband and wife, by mutual agreement, to set aside conjugal rights during a period devoted to prayer.[87] His position was counter to that of some Corinthians who rejected sexual intercourse. At the beginning of his discussion of marriage, the apostle quotes a slogan of that opposition group. He writes: "Regarding the matters about which you wrote: 'A man should not have sexual intimacy with a woman.'" The lack of proper punctuation in earlier translations has resulted in attributing to Paul a position that he rejected. The prevailing interpretation has been that of Tertullian, who presumed that Paul is here stating that "it is evil to have contact with a woman."[88] Translators of the New Revised Standard Version and the Revised English Bible have accepted my criticism of previous translations and now provide crucial quotation marks to distinguish Paul's outlook from that of a group within the Corinthian community who advocated complete sexual abstinence.[89]

Hirschel Revel is not indulging in overstatement when he asserts: "The voluntary renunciation of marriage is a conception utterly foreign to Judaism."[90] But the ancient Jews were much more positive toward sexuality than the mere avoidance of celibacy and monasticism. The many-splendored purposes of connubial love were extolled, and the extremes of undisciplined license and sexual deprivation were abhorred. A talmudic scholar summed up the position of ancient Judaism, studding it with biblical quotes:

> Any man who has no wife lives without joy, without blessing, and without goodness. Without joy, for it is written, "You shall rejoice in your house." Without blessing, for it is written, "Cause a blessing to rest on your house." Without goodness, for it is written, "It is not good that the man should be alone."[91]

Some leaders of the early Mormon church believed that Jesus emerges as a holier traveling preacher when viewed as married to his female companions. Not long after settling in Utah, Apostle Orson Hyde declared: "There was a marriage in Cana of

Galilee. . . . Jesus Christ was married on that occasion. If he was never married, his intimacy with Mary, Martha, and the other Mary also, who Jesus loved, must have been highly unbecoming and improper, to say the best of it."[92] The founder of the Utah Mormons, according to one of his wives, agreed with Hyde:

> Brigham Young, in one of his sermons . . . declared that "Jesus Christ was a practical polygamist; Mary and Martha, the sisters of Lazarus, were his plural wives, and Mary Magdalene was another. Also, the bridal feast at Cana of Galilee, where Jesus turned the water into wine, was on the occasion of one of his own marriages."[93]

Mormons continue to associate the Cana wedding with Jesus' own marriage. Ogdon Kraut reasons that if the wedding were not of someone in the family of Jesus' mother, why would she be anxious over the supply of wine becoming exhausted?[94] Donavan Joyce also believes that Jesus was the Cana bridegroom, and that it is "absolutely certain that Jesus was a married man."[95]

4. Jesus rebelled against his Jewish heritage in which marriage was expected of religious leaders.

PRO

Although Jesus was raised in a pious family of the Jewish community, some think he severed his ties with Judaism when he became mature. Accordingly, he expressed his nonconformity to the Hebrew doctrine of creation by rejecting marriage for himself. Max Thurian writes: "Christ did not experience marriage, physical love and sexual union. . . . Jesus Christ calls in question the system of creation and nature."[96] The Vatican has asserted that it is fallacious to presume that Jesus was influenced by the prevailing outlook on sexuality of his Jewish community. Its semiofficial journal stated: "Christ was anything but conditioned by the cultural and religious atmosphere of his time. . . . A 'married Christ' would not have made flower in the world the marvel of virginity."[97] That outlook is echoed by Catholic priest Peter Rinaldi who thinks that Jesus opposed what the Jews had established as the prerequisite for righteous adulthood. Rinaldi writes: "There is not a shred of evidence in the New Testament or in the early Christian writers that can be seriously invoked to prove that Jesus could have been married. . . . Both by temperament and choice Jesus set his course against ancient tradition."[98] Another Catholic, Sidney Callahan, treats marriage as a cultural confinement from which Jesus, "an abnormal Outsider," rebelled. She describes his liberation in this way:

> As a feminist I think Jesus' celibacy was needed to break open the 'normal' bondage of women, marriage, and family life. . . . The holy family should be one where the mother is not dependent on the father and the father doesn't impose marriage and spouse on dependent children. Marriage at puberty isn't such a hot idea either. . . . We need time and loneliness and rebellion.[99]

CON

Rudolf Bultmann, one of the most influential New Testament interpreters in the twentieth century, thinks that there is little biographical information about Jesus that is historically sound. Yet he admits: "It is at least clear that Jesus actually lived as a Jewish rabbi. . . . As such he disputes over questions of the Law with pupils and opponents."[100] A mishnaic injunction states categorically: "An unmarried man may not be a teacher."[101] Celibacy was not kosher in the Israelite religion, and Jesus grew up in that tradition.

Wendell Phillips writes in his biography about Jesus' participation in Jewish customs:

> From Luke 2:42, 51 we learn that when Jesus was on the threshold of adulthood he was the obedient son of Joseph. It is reasonable to assume that, like his brothers, who were married, as

we know from 1 Cor. 9:5, Jesus . . . would have expected his
father to . . . initiate similar arrangements for him. . . . The
unbiblical notion that Jesus was unmarried and a perpetual
virgin originated with the second century heretics Basilides and
Tatian.[102]

In the Hebrew patriarchy, it was the parents, especially the fathers, who were responsible for finding suitable mates for their
children. The marriage account of Isaac and Rebekah depicts customs that were typical throughout the biblical era. The betrothal
was initiated by the heads of two families. The fathers or their
agents negotiated the agreement, whereupon the boy's represen-
tative turned over the dowry payment to the girl's guardians. The
bridal couple played an insignificant role in the transaction. Isaac,
who was not consulted, simply "took Rebekah, and she became
his wife, and he loved her" (Gen. 24:67). Biblical sociologist
Roland de Vaux states: "The parents took all the decisions when
a marriage was being arranged. Neither the girl nor, often, the
youth was consulted."[103] Malina and Rohrbaugh assert: "Under
normal circumstances in the world of Jesus, individuals really did
not get married; rather families did. One family offered a male, the
other a female. Their wedding stood for the wedding of the larger
extended families."[104]

During the ancient period of Christianity, the Jewish custom of
parents arranging early marriage continued. A fourth-century
church manual enjoins:

Fathers: . . . at the time when your children are of marriageable
age, join them in wedlock and settle them together, lest in the
heat and fervor of their age their course of life become dissolute,
and you be required to give an account by the Lord God in the
day of judgment.[105]

Parents desired teenage marriage to maximize progeny for their
extended family as well as to provide a remedy for illicit sex. A

line in John Milton's famous poem shows that the latter purpose continued to be praised by Christians: "Hail wedded love. . . . By thee adulterous lust was driven from men."[106]

Since we know as a matter of fact that the apostles were married and traveled with their wives on Christian missions, Jesus evidently would not have objected to that mode of living. Of course, those apostles could have married before coming under Jesus' influence. If so, the impact of his marital status could not be fully measured until second generation Christians came of age. Had Jesus been a lifelong celibate and advised his disciples to adopt his lifestyle, then they would be expected to enjoin future members of "the body of Christ" to emulate the "Head." On the other hand, if Jesus had married it would be expected that the apostles would advise the church leadership in subsequent generations to follow that pattern. The latter situation seems to have been the case since there is no evidence of a celibate group of Christians in the century after the beginning of that community.

The Pastoral letters, which belong to the generation after the apostles, show marriage to have been expected of bishops, elders, and deacons.[107] Ascetics who advocated abstinence from marriage and certain foods were criticized as betraying the Christian doctrine of creation. A letter to Timothy affirms that "everything created by God is good and nothing is to be rejected, provided it is received with thanksgiving" (1 Tim. 4:2–4). An expectation of successful marriage for church officers is displayed in this question: "If someone does not know how to manage his own household, how can he care for God's church?" (1 Tim. 3:5) Assumed here is a close parallel between the oversight of one's family and the wider responsibility for one's Christian community. Since the local churches in which the officers served were house churches, the ability to carry out familial duties had a direct bearing on leadership ability in the "household of faith."[108]

Some time after the New Testament was completed, the Apostolic Canons were published in a manual of church discipline. One of the rules, which was not approved in Latin Christianity, reinforces the doctrine of the Pastoral letters. It states that any cleric "blasphemously misrepresents God's work of creation" who abstains from marriage, meat, or wine "out of abhorrence, forgetting that all things are exceedingly good, and that God made man male and female." Anyone who has such an outlook is told to mend his ways or be deposed from office and expelled from the church.[109] Another rule follows the Pastoral letters in requiring "that the bishop be a man who has one wife . . . and has brought up his children to revere God."[110]

Personal Reasons

1. Jesus was unwilling to ask
a spouse to share his lifestyle.

PRO

As a man of compassion Jesus would not have asked any woman to marry someone who would have "no place to lay his head" (Matt. 8:20). He practiced what he taught about counting the cost before tackling a difficult task.[111] Accordingly, Protestant biblical scholar Vernon McCasland thinks that Jesus did not want a mate to undergo the hardships he personally anticipated: "The daring role he assumed for himself had no place in it for a woman at his side. The uncertainty, the poverty, the danger, the implied final agony, were not the basis on which to found a marriage, to rear a family."[112]

Catholic biblical scholar Joseph Blenkinsopp suggests that "Jesus was celibate because he was too poor to marry."[113] It would have been unloving to a wife for him to have married, knowing the absence of living wages that would confront him as an unemployed craftsman. Similarly, religious journalist Louis Cassels writes: "Jesus chose a life of celibacy for a good and obvious reason; he could not support a wife and children while carrying on an unpaid itinerant ministry."[114]

CON

Those who speculate that Jesus voluntarily remained a bachelor because of his poverty as wandering teacher assume incorrectly that Jews did not marry early in life. Marriage was more of a family choice than an individual choice in Jesus' culture, as we have seen, and arranging marriages during the second decade of life was the norm.[115] In ancient Jewish betrothals "it was the word of the respective fathers rather than that of the parties themselves which gave binding validity to a promise of marriage, especially so as in many cases the parties themselves must have been minors."[116] There is no basis for presuming that marriage for ancient Jews was postponed until they had completed three decades of life.

The New Testament indicates that Jesus left the carpentry business and began to proclaim the gospel when he was "about thirty years old" (Luke 3:23), which would have been middle age in his culture. At the time when Jesus was likely to marry, poverty would not have been a problem. There is no evidence suggesting that construction workers in Galilee, a productive agricultural region, were not compensated adequately to support a family. Since Joseph and Jesus had the same occupation, it is likely that one could afford to marry as easily as the other. Meier judges that Jesus was probably no poorer than most of his fellow Nazarenes.[117]

Perhaps Jesus and his wife decided that she would not accompany him while he was itinerating from town to town. Akiba, who lived in the same era as Jesus, gained permission from his wife to leave for some years in order to travel about in connection with his rabbinical responsibilities.[118] Jesus' wife could have stayed in Nazareth to attend to pressing domestic responsibilities, such as child and/or parent care. Or, realizing that Jesus was alienated from his family, and that there were citizens of Nazareth who wanted to lynch him,[119] it is altogether possible that she separated from him for her self-protection. Or again, her health could have been too frail or her safety anxieties could have been too great for camping out with the traveling band. However, for much of the time that Jesus was away from Nazareth, his life was not one of continual movement from place to place. After leaving Nazareth, he settled in the fishing town of Capernaum. The earliest Gospel refers to Jesus' "home" there.[120]

2. Jesus was not heterosexually oriented.

PRO

American biblical scholar Morton Smith discovered in 1958 at the Mar Saba monastery in the Dead Sea region an excerpt from a manuscript that suggests that the Carpocratian sect thought Jesus engaged in a homosexual tryst. The excerpt may be from a letter by Clement of Alexandria, but its authenticity has not been proven.[121] The second century Carpocratians were known for their "licentious" behavior and were considered heretical.[122] Clement alleged that they desecrated the Agape, the Christian love-feast, by extinguishing the lamps and having intercourse with anyone who pleased them.[123] The Carpocratians were aware of the now lost scroll entitled the Secret Gospel of Mark, which associates Jesus' resurrection with male bonding. It states:

> The youth, looking upon him [Jesus] loved him and began to beseech him that he might be with him. And going out of the tomb they came into the house of the youth, for he was rich. After six days Jesus told him what to do and in the evening the youth comes to him wearing a linen cloth over his naked body. And he remained with him that night, for Jesus taught him the mystery of the kingdom of God.[124]

That youth might be identified with the one mentioned in Mark who fled naked in the middle of the night when Jesus was arrested in the garden of Gethsemane.[125]

Anglican bishop Hugh Montefiore suggested that Jesus did not marry because he had a homosexual personality orientation. If Jesus was "not by nature the marrying sort," as Montefiore delicately described the situation a generation ago, having such a disposition without practicing homosexuality would not have constituted sin.[126] Robinson, stimulated by that fellow Anglican priest, asks whether Jesus had a homosexual or a heterosexual tendency. He could have had either, Robinson thinks, even though the traditional answer has been neither.[127]

With regard to Jesus, John Boswell—a historian with a homosexual orientation—claims that "the only persons with whom the Gospels suggest he had any special relationship were men, especially Saint John, who carefully describes himself throughout his Gospel as the disciple whom Jesus loved."[128] Boswell points out that Aelred, a medieval homosexual monk, found an example of his passion in Jesus who allowed John "to recline on his breast as a sign of his special love."[129] Troy Perry, the founder of a gay denomination of Christians, also considers some of Jesus' behavior to be sexually suggestive.[130] Perry notes that Jesus constantly associated himself with a group of male disciples and occasionally had bodily contact with them. One Gospel states that at the Last Supper "there was leaning on Jesus' bosom one of his disciples," another Gospel states that he was kissed by a disciple after that final dinner.[131]

Tom Horner has written a book on homosexuality in the Bible that contains a chapter on Jesus' sexuality. Although Horner does not think there is enough evidence to prove Jesus was gay, "he was not the type of person who would have displayed any hostility toward those who might have had homosexual relationships." Jesus commended eunuchs who, according to Horner, often assumed passive roles as homosexual practitioners.[132] Horner also states:

> Everything that we read in the Gospels indicates that Jesus' intimate group of disciples consisted of either single men or men who did not consider their marriage vows the first loyalty of their lives. And with these men, or at least with some of

them, Jesus had a relationship that was unusually warm and intimate.[133]

Speculation has also been made that Jesus might have been bisexual. Rosemary Ruether portrays a person who was neither married nor celibate. She suggests: "Jesus' life shows close special friendships with both men and women that included physical tenderness. . . . He could love both John and Mary Magdalene, physically embrace and be embraced by them, because first of all he knew them as friends, not as sexual objects."[134] Methodist pastor James Conn has expressed a similar position. He said: "I've always assumed Jesus' relationship with Mary Magdalene was hands-on stuff. And I have always been intrigued by the closeness between Jesus and his beloved disciple, John. John was apparently young and strong and handsome."[135] United Church of Christ minister Bill Johnson likewise thinks that Jesus expressed himself sexually with both women and men. He explains Jesus' bisexuality in this way:

As the gynandrous personification of Spirit in human flesh, Jesus was the paradigm of male/female Godliness fully experiencing life on this physical plane. . . . Men and women who intimately shared his earthly sojourn could well have been a significant lesbian/gay/bisexual community.[136]

Danish filmmaker Jens Thorsen tried in several European countries to produce *The Many Faces of Jesus*. Thorsen fantasized that Jesus engaged in sexual activity with various women. His swinging Jesus also enjoyed the companionship and sexual favors of John. Because of protests, the pornographic film has not been licensed for public screening.[137]

CON

Jesus had close companions of both sexes who accompanied him as he visited Palestinian villages, but having good friends does not imply sexual liaisons with them. John reclined next to Jesus at the Last Supper, but that usual Roman practice of dining in a prone position should not be associated with sexual behavior. Likewise, Judas' kiss of Jesus was understood as a common greeting in ancient Palestine.[138] In a culture where homosexual liaisons were regarded as an "abomination" (Lev. 20:13), a physical contact implying such behavior would hardly have been the prearranged method for Judas to identify Jesus to the Jewish authorities.

After thoroughly reviewing the Carpocratians' claim that Jesus was gay, historical Jesus specialist John Crossan dismisses the matter in this way: "I see no evidence that Jesus and the youth are engaged in anything shocking. And I prefer to let the Carpocratians alone in salivating over the incident."[139] Raymond Brown, in his definitive commentary on the narratives pertaining to Jesus' last week in Jerusalem, does not think the reference to the unclothed youth in Gethsemane should be associated with homosexual conduct. Brown finds in the account of the youth abandoning his garment on being seized no more than an expression of his anxiety to escape from his captors.[140]

3. Jesus was an ascetic who sacrificed sexual happiness.

PRO

An anonymous Christian of the third century thought that Jesus, like an ascetic Platonist,[141] gratified only those sensual impulses that were necessary for individual survival. He asserted:

> Christ did not submit to discharging the sexual function, for regarding the desires of the flesh, he accepted some as necessary, while others, which were unnecessary, he did not submit to. For if the flesh were deprived of food, drink, and clothing, it would be destroyed; but being deprived of lawless desire, it suffers no harm.[142]

English novelist D. H. Lawrence depicted the historical Jesus as an ascetic who, like Plato, thought of his body as a tomb.[143] In pursuit of self-mortification, Jesus withdrew from embracing others in a sensual manner. He was reluctant to become vulnerable, thinking that love was a selfless giving to others. Lawrence thought that Jesus encouraged his disciples "to love with dead bodies."

Lawrence expressed his disdain for that imagined nonsensual founder of Christianity by writing a short novel that he entitled *The Escaped Cock*. It tells of the way in which Jesus reversed his pre-crucifixion lifestyle after he arose in the flesh. The Easter rejuvenation enabled him to overcome his former contempt for phallic activity. Realizing at last that love involves receiving as well as giving, Jesus accepts "the tender touch of life." A priestess who massages his crucifixion wounds stimulates this response:

> He crouched to her, and he felt the blaze of his manhood and his power rise up in his loins, magnificent. "I am risen!" . . . He untied the string of linen tunic, and slipped the garment down, till he saw the white glow of her white-gold breasts. And he touched them, and he felt his life go molten. "Father!" he said, "why did you hide this from me?" And he touched her with the poignancy of wonder, and the marvelous piercing transcendence of desire. "Lo!" he said, "this is beyond prayer." . . . So he knew her, and was one with her.[144]

Biblical interpreter Samuel Terrien assumes that Jesus renounced some basic pleasures of life:

> Jesus was known to have stood beyond sexual affection, intimacy, or attachment. . . . Allusions to his prolonged periods of fasting and reminiscences of his nocturnal watches in solitude devoted to prayer strongly support the view that he was both celibate and chaste.

Terrien thinks that Jesus was unmarried even though at that time "Jewish men in general and religious teachers in particular always took a wife."[145]

Crossan maintains that Jesus was "more like a Cynic philosopher than anything else." Crossan thinks Jesus fits Epictetus' description of the celibate Cynic who frees himself from the entanglement of a wife and a home.[146] In a similar manner, Gerd Theissen believes that the Jesus group did not marry because they were like the Cynics who were contemptuous of wives, families, and possessions.[147]

CON

E. P. Sanders, a leading New Testament historian, argues that scholars such as Crossan "make an enormous mistake" in presuming that teachers of the Palestinian Jews modeled themselves after Cynic philosophers rather than the Israelite prophets.[148] During the era of Jesus, there is virtually no evidence that those philosophers were influential in Palestine.

In an article titled "Asceticism," Homes Dudden states:

Jesus nowhere teaches . . . that the gratification of the natural cravings is fraught with sin. He does not recommend men to treat their bodies with contempt. He does not suggest that flight from the world and disengagement from physical conditions is sanctification. He does not say that those who, for duty's sake, renounce the world, are on a higher spiritual level than those who do their duty in the world. He does not hint that the only way of avoiding sin lies in an austere renunciation of all those things from which an occasion of sin might arise. . . . He never implied that the married attain a lower grade of perfection than the continent.[149]

Biblical interpreter Jean von Allmen asserts: "The New Testament knows nothing of the very considerable depreciation of marriage which the influence of an ascetic dualism is to introduce into the church."[150] What von Allmen states about the New Testament's approval of marital relations applies also to the Semitic scriptures—the Hebrew Bible and the Arabic Quran. The life of Muhammad displays that personal emphasis upon fasting and long periods of prayer need not curtail approval of sexual indulgence.

Regarding participation in earthly pleasures, the Semitic religions can be distinguished from Buddhism. Adolf Harnack, an acknowledged expert church historian, comments on Jesus' lifestyle: "It is certain that the disciples did not understand their master to be a world-shunning ascetic. . . . They did not send away their wives. . . . How differently things developed in Buddhism from the very start!"[151] Harnack was probably thinking of Siddhartha's leaving his wife and child permanently in order to pursue religion seriously.

Rainer Maria Rilke, the famed German poet, viewed Jesus as one who overcame ascetic impulses and expressed himself sexually. According to one poem, Jesus fathers a child by Magdalene named Anna. D. H. Lawrence's novella about the dawning of Jesus' sexual awareness after his crucifixion may have been influenced by Rilke's "Vision of Christ" poems a generation earlier.[152]

Prominent New Testament scholar Rudolf Bultmann has written:

> Jesus desires no asceticism; he requires only the strength for sacrifice. As little as he repudiates property as such does he reject marriage or demand sexual asceticism. The ideal of virginity . . . is entirely foreign to Jesus; he required only purity and the sanctity of marriage.[153]

Jesus was not a recluse who preferred dwelling apart from the common people. He went fishing with his companions and slept on a cushion in the boat.[154] Jesus described his lifestyle as different from that of wilderness dweller John the Baptizer, as a joyful wedding party is different from a gloomy funeral procession.[155] He ate and drank with women and men in the villages he visited

and was fascinated by children. In his teachings Jesus used connubial celebrations to illustrate the optimum life.[156] He first
"manifested his glory," according to John's Gospel, by contribut-
ing to the conviviality of a wedding in Cana.[157]

Episcopal priest Jeffery Cave said in a sermon:

> A married Jesus gives me some hope that intimacy and Chris-
> tianity go together, that we are not meant to go through life
> denying some of the impulses in us which are most human.
> While some of us may choose to live alone, . . . a married Jesus
> teaches us that the friendship and devotion and loyalty, which
> can only come within the intimacy of human relationships, are
> all values worth striving for.[158]

How true to human experience is the notion that the unmarried
person suffers more than the married? In Spanish folk literature
there is a tale about a harried husband who, after hearing a
preacher recount all the torments that Jesus endured, inquired if
Jesus was married. On being told that he never had a wife, the
married man concluded that Jesus could not have known the
depth of suffering.[159] In a similar vein, novelist Kingsley Amis has
stated that a celibate Jesus would have avoided what is for most
people the most testing of all human experiences—close ties with
spouse and children. Amis claims that the zenith and nadir of humanity are best disclosed in the person beset by the obligations of
marriage. Unconditional love of profound depth is expressed by
those who uphold for life their vows to be faithful "in plenty and
in want, in joy and in sorrow, in sickness and in health." Celibates
tend to delude themselves, Amis thinks, when they believe they
have renounced family responsibilities for the more demanding
call of God.[160]

These opinions fall short of demonstrating that the married life
as such is more burdensome than the single life and thereby is
more in accord with what is expected of disciples who have been
asked to take up their cross. They do illustrate, however, the ab-

surdity of the frequent claim by celibates that their way is in general more arduous than that of persons who live with the inevitable domestic conflict situations and discharge their duties as spouse, parent, and in-law. Considering the likelihood of divorce in one out of two American marriages, it may be at least as morally demanding for a spouse to achieve a permanent loving relationship as for a monk to muster the discipline to remain chaste.

Religious Reasons

1. Jesus abstained from marriage because he was preoccupied with a higher calling.

PRO

According to Luke, Jesus told his parents, "I must be about my Father's interests" (Luke 2:49), so he was determined even as a boy not to allow family matters to take priority. Ministering to his disciples was an all-consuming mission, so Jesus had no time for a conjugal companion. Marital affection would have drained off vital energy that could better have been placed on expressing his religious genius. Although Paul does not refer to Jesus' marital status, he makes this observation: "The unmarried man is concerned about the Lord's interests, how to please the Lord, but the married man is concerned about worldly affairs, how to please his wife" (1 Cor. 7:32–33).

Jesus separated from his Nazareth family in pursuit of his calling as a roving rabbi, and he recommended that his disciples free themselves from some members of their households who might hinder them from following him.[161] Edward Schillebeeckx, a Dutch Catholic theologian who was influential in the discussions of the Second Vatican Council, argues that Jesus needed domestic independence so that he could sell all he had for a great treasure.[162] Schillebeeckx asserts:

That whoever belongs to Jesus' group in a special way cannot do other than leave everything and give up married life is an authentic biblical fact. . . . In view of their joy on finding the "hidden pearl," some people cannot do other than live unmarried. This religious experience itself makes them unmarriageable, actually incapable of marriage; their heart is where their treasure is.[163]

Some Catholic leaders join some mystics of India in thinking that even moderate sexual experience makes it impossible to focus with profound clarity on God.[164] Accordingly, Pope Pius XII claimed: "Virginity is more excellent than marriage chiefly because . . . it is a supremely effective means for devoting oneself wholly to the service of God, while the heart of married persons will always remain more or less divided."[165] It follows that Jesus, whose religious commitment was greater than that of any other human, must have eschewed any diffusing sexual activity. The Second Vatican Council restated that pontiff's position on "the superiority of virginity" in an effort to motivate seminarians to consecrate themselves wholly to God.[166] Pope John Paul II has given that position this tribute: "Virginity or celibacy . . . is that pearl of great price which is preferred to every other value no matter how great, and hence must be sought as the only definitive value."[167]

Ernest Renan thought that Jesus' sexual impulses were sublimated into spiritual activity. Renan asserted, "Jesus never married. All his power of loving was spent on what he considered his heavenly vocation."[168] Renan may have been influenced by Friedrich Nietzsche, his contemporary, who believed that creative people find marital sexuality a fetter. Nietzsche quotes with approval what the Buddha allegedly said on renouncing his wife and family: "Close and oppressive is life in a house, a place of impurity; to leave the house is freedom."[169] Similarly, Catholic professor John Engelche states: "Like the Buddha, Jesus found marriage quite incompatible with the demands of his life's work and mission. Each made the great renunciation: the Buddha after, the Christ before, marriage."[170] After Siddhartha came to think of marriage as an entrapment, he permanently left his wife and infant and retreated to a forest hermitage. He found freedom for himself by breaking loose from family entanglements and living with male disciples for the rest of his long life.[171]

Richard McBrien borrows Sigmund Freud's sublimation theory to explain why Jesus did not marry. Freud had likened the psyche to a hydraulic system containing a limited quantity of energy; libidinous energy has to be shunted away from sexual outlets if higher cultural expressions are to be achieved. After pointing to the way in which celibate Francis of Assisi sublimated genital love into religious love, Freud commented: "The work of civilization has become increasingly the business of men. . . . What he employs for cultural aims he to a great extent withdraws from women and sexual life."[172] Presumably, men who work at demanding jobs are less uxorious. Accordingly, McBrien thinks that Jesus freely redirected his sexual impulses so that he could proclaim the reign of God with more vigor.[173]

Confirmed bachelor Bernard Shaw asserted:

The mere thought of Jesus as a married man is felt to be blasphemous by the most conventional believers; and even those of us to whom Jesus is no supernatural personage, but a prophet only as Mahomet was a prophet, feel that there was something more dignified in the bachelordom of Jesus than in the spectacle of Mahomet lying distracted on the floor of his harem whilst his wives stormed and squabbled and henpecked round him.

Shaw based his reason for a single Jesus on the Gospel saying, "Where your treasure is, there will your heart be also" (Luke 12:34). A married man, Shaw thought, tends to be constricted by having to make money for his family. Marriage is "incompatible with both the contemplative and adventurous life." For Shaw, being unmarried is not the same thing as being a celibate. Regarding Jesus, Shaw said: "He perceived that nobody could live the higher life unless money and sexual love were obtainable without sacrificing it." He thought Roman Catholic priests were faithful to earliest Christianity in assuming that marital attachment is a kind of "slavery."[174]

The famous medieval lover-made-eunuch Peter Abelard called a husband a "domesticated beast of burden," and commented: "What servitude is heavier for a man to bear than no longer to be master of even his own body? In short, what can be more trying in life than to be daily a prey to the cares of wife and children?"[175] From this assessment, it would follow that only a celibate Jesus could focus attention on his religious vocation.

Protestant minister Richard Cromie thinks that Jesus remained a bachelor because of responsibilities in the family in which he grew up. Cromie presumes that Joseph disappeared early in the life of Jesus, making the eldest son the de facto family head. He remained unmarried and delayed leaving Nazareth until he was thirty in order to support and help rear his siblings. Cromie believes that Jesus "captures the essential and sacrificing goodness of every son and daughter, who in choosing to remain at home to serve father or mother, younger brothers or sisters, gives up an individual married life in the process."[176]

The centrality of Jesus' duties to his immediate family is an unusual reason given in the present era for concluding that he never married. More common is the claim that Jesus liberated himself from all family ties. Baptist theologian Harvey Cox claims that Jesus rejected marriage for himself and cut himself off from other kinship ties out of allegiance to a new kind of human community that goes beyond family bonds.[177] Letha Scanzoni and Nancy Hardesty think Jesus "must have ached to share love in the most intimate way" but he did not marry because he "saw real virtue in devoting one's life to God without the encumbrances of family."[178] Reformed theologian Lewis Smedes believes that Jesus forsook one good for a greater good:

> Jesus did not experience genital sex. . . . For Jesus, an urge toward sexual love would be in the same category as a temptation to take up fishing for a living. . . . Neither of these would be a temptation to do evil; both would be a temptation to turn away from his supreme vocation.[179]

An alleged revelation called Urantia claims that Rebekah, the daughter of a wealthy Nazareth merchant, fell in love with Jesus when he was nineteen. She saw him as "a splendid specimen of robust and intellectual manhood." When her father attempted to arrange a marriage, Jesus made it clear that his paramount obligation was to rear the family of his Paradise Father, so "he could not consider marriage until that was accomplished." Although Rebekah was heartbroken, she followed him throughout the years of his public ministry and stood with the other women at the place of Jesus' crucifixion.[180]

Sun Myung Moon, influenced by the traditional Confucian values of Korea, places supreme importance on being married and having offspring. This founder of the "Moonies" thinks that Jesus, as the Second Adam, should have found a bride and propagated perfect children, to whom no original sin would have been transmitted.[181] Since Jesus had priorities other than getting married, he failed to produce sinless children who would begin a redeemed humanity. Moon proclaims that there now is a Third Adam; from him and his chosen Eve a new perfected creation is coming.[182] Moon is recognized by members of his sect as the messianic restorer of God's kingdom because he and his wife are the "true parents" who have propagated a model family.[183] Mrs. Hak Ja Han Moon states that Jesus did not realize his glorious destiny to take a wife and become true parents, but she along with her husband and their thirteen children have established "the first completed True Family."[184]

Some theologians think along the lines of Francis Bacon's epigram: "A single life doth well with churchmen, for charity will hardly water the ground where it must first fill a pool."[185] Catholic priest Gerard Sloyan explains Jesus' presumed unmarried status in this way: "In light of all we are told of his concentration on his mission . . . he did not have time for the demands of domestic life. His gypsy existence, the crowds, the never-ending requests for cures saw to that."[186] Tim Stafford also argues that being single matches up better with singleness of purpose:

> Consider Jesus. It is impossible to imagine a more single-minded person than he. Throughout his ministry he knew his business exactly. He could not be dissuaded from his agenda by the concerns of the crowds, the criticisms of the Pharisees, or the fears and hopes of his disciples. He "set his face" as he went toward Jerusalem to his own death. . . . But could Jesus have made these choices if he were married and had a family to care for? Perhaps; but certainly not so freely. . . . A single person can demonstrate with a remarkable clarity that he knows the reason he was created: to love and serve God and him only.[187]

CON

There was an occasion when Jesus declared his independence from his Nazareth family. They were concerned about his sanity and safety after his gospel provoked some hostility in the Galilean villages he visited.[188] When they attempted to take him home, he announced that his strongest ties were not with his physical family. He showed fondness for friends traveling with him by saying: "Here are my mother and my brothers! Whoever does the will of God is my brother and sister and mother" (Mark 3:35). Of course, this is not a disclaimer of having a particular mother, or brothers and sisters. In context, the saying means that when confronted with a conflict between following family advice and adhering to his spiritual convictions, he opted for the latter. Jesus believed that family ties are not the be-all and end-all of life, and that his followers should sever bonds that are incompatible with religious devotion. Lawrence Marshall offers this explanation of Jesus' dilemma arising from strained kinship ties:

> The reason of our Lord's breach with his family was that they were endeavoring to put a stop to his public ministry and were pronouncing it sheer madness on his part to carry on with it. Similarly the Christian disciple is called upon to resist and even to renounce his family only if they seek to interfere with what he solemnly believes to be the will of God.[189]

Judging from the full range of Jesus' teachings, he did not think that the love of God usually cut one off from family responsibilities. He asked a rich man if he had fulfilled, among others, the commandment to honor his parents.[190] Jesus was critical of those who allowed a religious offering to take precedence over supporting their parents.[191] Parental obligations should be kept secondary but they need not rival giving allegiance to God.

Jesus' teaching that his followers cannot be devoted to both God and money[192] has overtones for his view of marital sexuality. He did not mean that poverty was obligatory for discipleship, even though some monks gave it that interpretation. Jesus approved of tax collector Zacchaeus who announced that he had renounced extortion and was giving away part of his wealth.[193] What Zacchaeus abandoned was his obsession with accumulating money that was incompatible with the divine command to avoid greed. In a parallel way, it is not wrong to have a spouse but it is wrong to give a spouse ultimate priority in one's life.

Exegete Stuart Currie finds it instructive that the word "wife" is missing in the Gospels of Mark, Matthew, and Thomas from the lists of persons and things that Jesus' disciples are asked to leave.[194] Currie comments:

> Jesus was remembered to have set a high value upon marriage, confined though it is to this earthly scene; to have regarded it as constituted by a resolution of commitment to leave father and mother and stick to one's spouse until separated by death; to have spoken about the cost of discipleship in terms of the possibility of leaving any of a list of kindred among whom "wife" is conspicuously absent. . . . This relationship of husband and wife constitutes so special a bond that it is not mentioned in the same breath with filial, sibling, and parental ties. . . . Jesus was ready to see in this form of commitment if not a model at least a figure of or analogy to the commitment of discipleship, and in that virtually unqualified and unreserved allegiance if not a model at least a figure of and analogy to proper allegiance to God. . . . Marriage . . . combines not only the motif of permanence but also of a beginning requiring resolution and an involvement of the whole embodied person in a totality of sharing not equaled in other relationships. Children after all grow up and roles are reversed as the supported become supportive and then supporters. Sibling commitments are superseded by marriage.[195]

Since God is the ground of all love, the notion that piety generally involves renouncing affection for individual humans is a gross misunderstanding of Christian theology. Although Jesus taught that a slave cannot love two masters,[196] the Gospels do not suggest that Jesus' love of God was in any way diminished by his special love of particular men and women. Love is not like an exhaustible keg of beer that diminishes in accord with the number imbibing; rather, it multiplies when used to nourish intimate as well as ultimate relationships. Therapists Morton and Barbara Kelsey make this assessment:

Human beings are able to live without genital contact, but they are not able to live creatively without communication, love, affection and touch. Celibates who attempt to be equally committed to all people and/or avoid selective intimate relationships tend to become inhuman. We need a base of intimacy from which to go out to others. . . . People who live alone with little physical or emotional contact have a death rate in every major disease category in each age group at least 100 percent greater. . . . Relating to other human beings in depth is important not only for our religious health, but also for our psychic and physical health. And a relationship that is upbuilding and healing will be one in which some level of love is shared.[197]

Marriage counselors Howard and Charlotte Clinebell consider a loving marriage to be an ideal opportunity for achieving "spiritual experiences which transcend the marriage relationship."[198] They point out that the in-depth encounter, in New Testament terms, enables partners to discover that "God is love, and those who dwell in love dwell in God" (1 John 4:16). In the same Johannine passage from which that verse is quoted is another profound insight relevant to marriage: "Those who do not love a fellow-Christian whom they have seen are incapable of loving God whom they have not seen" (4:20).

Freud, the psychiatrist most associated with the sublimation theory, also admitted its defectiveness. He stated:

An abstinent artist is scarcely conceivable. . . . The production of the artist is probably powerfully stimulated by his sexual experience. On the whole I have not gained the impression that sexual abstinence helps to shape energetic, self-reliant men of action, nor original thinkers, bold pioneers and reformers; far more often it produces 'good' weaklings who later become lost in the crowd.[199]

In a section titled "A Contradiction in Freud's Theory of Culture," Wilhelm Reich says that his basic idea "that achievements result from sublimated sexual energy . . . is erroneous."[200]

To say Jesus could minister better unmarried makes as much sense as to hold that unmarried pediatricians or marriage counselors are more capable than those with spouses and children because they can spend more time in their profession. Theologian Rosemary Ruether comments:

> The oft-stated view that by withdrawing from an exclusive relationship with one person, one is freeing oneself to love and be the father of everyone, rests on a very peculiar view of the psychology of human relationships. . . . One loves and serves only in real and concrete situations and commitments.[201]

Paul overgeneralized when he claimed that a bachelor is more focused on pleasing God than a married man.[202] Manuel Galvez's claim from his study of Spanish priests that "all of them were obsessed by women"[203] may be an overstatement in the opposite direction. A former Catholic seminarian voices the forbidden fruit syndrome: "Celibacy, by its very prohibitions, guarantees a preoccupation with sexuality. You always want what you don't have or think you can't get."[204] Celibate Ignatius Hunt comments:

> The unmarried person who is not happy in his state can be deeply concerned about the other sex and spend a great deal of time thinking over the situation, formulating plans of compromise and thus not only lack the time to be "pleasing to God," but in extreme cases lose all sight of pleasing God.[205]

Paul failed to realize that the unmarried, as commonly as the married, may be selfish and have their minds on secular things. An anonymous fourth-century writer, critical of the apostle's assessment, comments that "we see virgins with their minds on the world and married people eager for the works of the Lord."[206] Jeremy Taylor, an outstanding early Anglican bishop, similarly observes that "a married man may spend as much time in devotion as any virgins or widows do." "Though marriage hath cares," he said, "yet the single life hath desires which are more troublesome and more dangerous."[207] Although Bacon advocated priestly celibacy, he believed that single men "are more cruel and hardhearted because their tenderness is not so oft called upon."[208]

Although some married persons make sex their primary concern, a case can be made that the happily married tend to be less consumed by sex than those who focus on avoiding sexual relationships. Philanderers and some celibates may be compared to gluttons and some dieters who share an obsession with foods. Casanova's memoirs and Jerome's letters would both rank high on a prurience scale. Hermit Jerome fantasized about sexual liaisons in this way:

> When I was living in the desert, how often did I fancy myself among the pleasures of Rome! . . . I often found myself in the midst of dancing girls. My face was pale and my frame chilled with fasting, yet my mind was burning with desire and the fires of lust kept bubbling up before me when my flesh was as good as dead.[209]

Many religious leaders of various cultures have not found marriage to conflict with full-time devotion to God. Akiba, for example, a renowned ancient rabbi, gave credit to his wife for transforming him from an ignorant shepherd to a Torah scholar.[210] Contrary to Shaw's prejudiced view of Muhammad, the wife with whom he spent most of his prophetic years spurred him on when he was doubtful of his religious calling. Wealthy Khadija gave her husband both psychological reassurance and material support. She was the first to be convinced of the genuineness of her husband's revelatory experiences, believing in him when he was not believing in himself.[211] After her death Muhammad did have multiple wives during the last decade of his life, but there is no indication that they distracted him from his aim to banish idolatry from Arabia.[212]

Protestant reformer John Calvin contemplated getting married for this reason: "In order to dedicate myself more completely to the Lord, being more relieved from the worries of daily life."[213] He renounced bachelorhood so that he would have more singularity in his Christian service. On the death of his wife, he wrote: "I have been deprived of the best companion of my life. . . . While she lived she was the faithful helper of my ministry."[214] According to the biographer of Richard Mather, an early New England Calvinist, his wife "had taken off from her husband all secular cares, so that he wholly devoted himself to his study, and to sacred imployments."[215] The life of Johann Sebastian Bach also illustrates that marriage is not necessarily a distraction from a Christian vocation. Marrying twice and having twenty children contributed to his happy home and to making him one of the greatest Christian musical composers, both in quality and in quantity.

2. Jesus was spiritually wed to his devotees.

PRO

Jesus opted for a surrogate marriage to his community of followers in lieu of becoming an actual husband. In discussing why his disciples did not fast like the disciples of John the Baptizer, he asked, "Can the wedding guests fast while the bridegroom is with them?" (Mark 2:19). The first explanation that Clement of Alexandria gives as to why Jesus did not engage in ordinary marriage is that "he had his own bride, the Church."[216] Clement was influenced by the Ephesian letter, which counsels: "Husbands, love your wives, just as Christ loved the church" (Eph. 5:25). Subsequently Jerome claimed, on the authority of Paul, that Jesus had a monogamistic relation with the church. Jerome wrote: "Christ in the flesh is a virgin; in the spirit he is once married."[217] That monk asked Eustochium to think of her relationship with Jesus as similar to that of the bride to the groom in the Song of Songs:

> Always allow the Bridegroom to play with you within. Do you pray? You speak to the Bridegroom. Do you read? He speaks to you. When sleep overtakes you, he will come from behind and put his hand through the hole of the door, and your heart shall be moved for him.[218]

Chrysostom, the most prominent Bishop of Constantinople, thought of Jesus as a divine bridegroom. Those who had dedicated themselves to become priests were married to him, so to marry an earthly woman would involve deserting their first spouse and committing adultery.[219] In recent decades Schillebeeckx has defended this reason for a celibate Jesus: "He enters into a virginal marriage with his church, his bride."[220]

CON

When Jesus referred to himself as a bridegroom, he was speaking as figuratively as when he called himself a shepherd.[221] Moreover, his disciples are compared by Jesus to wedding guests, not to the bride. Jesus chose the wedding metaphor to point to the quality of his relationship with his disciples. In contrast to those who were associated with gloomy John the Baptizer, Jesus accentuated joy and love. Whereas John emphasized fasting, Jesus celebrated feasting.[222]

3. Jesus remained virginal because sexual desire
and its gratification is defiling.

PRO

There are texts in Jesus' Bible that associate sexual intercourse with impurity. The most prominent illustration of this
in the Torah follows: "If a man lies with a woman and has an
emission of semen, both of them shall bathe in water, and be unclean until evening" (Lev. 15:18). In one of the psalms, a penitent
confesses: "I was brought forth in iniquity, / and in sin did my
mother conceive me" (51:5). Some church fathers have attempted
to use such verses from the Hebrew Bible to prove that coitus
pollutes holiness.[223] Impeccable Jesus could not have been involved in "original sin" that was concomitant with sexual expression.

"Omni coitus impurus" was a theme of Jerome, the scholarly
monk who translated the Bible into Latin. He derived his dictum
from what he alleged to be Jesus' lifestyle: "In view of the purity
of the body of Christ, all sexual intercourse is impure."[224] In order to teach abstinence, Jesus was born with a penis that he re-
strained from using for sexual purposes.[225] Jerome believed that
Jesus did not completely devalue marriage because of the need for
a "seed plot out of which virginity springs."[226] Just as lovely
pearls come from ugly oyster shells, so virgins come from shameful coitus.[227]

Jerome interpreted Jesus' saying about lustful looking being
tantamount to committing adultery to mean that Jesus was de-
nouncing sexual desire even by spouses for one another.[228] Pope
John Paul II championed Jerome's view of the inherent evil of
sexual desire when he stated: "Adultery in the heart is committed
not only because a man looks in a certain way at a woman who is
not his wife. . . . Even if he were to look that way at the woman
who is his wife, he would be committing the same adultery in his
heart."[229]

Bishop Augustine quoted Jesus' saying about lust to prove that libidinous craving comes from the inward prompting of the Devil.[230] Our indecent genitals remind us, Augustine maintained, that sexual desire is a shame as well as a sin.[231] The superlatively pure Jesus could not have had sexual desire and, unlike ordinary humans, there was no reason for him to blush.[232] Protestant theologian Emil Brunner has expressed Augustine's outlook in this comment:

> Man is not merely ashamed of the sexuality which is forbidden to him morally, but shame accompanies him even into the completely personal sex-relations in marriage. . . . We cannot think of our Lord as married, although we are not in the least jarred by the fact that he ate and drank like the rest of mankind.[233]

Augustine also appealed to a proof-text from the Book of Revelation to buttress his position on sexuality. It reads: "These are men who have kept their virginity and have not defiled themselves with women; they follow the Lamb wherever he goes; out of all people, they have been redeemed as first fruits for God and the Lamb" (Rev. 14:4–5). According to Augustine, those verses affirm Jesus' perpetual virginity: "Virgins follow the Lamb, because the flesh of the Lamb is also virginal. For he [Jesus] preserved it himself in his manhood what he did not take away from his mother in his conception and birth."[234] Subsequently, Thomas Aquinas and Pope Pius XII have followed this scriptural interpretation to magnify the status of consecrated virgins.[235]

A novel by classics scholar Robert Graves illustrates the Augustinian assumption that sexual and divine love are antithetical. Mary of Bethany becomes Jesus' bride, but he "chastely denied her the consummation of marriage."[236] She is disturbed by his aloofness because her passion for him burns like that of the Shulammite for Solomon. Jesus chides Mary for not interpreting the lovemaking of the Song of Songs allegorically. To explain his refusal to have sex, Jesus philosophizes: "Man is to woman as reason is to the bodily senses, as upper to lower, as right to left, as the Divine to the human."[237] Lazarus counsels his sister Mary that only by practicing "sexless wedlock" would husband and wife avoid death and live their promised thousand years in the Messianic realm. Lazarus offers this reassurance: "You are fortunate beyond all other brides that your husband by abstaining from the enjoyment of your body has devoted you to eternal life."[238]

Catholic Reginald Trevett has offered this explanation of how priests came to be celibate:

> As Christ withheld from his human nature the full gifts of hu-
> man integrity to which he was entitled, so we too must make
> the same renunciation, redeemed though we are by and in
> him, and equally entitled with him to the complete integrity of
> Adam before the Fall. Virginity in Eden had no merit. Passion
> was under the control of reason. Not in us, redeemed though
> we are. Our Lord could not experience this upsurge of pas-
> sion.[239]

CON

The common assumption that Jesus was a celibate is due, Clifford Howard thinks, "to the underlying Christian prejudice against the female as a source of defilement" that has been "ec-clesiastically implanted."[240] Otherwise, Howard asks, why would the pious acknowledge that Jesus satisfied hunger, thirst, and friendship urges that are typical of humans while repelling as sac-rilegious the notion that he engaged in sex?

In contrast to the viewpoint of some church leaders, the Bible does not indicate that sexual intercourse is morally unclean. The levitical regulation dealing with sexual cleanness, as Norman Snaith points out, "has nothing to do with ethical matters."[241] The Israelites were anxious over a possible connection between some bodily discharges and illness. As a precautionary disinfectant, bodies were washed after exposure to semen. It is illegitimate to deduce from such physical cleansing that coitus is sinful.

The psalmists had a hyperbolic way of expressing the deep-seated sinfulness of humans. When the psalmists' speak of wickedness from conception onward, or of lying at birth,[242] it is wrong to take their poetry literally. They were not dealing with congenital evil that is transmitted by sexual generation. The psalmists were rather reflecting the way in which humans start making wrong choices early in life.

A comment by ancient Rabbi Akiba displays that the licit gratification of sexual passion was not defiling. He was of the opinion that "all the scriptures are holy, but the Song of Songs is the Holy of Holies."[243] That Song tells of a bridal couple who are enthralled with lovemaking. The groom confesses to his bride, "You have ravished my heart by a glance of your eyes" (Song of Songs 4:9). Underlying the poems is the conviction that "through love's fulfillment in marriage human nature reaches the greatest heights of earthly experience."[244]

There is no evidence that the Song of Songs was originally intended as an allegory showing God's love for Israel, or that it was interpreted as such in first-century Palestine.[245] Those lyrics were probably collected to be sung at wedding celebrations.[246] The sentiments are similar to those found in other books that the Jews included in their corpus of holy books. For example, the Song is echoed in this poem:

Have pleasure with the wife of your youth!
A lovely deer, a graceful doe!
May her breasts always intoxicate you!
May you ever find rapture in loving her! (Prov. 5:18–19)

The Hebrew Bible's outlook on sexuality is similar to that of Zoroastrianism, the Persian religion that had considerable influence on the Jews after their liberation from exile by Persian King Cyrus. Zoroastrianism is centered in avoiding defilement, but the Creator provided marital sexuality for human enjoyment. John Hinnells explains the ancient Zoroastrian ethics in this way:

> People have a religious duty to expand God's material creation as well as to support his spiritual creation. A man should get married and have children. . . . To remain celibate is sinfully to refrain from this duty. . . . In Zoroastrian belief a monk is as great a sinner as a lecher—both deny what God wills.[247]

Most translations of Jesus' saying pertaining to sexual desire obscure his teaching. It should read: "You have heard the commandment, 'You shall not commit adultery,' but I say to you that anyone who looks longingly (*epithymia*) at another's spouse (*gune*) has already committed adultery within" (Matt. 5:27–28). *Epithymia* is usually mistranslated as "lust," which is associated with lechery. For example, Shakespeare describes lust as "savage, extreme, rude, cruel."[248] However, the Greek term is morally neutral, for Jesus tells his disciples, "I have eagerly (*epithymia*) desired to eat this Passover with you."[249] In the Septuagint *epithymein* was favorably used to refer to desiring one's beautiful wife and longing for God but unfavorably used to refer to craving another person's spouse.[250] The other Greek term deserving attention is *gyne*, which should be translated here as "wife" with "of another" understood. The "Great Bible" of the English Renaissance properly translates *gune* as "another man's wife." Jesus interrelated two of the Ten Commandments: coveting a neighbor's spouse is the first step toward the act of adultery. He was in accord with his heritage in which there is no suggestion that sexual desire per se is immoral. Such is displayed by this ancient Jewish teaching:

> You are not to say that only he is called adulterer who uses his body in the act. We find Scripture saying that even he who vi-

sualizes himself in the act of adultery is called adulterer. And the proof? The verse "The eye of the adulterer also waits for the twilight, saying 'No eye will see me.'" (Job 24:15)[251]

A saying attributed to Jesus suggests that Christians should be not be ashamed of their naked bodies. After his disciples asked, "When will you appear to us?" Jesus replied: "When you strip without being ashamed, and you take your clothes and put them under your feet like little children and trample them, then you will see the son of the living one and you will not be afraid."[252]

Lactantius, a rhetorician in the early Church, held that Jesus' criticism of sexual desire was related only to impulses that precede adulterous conduct. Sexual desire is sanctioned, Lactantius affirmed, when it is an urge to merge in holy wedlock.[253] A similar interpretation of Matthew 5:28 has recently been given by Eugene Boring: "This text does not deal with natural sexual desire and its associated fantasy, but with the intensional lustful look at the wife of another."[254]

David Mace has remarked regarding that saying of Jesus:

> He obviously did not mean that a young man seeking a wife should experience no feelings of sexual desire as he contemplated an eligible young woman. Nor did he mean that the wholesome pleasure a man might feel in admiring a beautiful woman, or the delight with which a woman might look upon a fine specimen of manhood, was evil in itself. What he meant, surely, was that the best way in which we can all safeguard ourselves from unfaithfulness is to refuse to let the imagination dwell upon the thought of a sexual relationship which if it actually took place would violate a marriage, our own or another's.[255]

Theologian Tom Driver writes regarding the Gospels: "The absence of all comment in them about Jesus' sexuality cannot be taken to imply that he had no sexual feelings." He further asserts:

> It is not shocking, to me at least, to imagine Jesus moved to love according to the flesh. I cannot imagine a human tenderness, which the Gospels show to be characteristic of Jesus, that is not fed in some degree by the springs of passion. The human alternative to sexual tenderness is not asexual tenderness but sexual fear. Jesus lived in his body, as other men do.[256]

Catholic theologian McBrien also finds no conflict between the doctrine of the sinlessness of Jesus and his having sexual desires and temptations. Neither does McBrien find the possibility that Jesus engaged in sexual activities inconsistent with Catholic doctrine.[257]

Regarding the passage in Revelation about virgins who are undefiled, at first glance it does look as though sin is associated with sexual intercourse and holiness with virginity. Yet biblical scholars now recognize that virtually all of the last book of the New Testament is symbolic, and they reject the literal interpretation of Augustine and others. Indeed, if the verses from Revelation 14 to which he appealed are taken literally, the contextual meaning would be that the "redeemed" at Judgment Day will be limited to 144,000 male virgins. What then might be their meaning?

Interpretations in Protestant and Roman Catholic commentaries are clarifying. George Caird writes on the treatment of "virgins" by the author of Revelation: "He is not disclosing in an unguarded moment his personal predilection for asceticism. . . . This is a symbol . . . for moral purity from the seductions of the great whore of Babylon and from that fornication which is idolatry."[258] In a similar manner Jesuit Jean D'Aragon notes: "The 144,000 whose foreheads bear the seal constitute the totality of the Christian people. . . . Virginity is a metaphor for fidelity to God."[259] Also, Hans von Campenhausen maintains that the "virgins" of Revelation symbolize those who risk martyrdom rather than reject their worship of Jesus.[260] Thus, the untarnished sexual virtue of youth who have not married is a fitting metaphor for picturing Christians who are innocent of worship at the pagan altars of Rome ("Babylon").

4. Jesus was not oriented toward preparing for a future generation because he believed that the earthly realm would soon end.

PRO

Since Jesus was the role model for Paul, and since the apostle was unmarried during his years as a Christian missionary, some assume that both men were celibate for the same basic reason. Paul discouraged marriage for those who had never married and re-marriage for those whose spouses had died.[261] His advice was primarily motivated by his belief that the end was near. When Paul wrote the Thessalonian and Corinthian letters he was convinced that human history would be completed in his own lifetime.[262] The expectation of an imminent end of the age is especially apparent in Paul's most extensive discussion of marriage. He thought he was living in the last years as well as in the first years of church history. Customary activities were shadowed by what he called "the impending crisis." He recommended that Christians should not alter their marital status because "the appointed time has grown short." Celebrating, mourning, buying, and marrying deserve little consideration in the brief span of time remaining.[263]

Some early Latin church leaders thought Jesus denounced the fruit of sexual activity because of the impending doomsday.[264] They based their judgment on this saying of Jesus: "Woe to those who are pregnant and to those who are nursing infants in those days" (Mark 13:17). Tertullian gave this interpretation: "There will be fulfilled the curse on those who are pregnant and who are nursing, that is, the married and the lustful—for to marriage belong the womb, the breasts, and the babies."[265] That church father thought that God's command to "reproduce and multiply" had been cancelled by Paul's announcement that the end time was nigh.[266] Taking the same position, Augustine appealed to a biblical saying about "a time to embrace and a time to refrain from embracing" (Eccles. 3:5). The sexual indulgence that was hallowed in the Old Testament period is no longer acceptable for the latter-day Christian saints.[267] Jerome and John Chrysostom announced that procreation was no longer a moral imperative because the earth was fully inhabited.[268]

In our own time Susanne Heine presumes that the Jesus group was homeless, propertyless, and spouseless because of their belief in the imminence of God's kingdom. She asks: "Is it worthwhile continuing to bring children into this world in order to hand them over to the suffering in which everything will soon come to an end?"[269]

Meier argues that both Jeremiah and Jesus were celibates because of their commitment to God's message of judgment. A prophecy of Jeremiah shows Meier that "the Old Testament was not lacking in at least one celibate." Contained there is this testimony:

> The word of Yahweh came to me: "Do not marry or have children in this place. I will tell you what is going to happen to the children born in this place and their parents: . . . They will perish by sword or famine." (Jer. 16:1–4)

Jeremiah's celibacy, Meier contends, was an embodiment of "imminent doom as punishment for the apostasy of God's people."[270]

In a similar way, scholar-pastor Carl Howie claims that "the early church modeled Jesus after Jeremiah. Jeremiah was one who specifically by his understanding of his calling did not marry, because he felt the world was coming to an end and the situation demanded that he should not marry."[271] Howie gives general expression of a position affirmed by the Presbyterian Church in the United States with which he has been associated. That denomination adopted a paper in which the claim is made that Jesus viewed marriage "as a dispensable reality, not a clue to the life of the Kingdom" because of the presumed imminent end of history. Jesus "declared that marriage is not the order of being in the Kingdom" and provided a "powerful example" of his alleged teaching by remaining unmarried.[272] (Those who are ministers in this denomination, which include myself, are not required to accept such positions.)

CON

According to Will Deming, in a recent dissertation, Paul viewed the dire threat of the end of history as "an impediment to initiating new marriages."[273] In light of his timetable, he expediently affirmed his personal preference for celibacy. We know that the apostle was at least nineteen hundred years in error.

Did Jesus share Paul's view that his culture's requirement could be suspended because of the presumed emergency situation? Early in the twentieth century scholars generally believed that Jesus was motivated by the apocalyptic view that doomsday was just around the corner. However, a substantial majority of current American scholars specializing in the historical Jesus do not view him as a proclaimer of the imminent end of the world.[274]

Jesus' warning of the maternal suffering accompanying some future persecution should not be used to show that he recommended celibacy in the rather peaceful situation that was then current. Don Cuppit criticizes the position that Jesus remained a celibate because of the nearness of the reign of God:

> I am not convinced that it is right that, in the interim period between the declaration that the End is nigh and the coming of the End, everything must grind to a halt. . . . Many people who learn that they have an incurable illness decide to pack the time they have with as much moral action and enjoyment of life as they can.[275]

As regards the parallel between Jesus and Jeremiah, there is no indication in ancient Jewish and in the earliest Christian literature that Jeremiah never married. That prophet was confronted with a Jerusalem citizenry who stubbornly believed that God would not allow their city to be destroyed. They would not listen to him when he urged his people to surrender to the invading Babylonians and thereby avert death by disease and by war. In a desperate attempt to get the Jerusalemites to change their military policy, Jeremiah dramatized their impending plight in nonverbal ways. For a time he walked about wearing an oxen yoke to portray the bondage that would come if they continued to resist the enemy. Deciding not to marry or remarry was also calculated to have a shock effect. From that symbolic action the lethargic public might take seriously the grim future, since to be without wife and children was a terrible disgrace. Such deprivation could obviously result in the extinction of one's family. Jeremiah's actions at the time of the siege of Jerusalem, and his emphasis upon not marrying "in this place," show the temporary nature of his sexual abstinence.[276] M. D. Goldman, professor of Semitic studies at the University of Melbourne, plausibly interprets several passages in Jeremiah's prophecy as alluding to his wife.[277] He purchased a plot of land,[278] indicating that he planned to settle down to normal life if he survived the destruction of Jerusalem. He probably intended to act himself on the advice that he gave to the exiles— to build homes, take wives, and bear children.[279] The city was destroyed and the Babylonian conflict was over not long after Jeremiah's peace demonstrations. When that tragedy had passed, there would have been no point in his continuing his protest, either by wearing the undesirable oxen yoke or by refraining from the desirable connubial yoke.

Prophet Zoroaster was the founder of a religion that influenced the apocalyptic motif of ancient Judaism. While he had strong ideas about the approaching end of history and the Paradise beyond, he was married to a woman named Hvovi and had children.[280]

5. Jesus believed that the angelic life should now be copied.

PRO

Jesus said to the Sadducees:

> Those who belong to this age marry and are given in marriage; but those who are considered worthy of a place in that age and in the resurrection from the dead neither marry nor are given in marriage. Indeed they cannot die anymore, because they are like angels. (Luke 20:34–36)

These words of Jesus to the Sadducees have occasionally been cited in the history of Christianity to justify celibacy. In the second century, Marcion presumed Jesus was here depreciating secularists who marry. He abases "those who belong to this age" and exalts the remainder who abstain. Only the latter are Christians, and hence they are those whom God accounts worthy of obtaining life after death.[281] In the third century, Cyprian praised virgins in this manner:

> That which we shall be, you have already begun to be. You already possess in this world the glory of the resurrection; you pass through the world without its contagion. In preserving virginal chastity you are the equals of the angels of God.[282]

Those words of Cyprian were quoted approvingly by Pope Pius XII.[283] Earlier in the twentieth century, Pope Pius XI advocated what he called the "angelic life" for priests. He reasoned: "Since God is a spirit, it is only fitting that he who dedicates and consecrates himself to God's service should in some ways divest himself of the body." Also, he asked regarding the priest:

> Ought he not to be obliged to live as far as possible like a pure spirit? The priest who ought to be entirely "about the Lord's

business," ought he not to be entirely detached from earthly things, so that his life be lived entirely in heaven?[284]

According to Jerome, Jesus' aim during his days in the flesh was to live the paradisal life of virginity and to enable holy men and women to "manifest themselves even in this life as angels."[285] Presuming angels to be sexless, Jerome implored earthly virgins to remain sexually inactive in order to get a head start on the heavenly life.[286] By austerities they can imitate Jesus who quenched the flame of passion, "and while in the body live as though out of it."[287] Jerome applied to the life after death the conclusion of one of Jesus' parables, which states that good soil brings forth three different yields: thirty, sixty and a hundredfold.[288] These represent, from least to greatest, pious spouses, chaste widows, and consecrated virgins. Thirty represents matrimony, Jerome claimed, because the Roman numeral XXX symbolizes the kissing and interlocking of husband and wife![289]

Otto Bochert questions why Jesus did not have a wife since he believed that marriage was the highest earthly state. He answers his inquiry in this way: "He was already living according to the laws of the fulfilled Kingdom of God, when there shall be no marriage, neither giving in marriage. He was already 'the Son of man which is in heaven' (John 3:13)."[290] Lucien Legrand likewise claims that Jesus and many of his followers refrained from sexual activity because life as sexless heavenly spirits had already begun to stir in them.[291]

CON

Only by an interpretive sleight of hand can Jesus' response to a question from the Sadducees be associated with celibacy. How strangely incongruous that those who profess to follow the Incarnate One should attempt to imitate angels, who by nature are not incarnate. Catholic philosopher Jacques Maritain, drawing on the medieval definition of "angel" as a bodyless mind, coined the term "angelism" to refer to futile attempts "to play the pure spirit" and detach oneself from the corporeal realm.[292] Apropos here is the reflection of Kent Nerburn on the nature of our humanity:

> We are neither animals nor angels. We are something else—we are humans—part spiritual and part physical, and those two parts are combined into one. A true sexuality acknowledges both these dimensions and tries to embrace them both in the act of love. . . . Having sex is what the animals do. Achieving mystical union is what the angels do. We alone can make love, where the physical and the spiritual commingle in a single, joyous act.[293]

Jesus' teaching pertains to his affirmation of a life after death in contrast to the Sadducees who rejected its possibility. He believed that resurrected humans are like angels in that they are incorporeal and neither reproduce nor die.[294] Clement of Alexandria rightly claimed that anyone examining the passage carefully would realize that Jesus was not denigrating marriage and exalting celibacy. Rather, he was criticizing those who assume that the afterlife would be simply an extension of life as now experienced, including marriage and propagation. Clement's point was that death and the need for reproduction is not a quality of the immortal life, although it is intrinsic to the organic realm.[295] By reductio ad absurdum logic, he argued that those who reject marriage on the claim that they are now living the nonphysical life of the resurrection should also avoid eating and drinking.[296]

Jesus' reply to the Sadducees can more properly be used to encourage marriage in this life than to authorize celibacy. Novelist D. H. Lawrence comments: "We may well believe that in heaven there is no marrying or giving in marriage. All this has to be fulfilled here, and if it is not fulfilled here, it will never be fulfilled."[297]

Maurice Wiles speculates that the love and joy that is associated with earthly marriage may become intensified in a heavenly realm:

Marriage represents the deepest form of personal relationship, the highest form of social experience which is open to us in this life. Within the limitations of our finite, human experience such a relationship can only be shared with one other person at one time. But need such a limitation apply to the life of heaven? Is it not more reasonable that the life of heaven should involve a going on from, rather that a drawing back from, the highest kind of personal relationship known to us? If this is so, the point of the saying of Jesus may be not that heaven involves a reversal of the words of God, "It is not good that man should be alone," but rather that a relationship which in this life necessarily involves exclusiveness finds in heaven an ultimate fulfillment in which the element of exclusiveness is done away. In epigrammatic form we might say that the real significance of the saying is not that in heaven we shall be married to nobody but rather that in heaven we shall be married to everybody.[298]

Ronald Goetz offers a similar interpretation of Jesus' comment on no marriage in God's fulfilled reign:

Our love for one another is set free from the finite bonds and limitations which presently constrain us. We are presently finite and cannot love everyone with the utter intimacy with which we can love one person in marriage. But if we are raised to the divine life, we can love with the universal, all-inclusive intimacy of God's own love. There is unbounded love in the kingdom of God. There is no need for the restriction of marriage. To this extent, there is free love in heaven. The Sadducees tragically underestimated the power of God's love.[299]

6. Jesus was too divine to marry.

PRO

Jesus, the incarnation of God, was the only sinless person who ever lived, and he would not have married a sinful woman. Philip

Schaff, an eminent church historian, writes: "The Son of God and Savior of the world was too far above all the daughters of Eve to find an equal companion among them, and in any case cannot be conceived as holding such relations."[300] Even if the assumption is made that bride selection was primarily a parental responsibility, Mary and Joseph would not have followed the prevailing custom because they recognized Jesus' unique holiness.

Expositor Eric Krell argues that since God cannot be married, "anyone created in the image of God is never in need of another [opposite] sex." Jesus, as the last Adam, was distinguished as "male and female in one personality." When Jesus is referred to as man in the New Testament, Krell contends, this should be interpreted to mean that he was human, not that he was male.[301] Hence, it is absurd to speak of that sexual neuter as being attracted to the opposite sex. Sexual passion began when the first Adam fell and shattered the divine image.

Charles Feinberg, dean of Talbot Theological Seminary, comments: "The idea of Jesus having sexual relations . . . challenges Christ's divinity and approximates blasphemy."[302] David Schuyler, Catholic dean of faculty at Chaminade College in Hawaii, has a similar position. He said: "Christ was not just a man, a member of a certain people and culture, subject to and following its normal pattern of life; He was the unique God-Man. . . . Christ presented to His followers the example of the ideal Son of God, undivided in heart, unmarried, and without earthly possessions."[303]

Jesus was a perfect divine Spirit, and marriage is not a part of the Spirit world. Theologian Paul Jewett states: "If Jesus was only and essentially a first-century Palestinian Jew, then in all likelihood he was married." But as "true God" he embodied the dominion of heaven where there is no sexual congress between husband and wife. Jesus did not continue practices of the earthly realm because "he is the heavenly bridegroom who, though taken from his bride for a time, will return to celebrate his nuptial feast at the consummation of all things."[304]

CON

On the theological level, there is no conflict between orthodox Christology and the historical possibility of Jesus having been married. Charles Davis, who until he became married, was Britain's leading Roman Catholic theologian, carefully reviewed the evidence for and against Jesus' alleged celibacy. From this he affirmed: "It is difficult to see that any inherent incompatibility between marriage and divine sonship excludes a married Jesus."[305] German Lutheran Christologist Wolfhart Pannenberg, while not dealing with whether Jesus did or did not marry, argues that Jesus' kinship with God cannot be separated from his complete self-dedication to God while engaging in concrete human activities. Pannenberg provides this clarifying judgment: "Jesus' divinity is not a second 'substance' in the man Jesus in addition to his humanity. . . . Precisely in his particular humanity Jesus is the Son of God."[306]

Canon Edwin Bennett claims that Jesus knew he was God during his public ministry. Such awareness did not mean that he set aside his sexuality, because that is not something humans have but something humans are. It follows, Bennett said, that "when God became a human person, he did not change any of that. He is not a freak." That Episcopalian priest speculates on the implications of his position: "I would be very surprised if Jesus never masturbated, for example; every boy does." Also, as a down-to-earth divine person, "Jesus might have been married and had two kids."[307]

The Book of Hebrews in the New Testament affirms that Jesus "was tempted in every respect as we are, yet without sin" (Heb. 4:15). This means that Jesus confronted a wide sampling of human moral and spiritual testing, but did not succumb to conduct that transgressed God's will. The Council of Chalcedon in the fifth century, which clarified the meaning of Jesus' divinity, stated that he is "one in being with us as far as his human-ness is concerned, like us in all respects except for sin."

Joseph Jeffers, an "Ambassadors of Yahweh" prophet, writes:

The Messiah was married. . . . "He had to resemble his brothers in every respect" (Heb. 2:17). . . . If he had not been a married man and experienced married life, physical and mental, he could not have obtained the experiences he needed to understand man and woman and then help them accordingly.[308]

Oscar Cullmann, a distinguished Christologist, also discusses the importance of assertions in Hebrews pertaining to Jesus. Cullmann points out that Christians have often not taken serious statements that Jesus "learned obedience" through exposure to the same conditions as other humans.[309] Also, Cullmann comments:

"We have not a high priest who is unable to sympathize with our weaknesses, but one who in every respect has been tempted as we are" (Heb. 4:15). The full significance of this description of Jesus' humanity is rarely appreciated. . . . This statement of Hebrews, which thus goes beyond the Synoptic reports of Jesus' being tempted, is perhaps the boldest assertion of the completely human character of Jesus in the New Testament. It . . . casts a special light on the life of Jesus, leading us to consider aspects of his life with which we are not acquainted.[310]

Richard Langsdale has written a historical novel in an attempt to illustrate Jesus' continual awareness of both his "God-nature" and his full humanity. In Langsdale's story, a young woman from Magdala with psychological troubles is healed by "Yisu." He subsequently strolls with Mary Magdalene along the Sea of Galilee, and his "Yahweh Spirit" sanctions falling in love with her. Jesus acknowledges: "With Mary I saw a whole new dimension of compassion, understanding, patience and forgiveness." His fellow Galileans encourage him to take Mary as his wife. Langsdale's Jesus reflects during the honeymoon:

Long ago and in another place I had watched my father Joseph hone and plane and mold the jointure of two olive boards until, with nod of perfection gained and satisfied, he closed the jointure and bound the olive wood from two parts into one. So here in this night I drew this Mary, this handicraft of God, into human jointure with myself, and through the night we honed the union to its height and depth and breadth of intended perfection. We two became one.[311]

In his openness and responsiveness to marital intercourse, Jesus experienced the full-orbed "breadth and length and height and depth" of love to which the New Testament refers, and he became more acutely conscious of being "filled with the very nature of God" (Eph. 3:18–19). Lutheran clergyman Langsdale's treatment of the way in which Jesus might have expressed sexual passion is in accord with the outlook of Martin Luther.[312] Jesus, as portrayed by Langsdale, had as much awareness of his divine Spirit in a pleasant bed as on a painful cross. His intimate love of a particular person did not diminish his love for others. On the contrary, he acknowledged, "My life with Mary has turned a new facet of this prism of love into focus."[313] That enriching experience is similar to that of Shakespeare's Juliet, who affirmed:

My bounty is as boundless as the sea,
My love as deep; the more I give to thee,
The more I have, for both are infinite.[314]

In one of Anthony Burgess's novels, Jesus marries Sara of Cana when he is twenty so that he can "know the whole life of a man." The narrator, who is portrayed as a first-century scholar, comments on Jesus: "We may suppose that he savoured the bodily joys as much as any other of us who have entered the blessed state, though I do not doubt that he suffered from woman's foolishness, capriciousness, and loquacity like the rest of us." Sara had three miscarriages in rapid succession and was killed by police at the Temple in Jerusalem when they were suppressing a riot.[315]

John Erskine, a distinguished American writer, suggests that

Jesus had a wife and children during those two decades of young manhood that are unmentioned in the Gospels. He speculates that the wedlock became a deadlock:

> It does not seem improbable that he did fall in love and had some experience of parenthood. . . . He understood women very well indeed, with the special understanding of a man who has been hurt by one of them. . . . I think he early met someone who charmed but who was unworthy, someone he idealized, and by whom he was cruelly disillusioned. . . . The Gospels indicate that Jesus had an extraordinary fondness for children, and a special understanding of the relation between father and son. It is evident that he exerted upon women of various temperaments a strong fascination. . . . The father of the prodigal son is not a portrait of Joseph, but the record of human yearning for a child. Whether these emotions in Jesus ever attached themselves to particular objects, the story does not say, but his character renders it for me utterly impossible that his youth and manhood could have been unmoved by warm, human emotions. . . . If he really took our nature upon him and was human, then he had our equipment of sex.[316]

FOUR

Women and Magdalene

His Relations with Women in General

✦ Jesus grew up in a culture in which women were held in low esteem. A few generations earlier, Jesus ben Sirach charged: "Woman is the origin of sin, and it is through her that we all die. . . . Out of clothes comes the moth, and out of woman comes wickedness. A man's wickedness is better than a woman's goodness; it is woman who brings shame and disgrace."[1] Generally subscribing to Sirach's misogyny in the generation before Jesus, influential Rabbi Hillel commented, "The more women, the more witch-crafts."[2] Later in the century in which Jesus lived, Josephus stated that "woman is in all things inferior to man."[3]

One of the most extraordinary ways in which Jesus differed from the men of his culture was in his companionship with women. In his study of Jesus' social environment, Joachim Jeremias notes that a male teacher attracting women disciples was "an unprecedented happening in the history of that time."[4] It was then customary for only young men to follow after a charismatic leader.

Women apparently joined Jesus' band without having been specially "called." According to Mark, both men and women "followed him" (Mark 1:17, 15:40–41), which occasionally involved them in proclaiming the gospel. They moved about the country with him, even though his day-to-day life was hazardous and often deficient in the customary amenities. In light of the ancient Jewish custom of women being married near the age of puberty, and in view of the danger that parents would surely have seen in allowing single daughters to live with men, it may be assumed that all of Jesus' women followers had married. Some may have been widows, but some were probably the wives of his male disciples. Luke reports that on one occasion Jesus sent out several dozen pairs of disciples into Palestine to proclaim the "reign of God" (Luke 10:1–9). It is likely that at least some of those who lodged "two by two" were husband and wife teams.

Married couples engaging in mission travel during Jesus' ministry may have influenced what became customary among the apostles and other Christian teachers.[5] In addition to providing for the needs of their spouses, the women probably functioned as evangelistic co-partners. Priscilla, for example, along with her husband, instructed the well-educated Apollos so that he would know the Christian tradition more accurately.[6] Early church leader Clement suggested that the apostles took wives along "that they might be their fellow-ministers in dealing with housewives. It was through them that the Lord's teaching penetrated also the women's quarters without any scandal being aroused."[7]

The position of the women who traveled with Jesus was no more demeaning than that of their leader, for Luke uses the same verb, *diakonein* (to wait on), to commend the ministry of both Jesus and the women with him.[8] The Gospels tell of some women, but no men, who ministered unto Jesus as he ministered unto others. For example, after Jesus assisted Peter's mother-in-law, she reciprocated by serving him and his disciples.[9]

One measure of greatness in Jesus' culture had been the number of servants/slaves under a person's control.[10] By word and deed Jesus attempted to show that greatness should rather be associated with assisting others. Although he did not rank individual men or women, his measure of preeminence was by service, not by sex. In this regard, he elevated the role of male servants who performed menial tasks.[11] Jesus encouraged his followers to counter the prevailing view: "You know that the recognized rulers in the world lord it over their subjects, and their great ones are tyrants; but it shall not be so with you" (Mark 10:42–43). Regarding himself, Jesus said, "I am among you as one who serves"

(Luke 22:27) and he illustrated those words in a concrete manner. Having stated that his mission in life was "not to be waited on but to wait on others" (Mark 10:45), he dramatized his humble role by washing his disciples' feet at the Last Supper.[12] The traditional role of women in washing men's feet is referred to in the Hebrew Bible as a handmaid's function.[13]

Even though Jesus commended the servant role, he countered a custom that the Jews shared with most traditional cultures, namely that a woman's fulfillment is inseparable from her domestic routines. He alarmed his friend Martha by encouraging her sister Mary to assume the position of a rabbinical student, properly a male role, rather than to prepare food.[14] He admired Mary's eagerness for learning and her realization that a woman could be something other than a homebody. Jesus also had high regard for the initiative of the Queen of Sheba who came to visit Solomon. In that gentile ruler he found a wisdom lacking in some of his fellow Jews.[15]

Realizing that women's self-esteem was being lessened by their constant identification with household cooking and water carrying, Jesus did not urge them to serve more. By encouraging food preparation and foot washing for men while commending scholarly pursuits for women, he was espousing a liberating switch in gender roles. Rosemary Ruether comments:

> The principles of Christian community are founded upon a role transformation between men and women, rulers and ruled. The ministry of the Church is not to be modeled on hierarchies of lordship, but on the diakonia of women and servants, while women are freed from exclusive identification with the service role, called to join the circle of disciples as equal members.[16]

The life of Jesus illustrates the artificiality of gender stereotypes. The Gospel writers describe the superlative model of Christian morality as having traits which traditionally have been at least as much associated with females as with males. Jesus is especially

noted for his tender emotions. The verb "to have compassion"—
the standard translation of a Greek term meaning "to be moved
in one's viscera"—is used in the New Testament exclusively with
respect to Jesus' teaching and life.[17] Weeping, a particular expression of the tender feelings, is also primarily associated in Western civilization with the female sex. "Jesus wept" (John 11:35)
sums up his grief response, and elsewhere in the New Testament
proof of his humanity is found in his "loud cries and tears"
(Heb. 5:7).

Devotion to children was a characteristic of Jesus, even though
it is another trait societies generally call feminine. Alarmed by violence directed toward the innocent in his nation, Jesus pictured his
role as a sheltering mother: "How often have I longed to gather
your children around me as a hen gathers her brood under her
wings, but you would not let me!" (Luke 13:34) He was no strut-
ting and fighting cock! Jesus also identified with children by an-
nouncing that cordiality to them was a way of receiving him.[18]

Jesus shared with women the trait of gentleness. He said: "Come
to me, all of you who are tired from carrying heavy loads, and I
will give you rest. Take my yoke upon you, and learn from me, because I am gentle and humble in spirit" (Matt. 11:28–29). Paul appealed to "the gentleness and kindness of Christ" (2 Cor. 10:1) in
writing to a congregation.

Suffering is another trait especially associated with women. Before the coming of modern medicine with its painkillers, excruci-
ating suffering was one of the dreads of childbirth. Inspired by the
suffering servant ideal of Isaiah, Jesus said, "The Son of Man must
undergo great sufferings" (Mark 8:31). He exemplifies par excel-
lence the traits of suffering and serving which traditionally have
been more associated with females than with males. Also, he
warned his followers that they would have to suffer like a woman
in labor.[19]

Turning to those traits commonly thought to be masculine, how
are they related to Jesus' personality? Aristotle claimed that men
by nature are more dominant, courageous, persevering, and ra-

tional than women.[20] "Bold, resolute, and open in conduct" is the definition that Webster gives for "manly." Jesus was noted for his leadership, fearlessness, powerfulness, and wisdom. Some left their work and possessions to become his disciples.[21] On encountering a storm at sea that frightened even seasoned fishermen, Jesus was not worried.[22]

The power within Jesus was physical as well as spiritual. For most of his adult life he was in a manual trade which required bodily strength. Since there were no power tools for sawing and drilling, his muscles were probably even more developed than those of carpenters today. When he became an itinerant teacher, he warned those who joined his band that stamina was needed for coping with hardships they would encounter.[23] Like a scoutmaster, he took his young disciples on a trek up the Lebanese mountains.[24] Jesus' assertiveness was conveyed by his denunciation of the exploitation by religious leaders. At the risk of his life, he combined verbal criticism with physical force to drive out those who were commercializing the temple in Jerusalem.[25]

In past times self-confidence has been associated more with males than with females. Jesus displayed assuredness in a superlative manner when he was on trial for his life. Pilate asked him if he thought of himself as a Jewish king. The Fourth Gospel represents Jesus as replying in this bold manner: "I am a king. For this I was born, and for this I have come into the world, to bear witness to the truth; and all who are on the side of truth listen to me" (John 18:37). The Roman procurator remarked, "Surely you know I have power to release you or to have you crucified." To this Jesus affirmed, "You would have no power over me unless it had been given you from above" (John 19:10–11).

In the masculine mystique of ancient Judaism, it was assumed that reasoning was principally possessed by males and that only they had the ability to become scholars. It was in accord with sex role expectations for Rabbi Jesus to have an intellectual command of his religious traditions and an ability to communicate fresh insights from that heritage. The keenness of his mind is well illustrated in his handling of criticisms after he drove moneychangers and animal sellers out of the temple. Inquiries were made with the purpose of embarrassing him regardless of his answer. Jesus cleverly responded to one loaded question about his authority by tossing back a question that his critics refused to answer. He then dealt astutely with a question involving giving to Caesar or God by replacing the either/or dilemma with both/and logic. According to Luke, the Jerusalem leaders conceded that Jesus won this battle of wits: "They were unable to catch him in anything he had to say in public; they were amazed at his answer and were silenced" (Luke 20:26).

In this survey of some of Jesus' traits, it can be seen that he was free of the pernicious gender polarization of human history. As Elisabeth Moltmann-Wendel rightly observes: "He had himself personally integrated so many male and female behavioral characteristics that one could consider him the first maturely integrated person."[26] Qualities that many cultures have considered feminine or masculine were harmoniously blended in his lifestyle. Jesus was both a brave, brainy, and brawny "he-man" and a sensitive, serving, and suffering "she-man"! He affectionately took children in his arms, but he also indignantly employed strong-arm tactics to drive out Temple hucksters. He surprised his companions by being both more "feminine" and more "masculine" than others.

The widespread double standard of sexual morality was rejected by Jesus. When some Pharisees charged that a woman had been detected in "the very act of adultery," Jesus was indignant that those men had apprehended only one of the liaison. The Jewish law to which they were appealing gave penalties to both parties.[27] It is ludicrous to presume that witnesses saw only one person engaging in sexual intercourse. Obviously the accusing men had indulgently winked at the male participant. Jesus admonished them: "Let him who is without sin among you be the first to throw a stone at her" (John 8:7). He spoke sternly to the hypocritical male accusers and gently to the adulterous woman, although he did not condone her behavior.[28] Jesus favored a single standard of mutual fidelity for men and women. Also, adultery was punished by Jewish law because another man's property was abused,[29] but Jesus was here concerned because a woman was abused.

Gentile as well as Jewish men would have been offended by Jesus' rejection of the double standard. For example, Cato the Elder, an influential early Roman statesman, remarked to some fellow males: "If you find your wife in adultery, you may kill her freely without a trial. But if you commit adultery . . . she has no right to raise a finger against you."[30] Throughout Western history men have demanded that women must be ladies while duplicitously accepting that "boys will be boys." Sexual harassment by males has been widely condoned in world cultures.

Jesus found more potential for repentance in outcasts, for sexual and other reasons, than in members of polite society.[31] One of the Pharisees (meaning "Separated Ones") named Simon was revolted by Jesus' acceptance of "a woman of the city, who was a sinner." Simon was shocked that Jesus did not shun her after being clued by her loose hair that her morals were also loose. But Jesus was pleased when she sensuously washed his feet and wiped them with her long hair. He defended her hospitable acts while he reclined at dinner and expressed appreciation for the way in which "she continued kissing his feet and scented them with ointment" (Luke 7:36–50).

Jesus rejected the principle of salvation by segregation from those of ill repute. He did not assume that purity was preserved by isolation from those who were morally infected. Jesus introduced the principle of befriending sexual offenders and other wrongdoers in order to bring out the best in each individual. He affirmed that his mission was to live not with the virtuous but with those who were aware of their moral sickness.[32] He aimed at extending the largest measure of trust possible to the marginalized in order to restore in them healthy self-confidence and awareness of being part of the religious community.

Women increased their sense of worth with Jesus' assistance as they regained physical, mental, and moral health. He dignified a hunchbacked woman by including her among God's chosen, calling her "a daughter of Abraham" (Luke 13:16). Jesus attempted to counteract economic discrimination against women; he denounced pious hypocrites who "devour widows' houses and for the sake of appearance say long prayers" (Mark 12:40). Empathy with various situations faced by women is revealed in a number of his parables: the ten bridesmaids, the woman working with yeast, and the widow confronting an unjust judge, for example.[33] In one parable he compared God to a woman in search of what she has lost, and told of her joy in finding it.[34]

"Jesus, the Sexy Man" is the startling chapter heading in a book attempting to relate sexuality to the founder of Christianity. Harlan Musser, a United Church of Christ minister, stimulates comparative reflection by this judgment: "Our Lord was as much a sex symbol to the people of his day as any singer, actor, politician, or personality to whom we so glibly apply this title today."[35] Jesus' consideration for and tenderness toward women may have sexually aroused some of them, but Musser's discussion of this interesting point is inadequate. Bruce Barton thinks that another factor in Jesus' appeal to women was "his life of outdoor living and the steel-like hardness of his nerves."[36]

Jewish scholar Claude Montefiore concluded from his thorough study of the Gospels: "There can be little doubt that in Jesus' attitude toward women we have a highly original and significant feature of his life and teaching."[37] The best illustration of the respect in which Jesus held women in comparison with his culture is found in his encounter with a person whom priests had pronounced untouchable. According to a law of Moses, persons who even touched something that had been in close contact with a menstruant were required to wash their body and clothing.[38] That law was honored in the era when Jesus lived; both Shammai and Hillel taught that the touch of a menstruating woman was contaminating, and an entire tract of the Mishnah is devoted to detecting her condition. There the taboo is expressed in this way: "The blood of a menstruant and the flesh of a corpse convey uncleanness."[39] Jesus disregarded that purification law of the Torah when he accepted a woman with "a flow of blood" who touched him.[40] He did not believe that religious defilement came from physical conditions. Giving personal encouragement to a stigmatized hemorrhaging woman was probably the main therapy he rendered. By addressing her as "daughter," Jesus included her in his new family that was not based on kinship ties.

The dominant motif of Leviticus, the book containing regulations about separating from menstruants, is that Israelites should be holy as God is holy.[41] The holiness code is concerned with removing blemished persons or animals from the community so they may not contaminate the righteous. Contained there, for example, is the only biblical law pertaining to homosexual conduct; the crime is assigned the death penalty.[42]

Rabbi Jacob Neusner faults Jesus for neglecting the purification theme and commends the Pharisees for emphasizing it.[43] Jesus was little concerned with the holiness code; for him the principal law might be stated: "Be compassionate as I your Sovereign God am compassionate" (Luke 6:36). Such suffering on behalf of others is especially associated in the Hebrew Bible with women, because the root of the word translated "compassion" (*racham*) literally means "movement in a womb" (*rechem*), hence "motherly concern."[44]

Jesus' disdain of his culture's tendency to withdraw from the "impure" is expressed in his parable of the Good Samaritan. It criticizes a Levitical law that warned priests to avoid being defiled by contact with a corpse.[45] The story tells of a priest and a Levite who avoided touching a bloody, half dead man whom they saw lying by the road. By contrast, an outsider was "moved with compassion" and took care of him.[46] Rather than erecting barriers against those presumed to be religiously contaminated, Jesus broke down dividing walls and made somebodies out of those who by social definition were nobodies. He replaced the exclusionary holiness orientation of Judaism with an inclusionary compassionate orientation. The teachings and actions of Jesus reflected a God "whose tender womb aches for the uninvited and the unloved: a compassionate parent, transcending gender, the Mother and Father of us all."[47]

Toward the end of Jesus' earthly life, an unnamed woman was singled out for exceptional praise. She stands in contrast to his disciples who had been uncomprehending when Jesus repeatedly warned them that he would be killed by the religious leaders of Judaism.[48] The woman anointed Jesus' head, an activity associated with coronations in Israel.[49] Intensely anticipated in Jesus' time was the coming of an anointed one like the victorious King David. This woman was the only person who discerned messianic qualities in Jesus even as he was being rejected by the Jerusalem authorities. Whereas bystanders snorted over her extravagant wasting of expensive ointment, Jesus responded in this appreciative way: "Wherever the good news is proclaimed in the whole world, what she has done will be told in remembrance of her" (Mark 14:9). John Crossan intriguingly suggests that this woman might have authored the Gospel now designated as "Mark."[50]

The accounts of Jesus' interactions with women show that D. H. Lawrence was wrong in claiming that Jesus was ever giving to women but was unable to receive from them. Both the story of the woman who washed his feet and the story of the woman who anointed his head display the mutuality of mature love. "Happiness lies more in giving than in getting" (Acts 20:35), Jesus taught, but that does not imply that he shunned the pleasure of receiving. Sheer altruism or selflessness was not idealized by Jesus, as it had been by Aristotle. That philosopher described the "great-souled" person as one who "is fond of conferring benefits, but ashamed to receive them, because the former is a mark of superiority and the latter of inferiority."[51]

Joseph Haroutunian is properly critical of the assumption that Jesus' love "flowed out of him as water from a spring . . . unmindful of any reciprocation." Haroutunian points out that some women and men called "sinners" in the Gospels aroused Jesus' affection:

Jesus not only loved but was also loved in return by the sinners. It is true that he did not love so that he might be loved in return. But it does not follow that he did not care whether he was loved or not. . . . Nothing but theological prejudice and confusion, accumulated through the centuries . . . would lead a man reading the accounts of Jesus' encounter with people to judge that his love was a one-way affair.[52]

The Fourth Gospel, while different from the Synoptics in many ways, reinforces their portrayal of Jesus' affirming attitude toward women. Gail O'Day points out that men do not have a monopoly on discipleship in the Gospel of John: "Women are Jesus' main conversation partners in three stories that reveal Jesus' identity and vocation and the nature of faithful discipleship (4:4–42, 7:53–8:11; 11:1–44)."[53] Raymond Brown also shows how John depicts "a community where in the things that really mattered in the following of Christ there was no difference between male and female." In its "gallery of heroes were the Samaritan woman who brought men to faith by her word and Mary Magdalene who proclaimed the good news of the risen Jesus."[54]

Jesus' words to a woman at a well in Samaria exceed in length any he directed to his disciples or family on any one occasion. His conversation with her illustrates the way in which he broke with cultural conventions, since he initiated it with one whom Jews would shun as a member of a despised Palestinian minority group. Although he was aware that the Samaritan woman was not married to her current sexual companion, Jesus did not treat her condescendingly. In his dialogue with her, he clarified his theology:

The woman said to him, . . . "Are you greater than our ancestor Jacob, who gave us this well from which he quenched his thirst?" . . . Jesus answered, "Everyone who drinks this water will get thirsty again, but no one who drinks the water I provide will ever be thirsty again; it will be a spring within them, a fountain of eternal life." "Sir," said the woman, "give me that water, so I may never be thirsty or have to keep coming here to draw water." . . . Jesus said, . . . "God is spirit, and those who worship God must worship him as he truly is." The woman continued, "I know that the Messiah is coming" (who is called Christ). "When he comes, he will explain everything." Jesus responded, "You have been talking to him all along." (John 4:11–26)

At that point, Jesus' male disciples joined him and were astonished to find him conversing with a woman. She then went back to her city, significantly leaving behind the water jug that represented the chores assigned to women. She told about Jesus and became an effective evangelist, since "many Samaritans from that city believed in him because of the woman's testimony" (John 4:39). They came to him while he was speaking about the fields being ripe for harvesting and saying that his disciples would reap what others had sowed. It appears that the writer of the Fourth Gospel features the Samaritan woman as an effective sower of the Gospel. In his influential article "Jesus Was a Feminist," Leonard Swidler argues that this episode with the Samaritan woman reinforces "Jesus' stress on the equal dignity of woman."[55]

The seriousness with which Jesus responded to women's concerns helps explain why there is no record of women being hostile to him. They reciprocated Jesus' respect for them; consequently the many caustic criticisms in the Gospels are all from males. An examination of Jesus' interaction with women shows that he made de facto their de jure status as equal creations with male humans in the "image of God." In his doctoral dissertation on women in the New Testament, Ben Witherington concludes:

We do not find negative remarks about the nature, abilities, and religious potential of women compared to men on the lips of Jesus in contrast to various Jewish authors. There is also reason to believe that Jesus' estimation of the worth and validity of a woman's word of testimony was higher than that of most of his

contemporaries. . . . Jesus appears to be a unique and sometimes radical reformer of the views of women and their roles
that were commonly held among his people.[56]

From a broader historical comparison, biblical exegete Walter
Wink gives this similar judgment:

In every single encounter with women in the four Gospels,
Jesus violated the mores of his time. . . . His behavior toward
women, while not fully "modern" or feminist or all it might
have been, is nevertheless astonishing, and, was without parallel in "civilized" societies since the rise of patriarchy roughly
three thousand years before his birth.[57]

His Relations with Magdalene in Particular

The best known of Jesus' female friends is Mary, from a place in
Galilee that has been traced to a fishing town later known as Mejdel.
In the Greek New Testament it is called Magdala, Magadan, or
Dalmanutha.[58] To distinguish this friend from other biblical
Marys, she is called Mary Magdalene in the New Testament, and
often simply Magdalene subsequently.

Mark informs his readers that Magdalene was among the
women who took care of Jesus' needs when he was in Galilee, and
that she accompanied him to Jerusalem. Luke includes Magdalene
among the women who received treatment (*therapeuo*) from
Jesus. In the parlance of ancient medicine, she was said to have been
healed when "seven demons" left her. "Demons" could refer to a
physical or mental disorder, and "seven" implies that it was serious.

Elisabeth Moltmann-Wendel perceptively imagines how Magdalene might have attained wholeness:

Jesus touched her, perhaps embraced her, made her get up, like
Peter's feverish mother-in-law or the person possessed by

demons. He spoke to her and she had a tangible feeling of nearness and contact. As he spoke, the spell left her. She again became herself, free to feel and decide, free once again to experience the world around her, free to enjoy herself and to learn to
live again.[59]

In the Synoptic Gospels, Magdalene leads the list of women associated with Jesus,[60] even as spokesperson Peter heads the list of
male disciples. That listing order suggests that Magdalene was recognized by her contemporaries as a special female companion of
Jesus. According to *The Sophia of Jesus Christ*, a second-century
writing, the disciples who traveled with Jesus included seven
women and twelve men. Jesus predicts in *Pistis Sophia*, a third-
century writing, that Magdalene and John will surpass the other
disciples.[61]

Magdalene has distinctiveness as the only friend of Jesus who
is mentioned in all four Gospels as being with him when he died.[62]
Whereas his other disciples were uncomprehending and deserted
him at the time of his trial and crucifixion,[63] she and some other
loyal women were with him until his agony was over. Having seen
where his body was hastily buried on the eve of a sabbath without the customary funeral perfumes, they returned with ointments
and spices at the dawn of the first day of the next week. Irishman
Eaton Barrett contrasts the faithfulness of these women with that
of Jesus' male disciples:

> Not she with trait'rous kiss her Savior stung,
> Not she denied him with unholy tongue;
> She, while apostles shrank, could danger brave,
> Last at his cross, and earliest at his grave.[64]

Although Magdalene had a notable place among Jesus' female
followers during his public ministry, she is most remembered for
her involvement in the Easter event. The Gospels do not tell of any
human witness to Jesus' rising from his tomb but they testify of

her witness to his first appearance after being crucified. Indeed, Magdalene is the only woman present in the resurrection stories of all four canonical Gospels. With regard to her prominence in John's Gospel's account, C. H. Dodd expresses the view of many scholars and laypersons when he calls it "the most humanly moving of all the stories of the risen Christ."[65] Commentator O'Day heightens Dodd's evaluation: "The conversation that takes place between Jesus and Mary at the tomb is one of the most poignant and artfully drawn scenes in all of scripture."[66]

What was the nature of that experience? The prevailing interpretation is that Magdalene, numbed by grief, came before dawn to the garden tomb where Jesus was buried. On seeing that its sealing stone had been rolled away, she concluded that Jesus' body had been removed and ran to tell other disciples of this. Some male disciples then rushed to the tomb and found there only the cloth in which Jesus' body had been wrapped. When Magdalene returned, she saw angels in the empty tomb who asked her why she was weeping. She was then greeted by Jesus, whom God had physically resurrected. Magdalene supposed the voice to be that of the gardener and frantically asked him of the whereabouts of Jesus' corpse. After Jesus addressed her as Mary, she called him Rabbouni, an affectionate way of referring to a rabbi, and went to announce to the disciples that she had seen Jesus. Magdalene stands out in the Gospels as the primary proclaimer of the Easter vindication.

Most Christians have believed that those present with Magdalene at that burial site could have discerned with their senses the material form of Jesus. The corpse of Jesus was supernaturally reanimated in a somewhat transformed state, according to the general belief, and the activity of that risen body changed Magdalene's fear into belief.

The main historical problem with interpreting the Magdalene story in a literal manner is that it clashes with the earliest record of Jesus' resurrection. Decades before the Gospel accounts were written, Paul wrote to Christians in Corinth about what had been transmitted to him pertaining to Jesus' life after death. The apostle did not mention his empty tomb and the angels there, or tell about disciples conversing with his revived body near his open grave. He rather wrote: "Even though we once knew Christ according to the flesh, we know him no longer in that way" (2 Cor. 5:16). If Paul received from other Christians a story of Jesus' physical resurrection, he did not find it convincing enough to repeat. For him, the certainty of Jesus' resurrection was based on his postmortem appearances to various individuals separately and to groups of people. After relating the core tradition of what happened after Jesus' death and burial, Paul testified from firsthand experience that Jesus appeared to him personally.[67] In the Greek New Testament, the verb "was seen" (*hophthen*) that the apostle uses to refer to those Easter events usually describes revelations occurring within persons.[68] Paul's usage of *hophthen* follows that of the Greek Septuagint: Job, for instance, confesses after encountering God in the whirlwind, "Now my eye sees you" (42:5). Isaiah says, "I saw Yahweh sitting upon a throne" (6:1). That sage and that prophet used a visual metaphor to describe a supra-empirical mystical experience.

Having established to his satisfaction the certainty of Jesus' resurrection, Paul tackles these questions: "How are the dead raised? With what kind of body do they come?" (1 Cor. 15:35) Paul assumes that the nonphysical mode of Jesus' life after death is similar to that of Christians who have died.[69] He realistically accepts the biological fact that the bodies of dead organisms decay irretrievably. The apostle frankly and plainly states that "flesh and blood cannot inherit the kingdom of God, nor does the perishable inherit the imperishable" (1 Cor. 15:50). He did not believe that a corpse or its residual dust could become a new material body. When Paul writes that the dusty children of Adam can be "raised a spiritual body" (1 Cor. 15:44), he is not referring to the physical skeleton and any flesh clinging to it. Rather, "spiritual body" means, in modern terminology, the self. If Paul's outlook is sound, as I think to be the case, then interpreters of Gospel stories should not scrutinize them to find historical data about a physically resurrected Jesus who later ascended into the sky. What is significant here is the internal insights, not the external sights, reported by particular disciples.

Magdalene's experience as told in the Fourth Gospel has some qualities that harmonize with Paul's experience. Her exclamation, "I have seen the Lord!" (John 20:18) parallels the apostle's testimony, "Have I not seen Jesus Christ our Lord?" (1 Cor. 9:1) Paul was probably referring to what is elsewhere described as his "vision" on the road to Damascus of the Jesus whom he was persecuting.[70]

More broadly, both Magdalene and Paul shared the usual prophetic way of experiencing the presence of God. Preceding such, there is a longing. An oracle of Jeremiah puts it this way: "'When you search for me, you will find me; if you seek me whole-heartedly I will let you find me,' says Yahweh" (Jer. 29:13–14). In each account of the Easter story, the yearning of Magdalene and her companions is highly significant.[71] In John's Gospel, Jesus asks Magdalene, "Whom are you seeking?" Mourners characteristically return to places that may spur memories of their loved one, hoping for something to fill their psychic emptiness.

Some have interpreted Magdalene's encounter with the resurrected Jesus as a hallucination triggered by grief. Celsus, a pagan living in the second century, attempted to debunk the most dramatic story of Jesus' resurrection by suggesting that it resulted in large part from "a hysterical woman." Celsus claimed that Magdalene and perhaps one other woman were so wrenched with grief at Jesus' failure that they hallucinated him risen from the dead by a sort of wishful thinking. This mistaking a fantasy for reality is not at all uncommon; indeed, it has happened to thousands. Just as possible, these deluded women wanted to impress the others—who had already the good sense to have abandoned him—by spreading their hallucinations about as "visions."[72]

Celsus also commented more broadly on the prevailing Christian outlook on life after death. Whereas some Christians realistically reject a physical resurrection, most "yearn for the restoration of their earthly body (as if there were nothing better than that to salvage!) in just the same form as it appeared during a man's life."[73] Celsus discerned that Christians generally presume that Jesus' resurrection was physical and that theirs would be likewise.

There is an abundance of data to support Celsus' comment about apparitions resulting from the loss of lovers. For example, the bride in the Song of Songs is emotionally exhausted by an imagined search for her beloved. Her fantasy happily concludes with a resumption of former embracing. "I held him and would not let him go," she testifies (3:4). Similar apparitions are found in contemporary studies of grief. Gnostic scholar Elaine Pagels, for instance, testifies of what happened after the accidental death of her young husband: "I became aware that, like many people who grieve, I was living in the presence of an invisible being—living, that is, with a vivid sense of someone who had died."[74] On the basis of his clinical research into the experiences of widows, psychiatrist Colin Parkes has documented that postmortem appearances of spouses are common in the early weeks after their deaths. "In the newly bereaved widow the perceptual element is very strong," Parkes comments. He evaluates the hallucinations as healthy rather than pathological, and notes that the recipients find them more comforting than disturbing. Sometimes the dead husband's presence is sensed internally, and not just nearby, causing the widow to see things through his eyes and adopt his sense of values.[75] Grief counselor William Worden reinforces Parkes and adds a philosophical teaser:

> Hallucinations of both the visual type and the auditory type . . . are a frequent experience of the bereaved. . . . With all the recent interest in mysticism and spirituality, it is interesting to speculate on whether these are really hallucinations or possibly some other kind of metaphysical phenomena.[76]

Ernest Renan, the famed nineteenth-century French biblical critic, gives Celsus' hallucination interpretation a positive and romantic twist. While treating the Easter appearance of Jesus as a product of Magdalene's imagination, Renan does not judge such as disparaging to its significance.[77] He provides this eloquent reconstruction of the occasion:

> Frantic with love, intoxicated with joy, Mary returned to the city. To the first disciples whom she met, she said: "I have seen him; he has spoken to me." Her greatly troubled mind, her broken and disconnected speech, caused some to think she was demented. . . . The glory of the resurrection belongs, then, to Mary of Magdala. After Jesus, it was Mary who has done the most in the founding of Christianity. The image created by her delicate sensibility still hovers before the world. Queen and patroness of idealists, Magdalene knew how to assert the vision of her passionate personality and convince everyone. Her grand feminine affirmation, "He is risen!" has become the basis of the faith of humanity. Away, feeble reason! Apply no cold analysis to this masterpiece of idealism.[78]

Renan summarizes the Easter experience tersely: "It was love that raised Jesus."[79]

Magdalene was among those who refused to allow Jesus' humiliating death to cause despair and loss of faith. She should be prominently included among those persons to whom historian Josephus refers. Of Jesus, he reported: "When Pilate condemned him to be crucified . . . those who loved him from the first did not cease."[80] Like Paul, Magdalene could appropriately ask: "Can anything separate us from the love of Christ? Can hardship or distress?" She could likewise declare with the apostle: "We are completely victorious through him who loved us; for I am certain that nothing in death or life . . . can come between us and his love" (Rom. 8:35, 37–39). Magdalene became absolutely convinced that Jesus was alive and that her bond of love with him was more personal and permanent than ever. She had come to believe that the triumphant Jesus was saying to his disciples, "I am with you always" (Matt. 28:20).

In the twentieth century, Greek novelist Nikos Kazantzakis accepted Renan's interpretation and elaborated on it.[81] Also, Jewish scholar Joseph Klausner quoted Renan's treatment of Magdalene and agreed that her vision, and the subsequent visions by the male apostles, had high significance. They help to explain why the memory of Jesus was preserved, in contrast to the memories of other messianic figures of that era.[82]

Jack Lundsom has suggested that Magdalene may have had in mind lyrics from the Song of Songs that were popular in her day. Those sentiments may have contributed to the Easter story in the Gospel of John. In the Hebrew song a forlorn maiden asks watchmen, "Have you found my true love?" (Song of Songs 3:3) Similarly, distraught Magdalene inquires of a presumed gardener, "Sir, if you have removed him, tell me where you have laid him" (John 20:15). Then, in both cases, the lost loved one is suddenly found. Both the Hebrew song and Magdalene's experience have overtones of rekindled love in a renewed Paradise.[83]

Over against the interpretations originating with Celsus, I suggest that Magdalene's Easter experience need not be understood as exclusively a self-induced hallucination. Her faith that God had raised Jesus from the dead may well have been produced by more than subjective longing. She may not have dreamed up the presence of Jesus, but neither was it a "bolt out of the blue" for which there was no inward preparation. Her close ties with Jesus over an extended period gave her a readiness to believe that the love she had known could not be destroyed. In the bewilderment following his death, Magdalene was probably desperately attempting to reconcile his crucifixion with what he had taught about his mission, human sin, and God's will. While trying to puzzle through all of this, she went to the place where she had last been with Jesus' dead body. There she had a deeply moving experience that may have resulted from a divine disclosure interacting with her troubled mind. The Gospel writer believed that Jesus' appearance in Magdalene's psyche was not illusory but was the revelation of a transcendent reality. After "seeing" an unclothed Jesus and "hearing" him call her name,[84] she became convinced that he was not dead but altogether alive, albeit in a different mode. Her weeping was mixed with joy as she came to realize that even in this life she could be in communion with one who is "the resurrection and the life" (John 11:25) and who, like a good shepherd, knows his own and calls them by their individual names.[85] In John's Gospel, Jesus possessively calls his disciples "mine" because they belong to his intimate inner circle.[86]

William Thompson argues more generally that our experience of the death of loved ones gives a clue to the resurrection accounts of the New Testament:

At such moments we seem to discover the transcendent power of life and love, which sustains our trust and gives us the capacity to "rise" above these deaths. . . . The transcendent power of life and love manifests itself through the greater openness and overcoming of closure. Our human capacity to hope against defeatism and to protest human misery . . . are echoes of the divine gift of life sustaining and renewing us. . . . Like us, in these (risen Jesus) encounters early Christian disciples experienced a foretaste of what resurrection life is.[87]

Lines of an Easter hymn from medieval France capture the ambiance of Magdalene's revelation:

O Mary, do not weep, look no further. . . . He is with you, he whom you love. You sought Jesus and found him. . . . You have true joy; the relief of your pain is hidden within you, and you do not know; you have it inside, and you look outside for the remedy to your languor.[88]

A judicious examination of the record of Magdalene's Easter experience is hindered by the widespread prejudice against hallucinations or visions, especially in the modern era. On both popular and scientific levels there is a tendency to assume that nothing positive and creative can result from such.

Contemporary Christian literalists seem to presume that what Magdalene saw at the garden tomb could have been captured by a camcorder, had such a device been in use then. For something to be a fact and not a fabrication to those trained in Western technology, it must be publicly observable to all present, whether religious or nonreligious. But metaphorical language is commonly used by those who wish to affirm that they have discovered the solution to something that had been puzzling. After struggling with a difficult geometry problem, for example, students may become enlightened and exclaim, "Now we see it!" Their senses may not have supplied them with any new physical data, but they may have gained real understanding. Likewise, Magdalene and others throughout church history have apparently experienced Jesus as a living presence in their lives. It is to sell out to the positivist dogma of the immaculate preception to accept the metaphysics that only what is observable by the senses can be true. By that standard, the biblical declaration that God is a rock is literal non-sense and is therefore untrue.

Surprisingly, some religionists as well as atheists cannot accept the reality of a person who lacks material substance. For example, a basic belief of fundamentalism is that human immortality is inseparable from an objective rising of buried physical remains. By way of countering that position, psychoanalyst Ana-Maria Rizzuto demonstrates that fantasy can be associated with true reality.[89] Renowned psychiatrist Robert Cole concludes that much can be learned of reality from spiritual experiences, and that those who claim to see or hear Jesus may be displaying one way through which divine revelation is given.[90] Some of those whom secularists describe as having a nervous breakdown may be having a theological breakthrough!

To interpret the New Testament's resurrection stories, Harvard theologian Gordon Kaufman uses the term hallucination, which he defines as "a nonpublic but privately extremely significant experience." Genuine insight on the continuity of God's nature and purposes have been communicated by the accounts of the experiences of Magdalene and others. Kaufman writes:

> It is because an event occurred—comprehensible on the human level as a series of "appearances" or "hallucinations" creative of and in the context of a new community of love and forgiveness—through which the earliest disciples came to discern a new and deeper meaning in the life and death of Jesus: that here was the definitive manifestation of the unfailing love of almighty God toward man.[91]

The changed nature of the relationship is expressed in Jesus' words to Magdalene, "Do not continue to hug me" (*me mou haptou*, John 20:17). The verb *haptou*, used only here in the Fourth Gospel, ranges in meaning in the New Testament, from "touching a garment" to "having intercourse with a partner."[92] The Greek verb tense here with the negative means to stop an action in which one had been engaged. The imperative, aptly rendered in Moffatt's translation as "Cease clinging to me," graphically conveys the traumatic transformation to which Magdalene was adjusting as her tie with Jesus became exclusively intangible. No longer could she take hold of him physically, for he was no longer incarnate. John Marsh offers this explanation: "What Jesus is doing and saying to Mary can be summed up thus: she is to cease from holding him, because the new relationship between Lord and worshipper will not be one of physical contact, though it will be a real personal relationship."[93] Magdalene was convinced that Jesus was alive and that her bond with him was more intimate and permanent than is possible in earthly associations.

The *me mou haptou* teaching not only provides assistance for a bewildered disciple in dealing with her trauma over Jesus' crucifixion but also helps any person who is mourning the loss of a close friend. Grief cannot be overcome if there is a persistent desire to cling to the past mode of personal encounter. A comforting way of internalizing the reality of death is by sublimating the urge to throw one's arms around a loved one. Physical intimacy can be transformed into an awareness of his or her spiritual presence. Even as Magdalene became convinced of Jesus' nearness and witnessed to that conviction, so grieving persons can return to productive activity in their communities while strengthened by the abiding personal, although nonphysical, companionship of the loved one.

Magdalene felt commissioned by a reimaged Jesus to proclaim his triumph over death to other disciples.[94] Rather than hoard privately the revelation that had transformed her sorrow into gladness, she spread the good news. However, when Magdalene and her female companions testified to Jesus' living presence, the male disciples initially dismissed their story as nonsense.[95] The prejudiced response is understandable when we realize that a woman's witness was unacceptable among the Jews.[96] Josephus wrote, "Let not the testimony of women be admitted."[97]

In the early centuries of Christianity, some church leaders acknowledged Magdalene's prominent position as an authoritative witness to the Easter triumph of Jesus. Susan Haskins, in the most thorough study ever conducted of Magdalene in history and in legend, tells how Jesus "chose a woman, Mary Magdalen, to be his 'first apostle,' in the true sense of the words."[98]

Magdalene's status may be compared to a woman named Junia or Julia in the earliest manuscripts of Paul's letter to the Romans. She and Andronicus—who is probably her husband—are described as "outstanding apostles." Paul also states that they are fellow Jews, that they became Christians before his conversion, and that they had been imprisoned with him.[99] Perhaps they were among the apostles whom Paul mentions elsewhere, in addition to those called the "Twelve," as having seen the risen Jesus.[100] John Chrysostom, the foremost leader of the Greek church in the fourth century, commented on Junia's position. Since he was an outspoken male supremacist, he was amazed that Paul addressed her by the highest title a Christian could have and commended her as being among the best of that group. Chrysostom wrote: "There is something great about being an apostle. But to be pre-eminent among the apostles—think what marvelous praise that is. . . . How great the wisdom of this woman must have been for her to have been found worthy of the title apostle!"[101] A medieval manuscript copier, who was unwilling to admit the possibility of women apostles, doctored the Greek text of Romans that had been transmitted to him. Junia is given the male ending Junias even though there is no record of Roman men with that name.

Hippolytus, in the third century, referred to the women at Jesus' tomb as "apostles."[102] In the Latin church, Magdalene was known as *apostola apostolorum* because she was called to proclaim the good news to the male apostles.[103] Peter Abelard, for example, gave her this tribute:

> The saint merits to be the first to be consoled by the Savior's resurrection, as his death had been a cause of sorrow and anguish to her. She is also called the apostle to the apostles, that is ambassadress of the ambassadors, as the Lord sent her to the apostles to announce the joy of the resurrection.[104]

Some church leaders may have recognized that Magdalene fulfilled better than Paul the criteria given by Jerusalem Christians for the office of apostle. To be certified for that position a person needed to have accompanied Jesus throughout his public ministry and to have witnessed his resurrection.[105] Paul's apostleship was in dispute because some Jewish Christians made an issue of his lack of one of the prime qualifications.[106]

The early status of Magdalene and her women companions was acknowledged in a comment of Protestant reformer John Calvin:

> He [Jesus] began with the women, and not only presented himself to be seen by them, but even gave them a commission to

announce the gospel to the apostles, so as to become their instructors. . . . [Jesus] bestowed on them [the women] distinguished honor, by taking away from men the apostolic office, and committing it to them for a short time.[107]

Gnostic Christians defended the high status of women in the band of disciples by pointing to Magdalene as the one who experienced Jesus' resurrection. The third-century Gospel of Mary portrays Peter as a jealous spokesperson, but Magdalene as an honest testifier. It contains this exchange:

Peter said to Mary, "Sister, we know that the Savior loved you more than the rest of women. Tell us the words of the Savior which you remember." . . . She said, "I saw the Lord in a vision. . . . He answered and said to me, 'Blessed are you, that you did not waver at the sight of me.'" . . . Peter questioned them [the apostles] about the Savior: "Did he really speak privately with a woman and not openly to us?" . . . Then Mary wept and said to Peter, . . . "Do you think that I thought this up myself in my heart, or that I am lying about the Savior?" Matthew said: "Peter, you have always been hot-tempered. Now I see you contending against the woman like the adversaries. But if the Savior made her worthy, who are you indeed to reject her? Surely the Savior knows her very well. That is why he loved her more than us."[108]

Elisabeth Moltmann-Wendel has compared the biblical and Gnostic accounts of Magdalene to the present Catholic treatment of women:

Testimony by witnesses both early and late indicates that Mary Magdalene, who played an important role among Jesus' followers, became one of the primary examples of this apostleship. As the Vatican today is agitated by such issues, so too

Peter, as predecessor of the popes, became insecure and angry that a woman should usurp what he regarded as a masculine position.[109]

When recent popes have issued their rationale for the prohibition of women priests, they have not considered the leadership role of some women in the early church. They claim that Roman Catholicism's refusal to ordain women is based on Jesus' example. Paul VI also stated that a priest must have a "natural resemblance" to the male Jesus. In claiming he was expressing fidelity to the Gospel, that pope contradicted the report of the commission he appointed that found no biblical basis for barring women from the priesthood.[110] John Paul II contends that Christ "by his free and sovereign choice—clearly attested to by the Gospel and by the church's constant tradition—entrusted only to men" the priesthood.[111] Thus, the basic rationale now offered by the pope for the ban on the ordination of women is the alleged authority of Jesus. In a letter to bishops on this subject, John Paul II asserts: "The church has always acknowledged as a perennial norm her Lord's way of acting in choosing the twelve men whom he made the foundations of his church."[112] If the Vatican would indeed use Jesus' example as its "perennial norm," the church might have more gender diversity in the priesthood. Jesuits Gerald O'Collins and Daniel Kendall demonstrate that the Gospels assigned Magdalene a lead role as bearer of the Easter faith but that prejudice against women throughout church history has deprecated that fact.[113]

Because of the close association of Jesus and Magdalene, some early Christians assumed that she was his wife. According to the Gospel of Philip, she was Jesus' "partner" (Greek, *koinonos*), or "spouse" (Coptic, *hotre*), and he kissed her often.[114] That Gospel also refers to Jesus as the offspring from the seed that "Joseph the carpenter planted." The "mystery of marriage" as it pertains to Jesus is described in this way: "The Lord is the Son of Man and the son of the Son of Man is he who is created through the Son of Man. The Son of Man received from God the capacity to create.

He also has the ability to beget."[115] The Gospel of Philip records a tradition that may be at least as old as the second century. Barbara Thiering bases her claim that Jesus married Magdalene on her plausible interpretation of the Gospel of Philip as well as on her bizarre interpretations of the Dead Sea Scrolls.[116]

The canonical Gospels can also be validly translated to show that Magdalene was Jesus' wife. In the New Testament *gune* most commonly means "wife." Journeying with Jesus and his male disciples, according to Luke, were some *gunai* "who provided for them out of their resources" (Luke 8:3). The three females named there are Magdalene, Susanna, and Joanna, the *gune* of Chuza. The first word of Jesus to Magdalene in John's Easter story was *gune*, and his question to Magdalene could be rendered, "Wife, why are you weeping?" Jesus' chief mourner wanted possession of Jesus' body for proper interment.[117] Unless she were the next of kin, it would have been inappropriate for her to claim his corpse. Moreover, she refers to Jesus as "my lord," a customary way for designating a husband in her culture.[118] Her desire to embrace Jesus would have also been proper only if he were her spouse.

The Jesus Seminar, a think tank devoted to historical analysis, concluded regarding Jesus' association with Magdalene:

> The Fellows of the Seminar were overwhelmingly of the opinion that Jesus did not advocate celibacy. A majority of the Fellows doubted, in fact, that Jesus himself was celibate. They regard it as probable that he had a special relationship with at least one woman, Mary of Magdala.[119]

Although Magdalene was the woman closest to Jesus in both the canonical and Gnostic Gospels of the first centuries of Christianity, her role was diminished in subsequent orthodox church tradition. No longer was she recognized as the woman whose companionship was so special that she helped anoint Jesus' dead body. Nor was she generally exalted as the one to whom the meaning of the resurrection was revealed and as one who shared the honored place of an evangelist. In a scholarly examination of the way Jesus' mother has been treated in history, Marina Warner shows how post-apostolic Christians were embarrassed by the way Magdalene eclipsed mother Mary in the earliest traditions.[120] For example, the New Testament says nothing about the risen Jesus' appearance to his mother.

Ruether points out that the earliest Christian historical tradition exalted Mary of Magdala, not Mary of Nazareth, but the former was later defamed and the latter was venerated.[121] The strange reversal of valuations is explained in this way:

> The suppression of the role of Mary Magdalene in the official church tradition may have something to do with the desire of the church to assign subordinate and conventional roles to women. . . . In the later church tradition Jesus again comes to have a faithful woman at his side, a woman who understands him from the beginning and remains loyal to him to the end, a woman who especially cooperates with him in the drama of salvation and mediates it to others. . . . By replacing Mary Magdalene with Mary, the mother, as the "woman who loved him," the church replaced a dangerously unconventional role model with a conventional role model.[122]

Some others have joined Ruether in arguing that Magdalene, the leading lady of the Gospels, was replaced by Jesus' mother as the faithful and understanding woman throughout his public ministry. Anglican Bishop John Spong gathers circumstantial evidence to support his view "that Jesus might well have been married, that Mary Magdalene, as the primary woman in the Gospel story itself, was Jesus' wife, and that this record was suppressed but not annihilated by the Christian church." Spong follows Ruether in this historical reconstruction: "By the turn of the first century there was in the life of the Christian church a clear need to remove Mary Magdalene . . . and to replace her with a sexless woman, the virgin mother."[123] Historian James Baker also finds evidence that

Magdalene's role as Jesus' partner was downplayed in the medieval era in order to boost the prestige of Jesus' mother.[124]

Another possible explanation can be given for the popular image of Magdalene in European culture. Some imaginative church scribe, who recognized that repentant prostitutes were more acceptable to Jesus than some respected religious authorities,[125] conflated the account of Magdalene with Luke's "sinful woman" story.[126] Woven in the Middle Ages was a tale of Magdalene who descended from a noble birth to a despicable life. According to Honorius of Autun, she was betrothed to John the son of Zebedee at her family's castle in Magdala. At the wedding feast in Cana, her groom forsook Magdalene in order to join Jesus' celibate band. Out of resentment "she became a common prostitute and of her own free will set up a brothel of sin and made it in truth a temple of demons, for seven devils entered into her and plagued her continually with foul desires." Eventually Jesus cast out those devils and "all things that she had willingly done before in the service of the flesh she now in sorrow turned to the service of the Lord."[127]

From the seventh century onward the fiction of Magdalene as a repentant whore became accepted as fact. Gregory the Great imagined that she devoted to Jesus the perfume she had acquired to use on her body to entice customers.[128] Magdalene became a central figure in the medieval church because of the treatment by that outstanding pope and because her sin of fornication was regarded as the most pervasive evil. According to a twelfth-century English sermon, Magdalene "is an example of penitence . . . that is what maketh the filthy clean."[129] "Magdalene homes" were established in various European countries as reformatories for "fallen" women.[130] The Magdalene Society of New York was founded in 1830 to provide "an asylum for females who have deviated from the paths of virtue."[131] The stigmatization of Magdalene in the Western tradition explains why her name is one of the least-common names for a girl while Mary is one of the most frequent.

In the art and literature of Western history, the identification of Magdalene with a former prostitute has persisted. William Blake suggested that she and the mother of Jesus had a similar past:

Was Jesus Born of a Virgin Pure
With narrow Soul and looks demure?
If he intended to take on Sin
The Mother should an Harlot been,
Just such a one as Magdalen
With seven devils in her Pen.[132]

In our own time, Franco Zeffirelli's film *Jesus of Nazareth* depicts Magdalene as one who had been a whore. Kahlil Gibran reconstructs this reminiscence that Magdalene might have had of Jesus:

I gazed at him, and my soul quivered within me, for he was beautiful. . . . He said, "You have many lovers, and yet I alone love you. . . . I see in you a beauty that shall not fade away, and in the autumn of your days that beauty shall not be afraid to gaze at itself in the mirror, and it shall not be offended. I, alone, love the unseen in you." On that day the sunset of his eyes slew the dragon in me, and I became a woman.[133]

The musical *Jesus Christ Superstar* has tantalized many theatergoers over the past generation, in part because of the role given Magdalene. Although baffled by Jesus, she massages him when he is tired and sings plaintively, "I don't know how to love him." Judas and others are alarmed that he would allow a woman of ill repute to stroke and kiss him, but Jesus is appreciative that she alone was attempting to give him what he needed. The youthful composers of the rock opera underscored some of the qualities of Jesus' humanizing sexuality.

Even though it affirms the gospel to imagine Jesus having intimate relations with a repentant prostitute, the historical likelihood of such being the relationship between Jesus and Magdalene is remote. After providing a scholarly review of the way Magdalene is treated in the Gospel, Jane Schaberg has this to say about the legend that Jesus lifted Mary from whoredom: "This identification fulfills the desire . . . to downgrade the Magdalene, as well as the desire to attach to female sexuality the notions of evil, repentance and mercy."[134]

More plausible is the recent view that Magdalene's position of prominence among the earliest disciples was denigrated in order to exalt a feminine model of the spiritual life who supposedly never engaged in sexual intercourse. The innocent Madonna without sexual desire stands out when contrasted to the "fallen" state of other women. Her pristine purity is most strikingly displayed when her opposite is one who indulges in shameless carnality. Haskins concludes:

> Christianity has offered, one could say imposed, two alternative feminine symbols, Mary the Virgin and Mary Magdalen, the whore. . . . From the early centuries of the Christian era, Mary Magdalen has, like the women she represents, been the scapegoat of the ecclesiastical institution, manipulated, controlled and, above all, misrepresented. . . . It is perhaps time to recognise the true feminine model, one which, according to the gospels, embodies strength, courage and independence, all feminine qualities which the Church has attempted to suppress by subordinating women to the model it has created, the passive virgin and mother.[135]

Haskins, an English Catholic, relates her scholarly treatment of Magdalene to a contemporary issue in her nation. During the past generation some outspoken Anglicans found Christian priestesses inconceivable. C. S. Lewis, for example, argued that only a male can represent God the Son, the Bridegroom of the Church.[136] Haskins cites Pope John Paul II's attempt to head off the ordination of women in the Church of England, which nevertheless was accomplished in 1994. She views the action of the Anglicans as no more shocking than Jesus' selection of Magdalene as the "Herald of the New Life." Haskins joins Lutheran clergyman John Damm who recognizes Magdalene as

> a full member of the revolutionary community created by the One who considered men and women equal. . . . Jesus valued her as a unique person in whom the life and power of God flowed with the same degree of intensity as it did in Peter, James or John.[137]

E. P. Sanders, the acclaimed New Testament scholar, has reviewed the passages pertaining to women in the Gospels. While recognizing that the authentic historical episodes usually treat Jesus' mother negatively, he states that "the women followers play an absolutely essential role." By way of placing this fact in its ancient context, Sanders comments: "History was then, as for centuries before and after, the history of males, and for the most part women play only supporting roles. For this one brief period, crucial to Christianity, Jesus' women followers are in the limelight."[138]

FIVE

Sexual Renunciation
in Western History

Pagan Asceticism

✦ Much of the sexual outlook in Western civilization has been fil-
tered through ancient philosophers who championed moral dualism and its concomitant asceticism. That theory and associated
practice is a legacy received mainly from the Greek culture. Only
after the pervasive impact of pagan asceticism is recognized can
one distinguish the distinctively different sexual viewpoint that
prevailed among participants in the biblical milieu.

Sexual asceticism can be traced to the Orphic cult at the dawn
of Western philosophy. Socrates used a pun in describing it: "The
body (*soma*) is the tomb (*sema*) of the soul."[1] The followers of the
legendary Orpheus also utilized a prison metaphor: "The body is
an enclosure in which the soul is incarcerated."[2] Orphic dualism
was adopted by Pythagoras, the first Greek to call himself a
philosopher. He was reported to have said, "Sexual pleasures
are always harmful and not conducive to health." Asked once
when a man should consort with a woman, he replied, "When you
want to lose what strength you have."[3] Empedocles, a pupil of
Pythagoras, denounced all forms of sexual relations.[4] Classics
authority E. R. Dodds, in discussing Empedocles, observes that
sexual asceticism not only originated in Greece but "was carried
by a Greek mind to its extreme theoretical limit."[5]

Democritus and Plato, Athenian admirers of Pythagoras, denounced sexual activity.[6] Plato referred to sexual desire as a dis-

eased part of the personality. In contrast to the appetite for food, which cannot be completely diverted if a person desires to survive, he pointed out that genital gratification is expendable. Plato pictured the well-balanced person as one who sublimates all his amorous energies in intellectual pursuits.[7] Greek philosophy specialist B. A. G. Fuller states that sex was for bachelor Plato "the arch-enemy of the life of the spirit."[8]

The Epicurean and Stoic schools were the most popular philosophic schools during the long Greco-Roman era. "Sexual intercourse has never done a man good," Epicurus said, "and he is lucky if it has not harmed him."[9] Lucretius, who championed Epicurus's philosophy in the Latin culture, asserted that sexual desire was a sickness that could not be cured by intercourse. A wise man should avoid it altogether, for it does not contribute to the ideal unruffled life. Lucretius described the problem of sex in this way: "At length when the pent-up desire has gone forth, there ensues a short pause in the burning passion; and then returns the same frenzy, then comes back the old madness."[10]

"Endure and abstain" was the motto of Epictetus and some other Stoics.[11] In a chapter titled "Concerning Asceticism," Epictetus taught that the impulse to indulge in sensual love should be counteracted by an opposing discipline of renunciation.[12] The Stoics continually believed that "the wise man is passionless (*apatheia*) and classified love, along with hatred, as irrational conditions to shun."[13]

In the first century before the Christian era, a cult related to Greek philosophy developed in the region of Alexandria. Combining asceticism with worship, this monastic community was called the Therapeutae. It was eclectic, the principal ingredients being Pythagoreanism, Platonism, and Stoicism. Celibacy was practiced by men and women who had left their spouses to purify themselves.[14] Influencing that movement were pagan Egyptian Serapis priests who devoted themselves to sexual and dietary austerities.[15]

During the first two centuries of the Christian era there flourished among the pagans a syncretism that is sometimes labeled

Neo-Pythagoreanism. Apollonius, Numenius, and Sextus were philosophers of that school. The celebrated Apollonius abstained from meat, wine, and women.[16] Numenius claimed that Pythagoras soundly believed that the physical stuff from which the world is created is evil and opposed to God. For Numenius, individual salvation consisted in abandoning sexual activity so as to liberate the soul from passion.[17] Plutarch, writing about the same time as Numenius, mentioned certain philosophers who abstained from wine and women in order "to honor God by their continence."[18]

Castration as a purity protector was given by Sextus this approval: "You may see men cutting off and casting away parts of their body in order that the rest may be strong; how much better to do this for the sake of chastity."[19] In the fourth century, Jerome commended that practice of some pagan Greeks: "The high priests of Athens to this day emasculate themselves."[20]

Dodds calls the last period of ancient philosophy the "age of anxiety" and he describes it in this way: "Contempt for the human condition and hatred of the body was a disease endemic in the entire culture of the period."[21] Plotinus, a leading Neoplatonist, held that the pure form of love "has no part in marriages."[22] Porphyry, a disciple of Plotinus, believed that sexual intercourse was defiling and that virginity was the sine qua non of purity.[23]

The church was nurtured under the wing of the ancient Jewish culture, but before the young community had come of age the destruction of the Jewish state shifted its center of influence away from Jerusalem. As the church moved westward and became predominantly Gentile, it attempted to assimilate some radically different Hellenistic ideas about the body and the nature of ideal manhood. Although church leaders generally denounced those who believed that the flesh was so contaminating that a perfect Jesus could not have been fully incarnate, they tended to read into the life of Jesus much of the widespread pagan asceticism. By the time the church was several centuries old it was permanently scarred by the stance of Mediterranean cults and philosophies that found no sanctity, and much mischief, in the physical. As Morton

Enslin sums up the situation: "Christianity did not make the world ascetic; rather the world in which Christianity found itself strove to make Christianity ascetic."[24]

Tertullian, the most influencial early Latin churchman, was embarrassed that pagans often did a better job of mortifying the flesh than Christians.[25] To stimulate Christians to at least match their competition, he reviewed some prominent Mediterranean practices of celibacy:

> We know about the Vestal Virgins, the virgins of Juno in a city of Achaia, those of Apollo at Delphi, of Athena and Artemis in certain other places. We know about others, also, who live a celibate life: the priests of that famous Egyptian bull [Serapis], for example, and those women who of their own accord, leave their husbands and grow old in the service of the African Ceres, renouncing forever all contact with men, even the kisses of their own sons.[26]

What Tertullian states about the Hellenic culture is supported in Joseph Swain's dissertation. His thesis: "The Greeks were particularly insistent upon the sexual purity of priests. There were innumerable cults which demanded the absolute chastity of the priest or priestess."[27] The assumption was widespread that cultic functionaries should imitate the sexual lifestyles of their deities. The Athenians crowned their city with the Parthenon in which the gold and ivory statue of virgin Athena was the center of adoration.

Roman orator Cicero told of the veneration of virginity in his culture. The most sacred office throughout Roman history was held by the virgins who were selected to be personifications of the virgin goddess Vesta.[28] Celibates were also associated with Mythraism, the popular mystery religion of the Roman empire and the chief rival of early Christianity.[29]

Christian hermitic and monastic life was introduced on the edge of the Egyptian desert by Anthony and Pachomius in the fourth century. Anthony had a powerful impact on Athanasius, Augustine, Jerome, and other major Christian leaders; he is mainly remembered by means of an adoring biography by Athanasius, the champion of trinitarian orthodoxy. Hermit Anthony so renounced his natural impulses that even eating necessary food after fasting filled him with shame.[30] He was sorely tempted when "the wretched devil even dared to masquerade as a woman by night."[31] Dodds points out that Athanasius' account of Anthony's life is similar to stories of the ascetic lives of Neoplatonic philosophers.[32]

Monastic developer Pachomius had been a priest in the Serapis cult before his conversion to Christianity.[33] Herbert Workman claims that the Stoic ideal of *apatheia* was a "powerful factor" in the evolution of Christian monasteries.[34] Going beyond moderating their natural impulses, the Christian monks aimed at passionlessness.[35] The practices of these Christians were so similar to those of the Therapeutae pagans in Egypt that fourth-century church historian Eusebius anachronistically identified the earlier community as Christian.[36]

After its early advocacy by a number of Greek and Roman philosophers, the theme of sexual renunciation has occasionally surfaced, with diminishing frequency, in the intellectual history of Western culture. Some of the leading modern European philosophers have continued to advocate sexual asceticism. Immanuel Kant, probably the most outstanding of all modern philosophers, found his life of celibacy gave him the detachment he needed for profound thought. He taught that sexual desire caused "the degradation of human nature, in that it gives rise to the preference of one sex to the other." Accordingly, "all strict moralists, and those who had pretensions to be regarded as saints, sought to suppress and extirpate it."[37]

Arthur Schopenhauer admired but did not practice sexual abstinence, calling it "the first step in asceticism or the denial of the will to live." He thought of Jesus as the "personification of the denial of the will to live" and considered celibacy as "the inmost

kernel of Christianity."[38] Friedrich Nietzsche, who was much influenced by Schopenhauer, wrote about some fellow bachelors in
this way:

> The philosopher abhors marriage, for he sees the married state
> as an obstacle to fulfillment. What great philosopher has ever
> been married? Heraclitus, Plato, Descartes, Spinoza, Leibniz,
> Kant, Schopenhauer—not one of them was married; moreover,
> it is impossible to imagine any of them married. . . . What, then,
> does the ascetic ideal betoken in a philosopher? . . . Asceticism
> provides him with the condition most favorable to the exercise
> of his intelligence.[39]

Christianity has not only been impacted by European philosophers but also by a strong tradition of celibacy in East Asian Religions. In the first century before the advent of Christianity, Greek
historian Alexander Polyhistor described Hindus, Buddhists, and
Jains who "think sexual relations are unnatural and unlawful."[40]
Egyptologist Flinders Petrie, who finds no encouragement of
celibacy in Egypt prior to the period of Indian influence, asserts:
"There is no difficulty in regarding India as the source of the entirely new ideal of asceticism in the West."[41] Apollonius, for example, claimed that his celibate-teetotaler-vegetarian lifestyle was
influenced by religious practices he observed and appreciated
while traveling in India.[42]

There is no evidence that church leaders were aware of Indian
religions until the beginning of the third-century. Clement of
Alexandria, the first Christian to mention Hinduism and Buddhism, claimed that they influenced Western asceticism.[43] Christians became aware of Indian renunciation of the flesh primarily
through Manichaeism. Mani, a third-century Persian, visited India during his formative years and assimilated much of Buddhist
monastic organization and morality into his cult. His three fundamental prohibitions were against eating meat, harming plant or
animal, and indulging in sexual intercourse.[44] Arthur Voobus, in

his survey of Syrian asceticism, states that the principles of Manichaean monasticism were borrowed from Buddhism and were "by no means inspired by the spirit of the New Testament."[45] As Christian monasticism developed in the fourth century in the West, it was heavily indebted to Manichaeism that had spread widely in the Mediterranean region.[46] Jovinian, a Christian adversary of Jerome and Augustine, charged that Catholics who exalted virginity over marriage were endorsing a doctrine of Manichaeism. Geoffrey Parrinder rightly points to one root of sexual asceticism in the church when he asserts:

> Christian monasticism and glorification of celibacy and perpetual virginity is foreign to the general spirit of the Bible, and no doubt is an intrusion from Manichee or even Buddhist sources, which brought in a conflict of matter and spirit that is unhebrew.[47]

Swami Bhaktipada, a Hare Krishna spiritual leader, endorses the reasons given by ancient and modern Indians for repressing sexual expression and advocates that practice for his disciples in the United States. He asserts:

> The face of a celibate is bright and charming. . . . A spiritual luster surrounds him because he's relishing the joy of no sex. . . . The retention of semen keeps the immune system strong. . . . When celibacy is strictly observed, sexual energy is converted into immense spiritual powers. "Celibacy is indispensable for self-realization," said Gandhi. . . . Without it, one can make little progress in God consciousness.[48]

The Virgin Mother

In the New Testament the circumstances of Jesus' birth are peripheral. No comment by Jesus pertaining to a miraculous conception is recorded, and the earliest Gospel does not even mention Jesus' birth. Marina Warner points out that the priority was soon shifted: "The New Testament itself was out of joint with the embattled desires and ideas of Christians for whom the virgin birth was a necessary precondition of Christ's divinity."[49]

The pillars of orthodoxy in the patristic era claimed that Jesus was discontinuous with humanity because his mother's womb was not fertilized by the sperm of a male. Justin Martyr, who had studied under Pythagorean and Platonist teachers, introduced ascetic philosophy into his biblical interpretations.[50] He contrasted the death brought by "virgin Eve" when she was seduced by "the logos of the serpent" with the benefits of virgin Mary who was impregnated by the overpowering logos of God.[51] In subsequent church teaching, ordinary women were identified with Eve who "fell" because of lustfulness; Ave was Gabriel's greeting for Mary because she, as the antithesis of Eva, had no sexual desire.[52]

Justin, who lived a century after the time of Jesus, was the first Christian on record to state unambiguously that Jesus was virginally conceived. Though he was aware that some Jewish Christians thought Jesus was the child of normal union,[53] Justin declared: "Christ is not man of men, begotten in the ordinary course of humanity."[54] He claimed a prophecy of Isaiah as the authority for his supernaturalism. The Greek translation of Isaiah 7:14 states that "a *parthenos* shall conceive." Assuming that the text originally had messianic reference and that the term *parthenos* refers only to a woman who had never experienced coitus, Justin argued with his Jewish adversary Trypho that Jesus must have been virginally conceived. In response, Trypho accurately pointed out that such a mode of birth was contrary to Jewish messianic expectations; that Isaiah was referring to an occurrence in the immediate future; and that the terminology pertained to a young woman, not to a virgin.[55]

Justin's argument for a virginal conception resulted from an eisegesis of Scripture, so where did it originate? This question was answered by Trypho when he accused Christians of adapting pagan birth stories of demigod heroes to aid in propagandizing their religion. He said: "In Greek mythology there is a story of how Perseus was born of Danae while she was a virgin when the one whom they call Zeus descended upon her in the form of a golden shower." Then Trypho chided: "You Christians ought to be ashamed to relate such things like the heathen. It would be better if you asserted that this Jesus is a human being of human parentage."[56] But Justin was far from being ashamed of the parallel, and he used it in defense of his doctrine. He asserted: "When we declare that the Logos, who is the first offspring of God, was born without sexual intercourse . . . we introduce nothing different from your view about those called sons of Zeus."[57] Justin thought he was strengthening the appeal of Christianity in the gentile world by admitting that there is really nothing unique about a virginally conceived person. Actually he was placing Christianity on a level with superstitions that many reasonable persons had discarded.

Tertullian, writing around 200 C.E., followed Justin's line of defense by establishing a tie with Hellenistic legends of miraculous conceptions. The manner of Jesus' birth is described in this way:

> The Son of God has a mother touched by no impurity. . . . When a ray is projected from the sun, it is a portion of the whole. . . . This ray of God . . . entered into a certain virgin, and, in her womb fashioned into flesh, is born, man mingled with God.[58]

Tertullian acknowledged that his treatment of Jesus' virginal conception was similar to pagan stories of unnatural liaisons. The parallel he may have had in mind is the myth of sun god Apollo siring Alexander the Great. A divine ray that penetrated his mother caused her pregnancy. Plutarch tells of the conception:

> The night before the marriage was consummated, the bride dreamed that there was a clap of thunder, that a bolt fell upon her womb, and that from the stroke a great fire was kindled,

which broke into flames that went out in all directions and then was extinguished.[59]

Tertullian makes this strange deduction about the presumed celibacy of Jesus: "Christ was himself a virgin in the flesh, in that he was born of a virgin's flesh."[60]

The Jewish scriptures were used in quirky ways to prove Jesus' virginal conception. According to Origen, the virginal conception of Jesus is prefigured in the prophecy of the suffering servant in Isaiah. "Like a root out of dry ground" (Isa. 53:2) was interpreted to refer to Mary's virginal womb that was not moistened with semen.[61] Gregory of Nyssa, an outstanding Greek church father, treated Miriam, the sister of Moses, as the archetype of the New Testament woman with the same name. He found evidence of Miriam's sexual restraint in the description of a dance celebration after Moses led the Israelites across the exodus sea.[62] Gregory took the comment that she played on her tambourine to mean allegorically that she beat down and killed her body's sexual desire.[63]

By treating Mary's conception as an unnatural occurrence, the church fathers magnified out of proportion the significance of Jesus' nativity in the life of earliest Christianity. In the creeds of the post-apostolic church, the mode of Jesus' birth usually has as significant a place as his sufferings and resurrection. That most important fourth-century Nicene Creed implies that there is nothing worth affirming about Jesus' earthly life except his virginal birth and his manner of death. In the New Testament the uniqueness of Jesus is bound up with his way of life, which incarnated love, justice, and freedom; but orthodoxy has emphasized his being born in a manner that was removed from the so-called tainted sensual pleasures and the corrupted sperm of Adam. The eminent theologian Athanasius articulated the settled outlook of the fourth-century church when he stated that the Logos took a human body "directly from a spotless, stainless virgin, without the agency of human father—a pure body, untainted by intercourse with man."[64]

In all major branches of Eastern Orthodoxy and Latin Catholicism, the Athanasian position on Mary has been declared to be true. That position is also widely accepted in Protestantism even to the present era. Reformed theologian Karl Barth, for example, asserts: "The event of sex cannot be considered at all as the sign of the divine agape which seeks not its own and never fails. . . . If Christ were the son of a male He would be a sinner like all the rest."[65]

Some of the later church fathers even refused to accept the New Testament claim that Joseph had sex with Mary after Jesus was born.[66] To justify their contention, they drew on an apocryphal story that portrays Joseph as an aged widower when he married Mary. Accordingly, Jesus' brothers and sisters are regarded as step-siblings from Joseph's first marriage. Moreover, to show that Mary was not only a virgin after the birth of Jesus but had an unruptured hymen during her delivery, a conversation between Mary's midwife and Salome is recorded. When the latter is informed that Mary did not lose her virginity when Jesus was born, Salome confirmed the truth of the midwife's report by personally investigating.[67] Incidentally, if Mary had a postpartum unruptured hymen it would be easy to believe that Mary could have retained that sign of virginity after having intercourse. If virginity can be miraculously preserved after an infant's head of several inches in diameter emerges, the entrance of a much smaller penis should not cause a membrane to tear.

In an attempt to make a supernatural birth by Mary more plausible, Jerome told of a tradition pertaining to Siddhartha that he regarded as true. Prior to the Christian era some Buddhists recorded a story of Queen Maya, who was void of sexual desire even though married. She became impregnated by a divine power, symbolized by the tusk of a white elephant entering her right side. The infant who would become the Buddha was later miraculously born from the same place where the penetration had been made.[68] Jerome thought skeptics should be persuaded by this parallel attestation that a woman could conceive and deliver in an unnatural manner.[69]

Jerome was offended by the nerve of Helvidius, a scholarly contemporary, who contended that marital sexuality was as holy as virginal abstinence and cited as proof holy Mary, who had numerous normal pregnancies.[70] Helvidius pointed out that Jesus is called Mary's "first-born" (*prototokos*), while Luke uses another term (*monogenes*) to refer to a person who procreates only one child.[71] In response, Jerome alleged that the Song of Songs contains a prophecy of Mary's unbroken hymen.[72] The bride in that Song is associated with "a fountain sealed" (4:12). Jerome's innovative mind linked the passing of Jesus through a closed vagina with his supernaturally moving through a closed door after his resurrection.[73] Realizing that even an old man with sexual experience might attempt to have sex with a young wife, Jerome declared that Joseph was a lifelong virgin.[74] Consequently, Jesus did not have even step-siblings; the brothers and sisters of Jesus who are referred to in the Gospels were really cousins![75] In spite of Paul's comment to the contrary, Jerome states that "James, the brother of the Lord . . . was distinguished by perpetual virginity."[76] Also, in spite of the Bible's statement that Adam and Eve were clinging together as "one flesh," while in the Eden paradise, Jerome maintained that they were virgins.[77]

In the Catholic tradition, Jerome has been respected as an authoritative interpreter of the Bible even though he often manhandled it.[78] For example, he must have known that he was reversing the creation story in claiming that Adam and Eve were virginal before they ate the forbidden fruit and did not marry until after they were cast out of Paradise.[79] Catholic tradition has, at least until recently, regarded him as not only an excellent Latin translator but as a great exegete. The Jerome Biblical Commentary editors, for example, refer to him as "the foremost Scripture scholar among the Church Fathers, a pioneer in biblical criticism."[80] However, his prejudice has been detected by John Kelly, who notes in his biography: "At the heart of his teaching lay the conviction that chastity was the quintessence of the gospel message, and that its supreme exemplification and proof was Mary, the virgin mother of the virgin Saviour."[81]

From the fifth century onward, "Mother of God" has been a principal title by which Jesus' mother has been honored among Catholics.[82] Gordon Laing argues convincingly that the worship of Artemis (or Diana), "the virgin goddess and the immaculate one," at the grand Ephesian temple contributed to the veneration of Mary. Significantly, Artemis and Mary were both called the "Queen of Heaven," and Mary was designated "Mother of God" (*Theotokos*) at the ecumenical council held at Ephesus in 431.[83]

This hyper-veneration of Mary also contains overtones of another pagan cult from Asia Minor that had centuries earlier become entrenched in Roman culture. The religion was centered in Cybele, who was worshiped as the great mother of the gods and as the one who provides fertility to the earth. Attis, her associate, was sometimes regarded as her virginally conceived son. The most distinctive feature of the myth of Attis is that he slashed off his testes to show abhorrence of Venus and devotion to Cybele.[84] Accordingly, the priests of the "Magna Mater" were expected to attain perfection by emasculating themselves.[85] Beginning in the third century after Christ, there was an annual commemoration at the spring equinox of the bloody death of Attis. Following this, the next day, was the Hilaria, a joyful celebration of Attis's resurrection.[86]

Hoffman Hayes relates developments in church history to the Cybele-Attis cult:

There is a similarity between the goddess Cybele with her eunuch priests and the later worship of the Virgin Mary sustained by a celibate clergy. The widespread worship of Mary retained the all-giving earth mother but removed the dangerous sexual qualities by making her a permanent virgin. And indeed the carefully desexualized figure of Christ is more than a little reminiscent of Attis.[87]

Augustine believed that Mary was "a virgin before, during, and after Jesus' birth" and drew on the Hebrew Bible for support. He allegorized this prophecy of Ezekiel: "This gate shall remain shut, it shall not be opened, and no man shall pass through it; because the Sovereign God of Israel has entered by it" (44:2). Augustine interpreted that description of the restored Jerusalem Temple as referring to Joseph not trespassing into his wife's taboo genitals.[88] Mary's perpetual virginity was declared by the Chalcedon Council, and in 649 the Lateran Council made it a doctrine of Roman Catholicism.

Aquinas, some centuries later, affirmed regarding Mary that there was no "unlocking of the enclosure of virginal purity,"[89] in spite of the reference in Luke to Jesus "opening the womb" (Luke 2:23). That preeminent theologian of Roman Catholicism shared Jerome's anger toward Helvidius's position. Aquinas wrote:

> Without any hesitation we must abhor the error of Helvidius, who dared to assert that Christ's mother, after his birth, was carnally known by Joseph, and bore other children. . . . This error is an insult to the Holy Spirit, whose shrine was the virginal womb, wherein he had formed the flesh of Christ. Thus it was unbecoming that it should be desecrated by intercourse with man.[90]

Aquinas borrowed Greek biological theory in order to explain how virginal conception saved Jesus from original sin.[91] The ancient Greeks believed the sperm alone conveyed the nonmaterial intelligible form of humanness to offspring and that woman merely provided the moist matter and receptacle for incubating the seed. A drama of Aeschylus, for example, contains these lines: "The so-called offspring is not produced by the mother. She is no more than the nurse, as it were, of the newly conceived fetus. It is the male who is the author of its being."[92] Hence, a virginally conceived Jesus could not inherit sin, according to Aquinas, for a mother could not transmit character qualities to her child. From the Latin fathers onward it has been a basic dogma in European Christianity that sin and guilt have been congenitally transmitted from "fallen" Adam.

Ever since ovulation was discovered in 1827, scientists have recognized that both male and female contribute equally to the genetic characteristics of their offspring. That new knowledge may have had some influence on Pope Pius IX, who announced in 1854 the Dogma of Mary's Immaculate Conception. The "infallible" declaration is interpreted to mean that all taint of original sin was miraculously removed from Mary at the moment of her conception, that she was liberated from sexual desire, and that she was made incapable of sinning.[93] Being more pure than angels, this unique woman could not infect the fruit of her womb, even though all other mothers and fathers transmit sinfulness to their children. Pius attempted to rewrite history by stating that his dogma "always existed in the church." Ironically, what is now a mandatory belief in Roman Catholicism was rejected as unsound by Aquinas, the most influential medieval contributor to the adoration of Mary.[94]

Henry Morris, a leading polemicist for American fundamentalism, has attempted to resolve the Christological dilemma precipitated by modern genetics. To prevent the transmission of a sinful nature into Jesus, he claims the zygote nurtured in Mary's womb was "formed neither of the seed of the man nor the egg of the woman."[95] To save Jesus from the alleged corruption of fallen humanity that would have been conveyed by the chromosomes of either male or female parent, Moore presumes that God directly created *ex nihilo* the perfect zygote for the second Adam. Even though Jesus lacked real human parents, Mary provided the surrogate uterus for God's fertile implant.

Mary Baker Eddy, the founder of the Christian Science church, believed that physical sexuality is metaphysically unreal. She admired Jesus' "Virgin-mother" and called Jesus "the offspring of Mary's self-conscious communion with God." She thought of his parthenogenesis as a step toward all people becoming exclusively God's incorporeal children.[96] Eddy wrote: "When we understand man's true birthright, that he is 'born, not . . . of the will of the flesh, nor of the will of man, but of God,' we shall . . . regard him as spiritual, and not material."[97]

Catholic theologian Jane Schaberg treats the asexual Mary of church history as a tool of entrenched sexism. Schaberg perceptively writes:

> Defined as wholly unique, she is set up as a model of womanhood that is unattainable. As the male projection of idealized femininity, a patriarchal construction, she is the good woman, stripped of all dangerous elements; she receives worship, not equality. . . . The shadow side of the glorification of the passive and dependent Virgin Mary is the denigration of women. Carl Jung comments that the consequence of increasing Mariolatry in the later Middle Ages was the witch hunt. The Mary myth reduces woman to something less than a whole human being.[98]

Her Virgin Son

The assumption that sexual abstinence is prerequisite to sublime purity was a pagan outlook shared by many common people and intellectuals of the Greco-Roman world, and that viewpoint was projected onto earliest Christianity. Foremost among those advocating this outlook was Tatian, who learned from his teacher, Justin Martyr, a mixture of Christianity and Greek asceticism.[99] He was noted for his Harmony of the Four Gospels and for the Encratites (meaning "the Continent Ones"), a school he founded that prohibited coitus, intoxicants, and meats.[100] Tatian taught that woman is entirely a creation of the Devil, but man is only halfway so; above the waist he is a creation of God, but his belly and below is made by the Devil.[101] Believing that sexual intercourse was an invention of the Devil, he judged anyone who attempted to combine being married with being Christian as trying to serve two masters.[102] Tatian and his followers, according to Clement, "proudly say that they are imitating the Lord who neither married nor had any possession in this world, boasting that they understand the Gospel better than anyone else."[103] Significantly, the first propaganda that Jesus was a celibate came from Tatian, who was later declared to be a heretic.

Tatian altered the text of the Gospels so that Christians would worship a figure who was separated from his Jewish heritage and fleshly associations.[104] By bending the meaning of the New Testament in a pernicious manner, it appeared that "the price of eternal life is virginity."[105] Tatian's sexual asceticism was well publicized by his Harmony, which was one of the most widely used books in the church. Armed with Jesus as the paradigm of virginity, the Encratites spread widely, especially in Tatian's home region of Syria.

Marcion, also one of the influential Christians of the second century, associated sex with evil. Since physical contact with a woman is defiling, Jesus could not have come from a fetus in the uterus. Avoiding reference to Jesus' conception, birth, and maturation, Marcion's gospel began with an adult who descended angel-like from heaven.[106] Jesus' comment that his mother was those who did God's will was interpreted by Marcion to mean that Jesus was unattached to any woman.[107] Believing that the immortal soul could best be emancipated from its carnal dungeon by crushing erotic passion, Marcion imposed the stringent requirement of sexual abstinence on his followers.[108] Clement traces Marcion's disdainful attitude toward conjugal relations to pagan philosophers. To demonstrate the similarity between the outlook of Marcion and Plato, he quotes at length from Plato's dialogues. For example, Clement finds one speaker in the Republic referring to sexual passion in this way: "It is with greatest joy that I escaped from it—as if I had escaped from a wild and raging tyrant."[109] Clement concludes: "I have shown clearly enough that Marcion took from Plato the starting-point of his strange doctrines."[110] Although orthodox Christianity rejected Marcion's extreme form of sexual asceticism, it did perpetuate celibacy for a holier class of Christians.

Late in the second century, Bishop Irenaeus developed Justin's typology, treating Jesus and Mary as Adam and Eve in reverse. Jesus, like Adam, was made from "untilled and yet virgin soil."[111] Had Adam been obedient and abstained from sex, he would not have lost Paradise. By contrast, Jesus' resolve to remain virginal became the most significant decision in world history. "As the human race fell into bondage to death by means of a virgin," Irenaeus writes, "so it is rescued by a virgin, virginal disobedience having been balanced in the opposite scale by virginal obedience.[112] Jesus and his mother, unlike Adam and Eve, never indulged in sex and thereby restored corrupt mankind to the good graces of God.[113]

Origen had this to say about the two immaculately pure figures of Christianity: "Jesus was the first-fruit among men of the purity which consists in virginity, and Mary among women."[114] Origen had himself castrated because he thought Jesus had advised such. He believed that the elimination of sexual functioning was the foremost of living sacrifices pleasing to God.[115] Eusebius states: "Origen did a thing that provided the fullest proof of a mind youthful and immature, but at the same time of faith and self-mastery. The saying 'there are eunuchs who made themselves eunuchs for the kingdom of heaven's sake' he took in an absurdly literal sense." Eusebius also records that young Origen was then teaching a class that included females.[116] Perhaps his mutilation was an attempt to eliminate the troublesome excitement caused by some girls in the mixed group. Later Origen deplored his act when he realized that his motivation for using the scalpel came from a pagan source. He acknowledged that Sextus had recommended the cutting off of genitals as a protection against fornication.[117]

Self-castration was occasionally practiced by Christians in the century following Origen, necessitating its prohibition by church law.[118] Leontius, a fourth-century Syrian, castrated himself to relieve his guilt for living intimately with a woman named Eustolia and later he became the bishop of Antioch.[119] The perverted piety of self-gelding was so much a problem that the first canon of the ecumenical council at Nicea in 325 was to prohibit such emasculation in the future. Beginning in the sixteenth century, Vatican officials castrated boys who had been trained for the Sistine choir, enabling them to continue to sing soprano for many years. That practice, possibly justified by a literal interpretation of Jesus' eunuch saying, was discontinued in the twentieth century when women were at last considered worthy to sing on the premises of the Vatican.[120]

From the third century onward it was firmly believed that Jesus and his apostles were celibates, even though the New Testament says nothing about a celibate Jesus and states that wives traveled with the apostles, including Peter who was the "rock" on whom the church was built.[121] Catholic theologian Uta Ranke-Heinemann writes: "Christians did not invent reverence for virginity, which in no way comes from Jesus. Rather, Christians adapted themselves to their environment." The social environment to which she refers was predominantly influenced by the Stoics, but also in it were some other body-hating ascetics.[122] Protestant theologian Emil Brunner has assessed in a similar way the causal relationship between ancient pagan asceticism and early Christianity. He writes:

> Through Platonic Hellenistic mysticism the idea penetrated into the early church that the sex element, as such, is something low, and unworthy of intelligent man, an idea which . . . is in absolute opposition to the biblical idea of creation.[123]

In the fourth century, some church fathers replaced martyrdom with virginity as the supreme virtue. Methodius even went so far as to claim that virgins, "not bearing the pains of the body for a little moment of time but enduring them through all their life," imitate Jesus better than the martyrs of the church.[124] That church leader glibly believed that the single person necessarily suffers more than the married person and that Jesus, who carried the most painful burden possible, must have been a lifelong virgin. With the rise of monasticism, celibacy gradually became a hallmark of the holier life. The monks assumed that pain was purer than pleasure, so much attention was given to ridding life of all fleshly satisfactions except those essential for individual survival.

The sermons of Bishop Ambrose had enormous influence on the moral outlook of Latin Christians. He believed that the path of holiness involved copying the way in which Jesus subdued sexuality. "The ministerial office must be kept pure and unspotted, and must not be defiled by coitus," was Ambrose's dictum.[125] In the best scholarly treatment of Ambrose's asceticism, Peter Brown writes:

> The absence of sexual desire in the circumstances of Christ's own conception and in Christ's own human flesh was not, for Ambrose, simply a prodigy, incapable of imitation by others. Rather, Christ's sexless birth and unstirred body acted as a bridge between the present, fallen state of the human body and its future, glorious transformation at the Resurrection. Christ's flesh was a magnetically attractive token of human nature as it should be. A body "unscarred" by the double taint of a sexual origin and of sexual impulses stood for human flesh as it should be.[126]

Augustine came to hear Ambrose preach at the Milan cathedral, and these sermons contributed significantly to Augustine's famous conversion experience.[127] Like a reformed alcoholic, he shifted from sexual addiction to total abstinence and came to view even moderate sexual desire as a product of the devil's workshop. In his biblical interpretations, Augustine contrasted the virtue of those who suppressed sexual desire with the vice of those who expressed it. He believed that God effected in Mary a single exception to the rest of humanity by miraculously enabling her to become fertilized without the contaminated semen of Adam's descendants.[128] So as to avoid any suggestion of a passion arousal in Mary, Augustine fancifully thought of Gabriel impregnating her through her ears.[129] Unlike the first Adam before his Fall who was "able not to sin," and after his Fall was "not able not to sin," Jesus, the last Adam, was "not able to sin."[130]

In his scheme of sin and salvation, Augustine regarded man's unruly penis as proof of his being conceived in iniquity and there-fore normally destined for infernal torments.[131] Woven into the fabric of Augustine's thought was the Stoic ideal of *apatheia*. He believed that the closest approximation to passionlessness in the earthly society is consecrated virginity.

Augustine defended this logic: since sexual desire pollutes sub-lime purity, and since Jesus was perfect, ergo he could not have had sexual desire.[132] The lustless Savior rescues some who would otherwise receive their just damnation. Those few whom God elects should show their appreciation by attempting to imitate the lifestyle which Jesus allegedly had. Augustine claimed that if the virtuous Israelites had lived after the advent of Jesus "they would have immediately made themselves eunuchs for the kingdom of heaven's sake."[133] Celibacy was advocated for all, and Augustine cheerfully accepted the prospect that human history would quickly end if everyone took his advice.[134]

The influence of Augustine can be illustrated in the marital sta-tus of the bishops of Rome. Peter and a number of the subsequent popes of early church history were married, but after Augustine there were only several popes who married.[135] Ninth-century Adrian II was the last married pope.

Augustine virtually equated sex with sin, setting the pattern for the Christian conscience that has prevailed for nearly sixteen cen-turies. By way of separating his views on sexuality from those of the early church, historian Vern Bullough states that "what we call Christian attitudes toward sex are really Augustinian attitudes."[136]

As a result of the excesses of Christianity in Augustine's era, "the very mention of Christ and sex in one breath" was rejected. Robert Keable continues: "The conception of Jesus even falling in love, let alone marrying, seemed to churchmen then, as it would seem to them today, merely blasphemous."[137] Margaret Maxey comments:

> It is from Augustine the Christian theologian—not Augustine the repentant father of an illegitimate son, or unfaithful lover of a mistress—that Christians have inherited a theology of human sexuality, or marriage, or virginity, and summarily of woman.[138]

Owing to Augustine's long shadow, Christians from his time onward have tended to think of the sinless Jesus as one who was tempted in every respect as we are, except for sex. The Second Council of Constantinople in the sixth century condemned Theodore of Mopsuestia, who maintained that Jesus was disturbed in earlier life by carnal desires.[139] Presumably, Jesus had only one of the two basic human drives. When he had hunger pangs in the wilderness testing area after his baptism, he resisted the food temptation by saying, "One does not live by bread alone" (Luke 4:4). But Jesus was so impervious to sexual temptation that the Devil did not bother to attempt to charm him by offering a voluptuous woman. Jesus was unlike twelfth-century celibate Bernard of Clairvaux, who had an erection while admiring a girl. Associating sexual desire with the fire of hell, he threw himself into an icy pond to extinguish his burning concupiscence.[140]

Augustine thought "pudenda" (from the Latin verb *pudere*, to feel shame) was an appropriate way to refer to the genitals.[141] The shame comes from involuntary erections which are not under rational control.[142] When medieval artists depicted Jesus' crucifixion, they had to find a way to disassociate Jesus from the shameful genitals. The Gospels informed them that he had been stripped of even his undergarment before he was nailed to the cross.[143]

Some artists painted a naked groin without genitalia, while others added a loincloth. Maerten van Heemskerck, an iconoclastic Renaissance artist, resisted the Augustinian tradition that regarded the rebellious phallus as "exhibit A" of man's sinfulness. Desiring to show Jesus as a complete and virile man, he exhibited him with a crown of thorns and an erect penis. Several of Heemskerck's paintings have been published by art historian Leo Steinberg, who demonstrates that the erections symbolize Christ's "resur-erection."[144]

Aquinas regarded Augustine as the definitive voice of Christian truth. Like his mentor, Aquinas preferred the celibate life because it is "unseared by the heat of sexual desire which is experienced in achieving the greatest bodily pleasure which is that of conjugal intercourse."[145] That awareness did not come from firsthand experience; the virginal Dominican monk relied on Augustine who confessed his robust sexual experience as a young man. Aquinas quotes as authoritative this judgment of Augustine: "I feel that nothing so casts down the manly mind from its heights as the fondling of women and those bodily contacts which belong to the married state."[146]

Jacob Burckhardt, the distinguished Swiss historian, was among those who viewed early Christianity through the lens of Augustine. He wrote in the nineteenth century: "Sensual enjoyment is a direct contradiction of Christianity. . . . Asceticism and its complete realization in the monastic life is the New Testament taken literally."[147]

Pioneer existentialist Søren Kierkegaard believed that Christians should oppose marriage because it is designed to continue normal worldly activities.[148] He therefore suppressed his ardent desire to marry his fiancée and remained a celibate.[149] Kierkegaard gave this rationale in support of opting for the single status: "To love God a man must give up all egoism, and first and foremost the potentiated egoism of the propagation of the species, the giving of life. . . . So God wishes to have celibacy because he wishes to be loved."[150] A Danish Lutheran, Kierkegaard ap-

proved of Martin Luther's rejection of a marital distinction between clergy and laity. He applied the doctrine of the priesthood
of all believers in this manner: "It is not that the priest should be
unmarried, but that the Christian should be unmarried."[151] He
appealed to the alleged celibacy of Jesus as his ultimate support:
"Christianity recommends the single state, which the Pattern exemplifies. . . . I am unable to comprehend how it can occur to any
man to unite being a Christian with being married."[152]

Throughout most of its history, the church has perverted the
biblical treatment of sexuality. Cardinal James Gibbons, for example, asserted that Jesus chose his mother and his apostles on the
basis of their virginity. Moreover, after ascending on high, he selected a large band of virgin angels to surround his throne. That
distinguished American Catholic concluded his amazing distortion thus: "Not only did our Lord thus manifest while on earth a
marked predilection for virgins, but he exhibits the same preference for them in heaven."[153] According to the New Testament, as
we have noted, most of the apostles were married and church officers were expected to marry, but that does not prevent Catholic
theologian J. W. Rehage from asserting that "many of the early
clergy practiced celibacy by choice, after the example of Christ and
most of the apostles."[154]

Pope Paul VI, while advocating the imitation of the alleged celibate Jesus, asserted that priests "will be more perfect the more free
the sacred minister is from the bonds of flesh and blood."[155]
Catholic theologian Anthony Padovano finds astonishing that the
pope seems to reject the doctrine of the incarnation. He asks,
"Should we not conclude that God should have become an angelic
spirit to lead us rather than a human being? Would the priesthood
fare better if it were made up of angels rather than people?"[156]

Many Christians have been enraged by Nikos Kazantzakis's
The Last Temptation of Christ, which portrays Jesus as being
tempted to marry Magdalene even though he emerges unscathed
from that desire. To guard the faithful from reading the story of

mutual erotic affection, the Vatican placed the book on its Index of books with doctrinal errors. The final scene of the novel reveals the lead motif: "The moment he cried ELI ELI and fainted, temptation had captured him for a split second and led him astray. The joys, marriages and children were lies . . . illusions sent by the Devil."[157]

Catholic writer Joan Ohanneson questions if Christians have yet overcome one of the earliest doctrinal errors of the church:

> Docetism, which stated that Jesus only "seemed" to have a body, was early condemned as a heresy. But has it disappeared? In our day, that Docetism lingers on in regard to Jesus' sexuality. This means that Christians are not sure about the humanity of him whom they call True Man. And this uncertainty confuses us about what it means for us to be human. One of the signs of this confusion is the chaos in sexual mores at the present time, which the Church has not been able to overcome and which it has actually helped bring about. . . . Despite the fact that biblical theology affirms that everything is created good, the most gnawing heresy in Christianity continues to be that the sensual is evil and that decontamination is effected by pommeling the pleasure drive to death.[158]

Lest one think there were no voices countering those who advocated sexual renunciation for church leaders, some balance needs be given by looking at another component of European history. One of the most abiding contributions of the Protestant Reformation was a deescalation of the medieval crusade against sex. Martin Luther held that sexual indulgence between a man and woman who were closely associated was as inevitable as the burning of dry straw when ignited.[159] He also maintained that men consort with prostitutes when deprived of wives.[160] This outlook lends some credence to the contemporary rumors regarding Luther's incontinence prior to his public renunciation of his priestly vows in his fifth decade of life.[161] According to the "table talk" recorded by one of his disciples, Luther assumed that Jesus fully expressed his sexual impulses with some women companions.[162]

Anglicans, from 1563 onward, have been bound by a creedal statement that moderates medieval excesses. Regarding clerical celibacy, article thirty-two states:

> Bishops, priests, and deacons are not commanded by God's law either to vow the estate of single life or to abstain from marriage: therefore it is lawful for them, as for all other Christian men, to marry at their own discretion, as they shall judge the same to serve better to godliness.

John Calvin, in the second generation of Protestant Reformers, sarcastically but accurately noted:

> It was later than the apostles that men lit upon the remarkable piece of wisdom that the priests of the Lord are defiled if they have intercourse with their lawful wives. At last it went so far that Pope Siricus had no hesitation about calling marriage "an uncleanness of the flesh, in which no one can please God." What, then, will happen to the unfortunate apostles, who persisted in this impurity until their death?[163]

The treatment of marriage by Charles Hodge, the most influential nineteenth-century American Calvinist, well represents the Protestant appeal to biblical authority and human experience. Regarding celibacy, Hodge wrote:

> The doctrine which degrades marriage by making it a less holy state, has its foundation in Manichaeism or Gnosticism. It assumes that evil is essentially connected with matter; that sin has its seat and source in the body; that holiness is attainable only through asceticism and neglecting the body. . . . Our Lord more than once quotes and enforces the original law given in

Gen. 2:24, that a man shall "leave his father and his mother, and shall cleave unto his wife, and they shall be one flesh." . . . It is thus taught that the marriage relation is the most intimate and sacred that can exist on earth, to which all other human relations must be sacrificed. We accordingly find that from the beginning, with rare exceptions, patriarchs, prophets, apostles, confessors, and martyrs, have been married men. . . . The teaching of Scripture as to the sanctity of marriage is confirmed by the experience of the world. It is only in the marriage state that some of the purest, most disinterested, and most elevated principles of our nature are called into exercise. All that concerns filial piety, and parental and especially maternal affection, depends on marriage for its very existence. . . . It is in the bosom of the family that there is a constant call for acts of kindness, of self-denial, of forbearance, and of love. . . . There has been no more prolific source of evil to the church than the unscriptural notion of the special virtue of virginity and the enforced celibacy of the clergy and monastic vows, to which that notion has given rise.[164]

SIX

Significance of the Topic

Historical Consequences

✦ We examined a bewildering variety of responses to these historical questions: Did Jesus and his mother remain virginal? Did Jesus remain a bachelor or did he marry? The lack of explicit information regarding the way Jesus expressed or contained his sexuality accounts for the difficulty of this probe. Different individuals and sects have thought of him as a celibate, a monogamist, a polygamist, a self-made eunuch, a gay lover, a bisexual, or a philanderer. Only the first two possibilities have been given much serious attention. The second type can be subdivided into those who conjecture that he lived with one wife throughout his adult life, or that he was a widower who remarried, or that he did not remarry after his wife deserted him or died. To shed light on these issues, information about sexual practices in ancient Judaism has been presented and related to the earliest data that we have about the life of Jesus.

From the opening pages of Hebrew Scriptures onward, a prominent theme is the sanctity of marriage as a part of the creation order. According to the Garden of Eden story, the solitary state is the first thing God pronounces undesirable. The male or female composer of that story believed that the unmarried state is deficient and that sex should be used for mutual fulfillment. The second chapter of Genesis tells of the ecstasy that comes when loneliness is relieved by companionship. Sexual relations between those "joined by God" is a necessary good, not a necessary evil. Masculine and feminine interdependence are exquisitely expressed in the world's best-known story. The notion of a historical "fall" of a primal couple that left humans in irreparable depravity is not found in the Hebrew Bible. The doctrine of precipitous plunge into the abyss of damnation by those who had defaced the "image of God" was introduced after the biblical period was completed.[1]

Sociological practice in the biblical culture with respect to marriage was in accord with the creation story. The burning love between a couple was admired by the poets of ancient Israel. Their loveliest song was entitled "The Song of Songs," using the Hebrew idiom for expressing superlative degree. It can be viewed as an expansion of the concluding portion of the second chapter of Genesis, for both tell of naked wedded partners clinging together without shame.[2] The ardent lovers savor every part of each other's bodies. The lyrics affirm that humans are created for close companionship that can be found through intimate man and woman relationships. The two become one flesh not primarily to reproduce, but to express their mutual love. The fact that procreation is not mentioned in the Song indicates that the bond between the lovers has an intrinsic value apart from breeding capabilities.

This monogamous bonding is "till death do us part." Near the end of the Song of Songs, the theme of steadfast love leaps to a blaze. The couple exchange these vows:

> Stamp me as a seal upon your heart,
> For love is as strong as death,
> And passion is as unyielding as the grave.
> Its flashes are bolts of lightning,
> A holy flame.
> Raging rivers cannot quench love,
> Nor can floods drown it. (Song of Sol. 8:6–7)

Sex was not idolized in ancient Israel as something ultimate—as in the fertility cults of Canaan—nor was it debased as something devilish, as in some other pagan cults. Marriage was considered a sacred obligation in Judaism and was fulfilled at an early age. Emphasis was on romance within marriage, which explains why the Talmud recommends sexual intercourse as the way to begin the holy Sabbath.[3]

Biblical religion does not attempt to affirm the supremacy of the spiritual by depreciating the physical. Its leaders lived on the boundary where the divine percolates through matter. The stuff of their humanity is essentially neither spirit nor flesh. Biblical men and women are represented as having spirited bodies. The Latin term *spiritus* means "breath," and is associated with liveliness and energy. The spirit in bodies was not thought of as a separate substance grafted onto life; rather, it made its possessors enthusiastic participants in the sensuous aspects of life.[4]

Over the many centuries of biblical history, there was no instance of lifelong celibacy. Since marriage was expected of every Jewish adult, individual marital status was generally not considered noteworthy in the Bible even for major personalities, and we know of some marriages only incidentally. The documentary silence on the marital status of various persons in the Old and New Testaments should be interpreted to mean that they were in all probability married. The burden of proof rests upon those who maintain that such persons deviated from the sanctioned pattern of behavior.

Jesus gave emphatic approval to the view of marriage expressed in the Eden account. When asked for his opinion on the subject, he quoted from that story of "one flesh" wholeness and said, in effect, that his position was that man and woman were made for permanent marital companionship.[5] He focused on psychological unity rather than biological reproduction when he discussed the matter.

The alleged New Testament evidence for Jesus' celibacy has been weighed and found wanting. The apostle Paul, who provides the earliest record of Jesus and who personally thought at one period of his life that the single were not obligated to marry, did not point to Jesus as a model for the unmarried. In First Corinthians, where appeal is made to the teaching of Jesus more frequently than in any other New Testament letter, the apostle explicitly stated that he knew nothing of Jesus' position on celibacy.[6] Also in that letter Paul mentioned in passing that travel with wives was the standard practice of the apostles.[7] Is it likely that this would have been the case if Jesus had been single and had expected the devout to follow his example? Moreover, in the Pastoral Letters, marriage is laid down as a qualification for those who hold a church office. Bishops, deacons, and elders (*presbyteroi*, from which "priests" later derived) were required to be husbands.[8] This requirement is unaccountable had not Jesus and his apostles been married.

What can be said regarding Jesus' practices relevant to wedlock? The Gospels describe him as one with human passions like other humans. Such qualities as love, joy, serenity, patience, humility, forgiveness, and faithful companionship—which he expressed in an abundant manner—are also basic ingredients of ideal marriage. In comparison to John the Baptizer, Jesus indulged more in satisfying fleshly appetites, and some of his contemporaries made that behavior an excuse for slander.[9] Moreover, Jesus expressed no antipathy toward women or marital sexuality that might have precluded his becoming married.

Marriages in ancient Palestine, like traditional marriages in most cultures throughout the world, were by parental arrangement. Assuming that Joseph discharged his duty as a righteous Jewish father, he must have arranged for Jesus' betrothal. Sometime during the decade following Jesus' boyhood experience with his parents in the Jerusalem Temple, about which there is no historical record, Jesus probably married. Also, the likelihood of his having offspring would be similar to that of others in his culture. The absence of any mention of such family members would indicate that they, unlike Jesus' brother James, did not become a prominent part of the early Christian community.

In the mid-twentieth century an ancient Christian scroll was discovered in Egypt that may shed fresh light on Jesus' marital status. If the Gospel of Philip preserves an authentic tradition, as it well may, then Jesus was married to Mary Magdalene. Since the term for "woman" used in the Greek of the New Testament can also mean "wife," it is probable that Magdalene was his wife and that she belonged to that group of wives who are mentioned in the canonical Gospels as traveling in Jesus' band. However, he may have married some other woman who remained in Nazareth by mutual agreement when he traveled. It is considerably more risky to attempt to identify whom Jesus married than it is to affirm that he married.

For only a small portion of Jesus' life span do we have any biographical information, so little can be stated about his life that goes beyond the realm of historical probability. Due to the paucity of documentary sources, it cannot even be definitely asserted that Jesus received schooling in his hometown. Hence, to say that Jesus probably married or that he probably received some formal education is as strong a statement as can be made. Examination of Hebrew mores and the New Testament show that the weight of the evidence is on the side of Jesus having engaged in marital sexuality. There are respected scholars in the Protestant, Roman Catholic, and Jewish faiths who have accepted this position.

If Jesus married, why is it that the opposite assumption has prevailed through most of Christian history? The mind/soul–body dualism of Greek philosophy infiltrated Gentile Christianity in the post-apostolic era and has been largely responsible for the tradition that Jesus was perpetually virginal. Regarding the corruption of Christology by such dualism, a second-century Christian sternly warned: "Many deceivers have gone out into the world, those who will not acknowledge the coming of Jesus Christ in the flesh; any such person is the deceiver and the antichrist!"[10] Those early heretics believed in a divine Jesus but did not accept that he passed through puberty and experienced fleshly desires.

Asceticism, the practical by-product of that dualistic intellectual outlook, maintains that bodily appetites should be severely repressed for the health of the soul. As this aspect of the Greco-Roman civilization is not admired in modern culture, little attention has been given to its influence. From the Renaissance to the present day, the ancient Greeks have been associated with a balanced ethic—"nothing overmuch." Of course, that rational moral mean can be traced from Homer onward. But an extreme ethic was popular among others in the Greco-Roman culture who drew on the views of the Pythagoreans, Platonists, and Stoics. Philosophers such as Cicero, Philo, and Plotinus—all scathing in their denunciation of physical pleasure—had a powerful impact on what came to be known as the Christian ethic.

The asceticism of respected intellectuals, coupled with the popular veneration for virginity in cults of the Mediterranean area, partially eclipsed the biblical emphasis on spirit-body integration and on the sanctity of the physical. Political and military factors quickened the impact of pagan values on the church. Christianity was nurtured under the wing of the Hebrew culture, but before the fledgling was fully mature the destruction of the Jewish state cut the early church off from its native habitat. Historian Peter Brown tells of the consequences:

> By 150 A.D., we stand at the beginning of an irreparable parting of the ways. The nature of the leadership acceptable in Judaism and that current in the Christian churches had begun to diverge precisely on the issue of marriage and continence.[11]

The abrupt movement of the church's center of gravity to the Gentile world caused some radically different mores to be assimilated. Many Gentile Christians had been reared in a milieu in which sexual intercourse was regarded as defiling to sublime purity.

Christianity is like a river with Jesus at the headwater. The source contained "living water" that sprang up from the Hebrew soil where high valuation was given to sexual coupling. As the stream flowed from the Galilean hills it combined with other streams from which both enrichment and contamination was received. The Greek philosophical stream enabled a rational systematic theology to develop, but it also carried some soma deprivations. From the Tiber of Rome came not only the doctrine of natural law but also cults that revered the Vestal Virgins and designated the celibate high priest of Jupiter as *pontifex maximus*. From the Nile came the desert hermits whose constant fasting included abstaining from sex. The Ganges of India also trickled into Christianity, encouraging the sublimation of sexual energies. The river of church traditions became so mixed that some of the quality of the original flow was lost.

By the end of the ancient Roman era, Christians generally believed that all the major characters of the Old and New Testament were celibates unless they were explicitly associated with spouses and/or children. Elijah among the prophets and John among the apostles were the "virgins" most frequently praised. Others commended as having this supposed highest good were Miriam, Joshua, Elisha, Jeremiah, and Daniel in the Old Testament. Joseph, John the Baptizer, Barnabas, Timothy, Paul, and all the other apostles—except Peter—were held to be celibates. The other outstanding personalities—such as Peter, the Hebrew patriarchs, Moses, Deborah, Samuel, David, Solomon, Job, Isaiah, and Ezekiel—would probably also have been deemed virgins if there had not been a scriptural remark about a spouse or a child who belonged to that person.

In orthodoxy, Jesus became the model for virginity among males and Mary among females. Bishop Irenaeus interpreted Jesus and his mother as the anti-types of Adam and his wife. According to that influential church father, our first parents lived in an unconsummated marriage until they sinned but Jesus and Mary never engaged in sex. In the third century, the earlier tradition held by some Christians that Jesus married was squelched and the speculation that he was perpetually virginal coagulated into unquestioned belief.

Augustine and Aquinas, the main pillars of medieval orthodoxy, differed little from each other in their sexual asceticism. Both damned marriage with faint praise by making invidious comparisons of its lower good to the higher good of virginity. They believed that marriage was a concession to human weakness and that the curse of sexual desire had been perpetuated throughout history from the aboriginal disobedient Adam and Eve. Augustine, who strongly influenced the spread of the monastic movement, looked to virginal Mary and Jesus as exemplars of this alleged holier way of life. Augustine followed his mentor Ambrose who had said: "By Mary's example all are summoned to the cult of virginity."[12] According to Augustine, her example was exceeded only by that of Jesus: "We are to contemplate in Christ himself the chief instruction and pattern of virginal purity."[13]

Edward Schillebeeckx traces the evolution of priestly celibacy in this way:

> In ancient times, the Eastern and Western Churches of the first ten centuries never thought of making celibacy a condition of entering the ministry: both married and unmarried men were welcome as ministers. From the fourth century on, church law, which was at that time new, contained a lex continentiae . . . forbidding sexual intercourse during the night before communicating the eucharist. . . . [When] the Western churches began to celebrate the eucharist daily, in practice this abstinence became a permanent condition for married priests.[14]

Around 305, the Council of Elvira in Spain acted in tacit opposition to Jesus who announced: "What God has joined, let no one separate" (Mark 10:9). Canon 33 of the Council was the first attempt to legislate that the sexual and the sacred are incompatible. It declared: "All who have a position in the ministry are ordered to abstain completely from their wives and not to have children. Whoever does so shall be expelled from his rank among the clergy."

The celibate ideal caused abiding troubles in the Middle Ages. Christians were exhorted to emulate the discarnate angels. It was, of course, an impossibility for creatures of flesh, but the bishops thought that those in sacred orders should at least attempt it. From the fourth century onward, church councils denounced clergy in the major orders who were allegedly soiling the sacraments by having sexual relations with their wives. An attempt was made to apply the Elvira regional council decision to the whole church when the first ecumenical council met at Nicea. It was rejected because Bishop Paphnutius argued that sexual intercourse within marriage was chastity;[15] in support of his position he quoted this relevant verse from the New Testament: "Let marriage be held in honor among all" (Heb. 13:14).

Fourth-century Pope Damasus urged priestly celibacy, judging that "intercourse is defilement" (*commixtio pollutio est*).[16] In 1049 Pope Leo IX sold the wives of clergymen into slavery.[17] But not until Pope Innocent II in the twelfth century was there a decree nullifying current or future clerical marriage.[18]

One effect of that greatest divorce act in history was to increase fornication and inverted forms of eroticism. James Cleugh has shown that unmarried clergy frequently obtained their sexual pleasure by masochism and sadism. The thesis of his lengthy disclosures is that "the remarkable proliferation of sexual perversions among the clergy of the Christian Middle Ages, especially the monks, from flagellation and sodomy to bestiality, was directly due to the senseless enforcement of celibacy."[19] John Boswell points out that the ban on clerical marriage was accompanied by more tolerance toward gay practice.[20] He states, "The approach to sexuality adopted by early twelfth-century theologians effectively 'decriminalized' homosexual relations altogether."[21]

Gordon Taylor describes the medieval outlook:

> In the eyes of the church, for a priest to marry was a worse crime than to keep a mistress, and to keep a mistress was worse than to engage in random fornication—a judgment which completely reverses secular conceptions of morality, which attach importance to the quality and durability of personal relationships.[22]

Eric Fuchs writes regarding the Renaissance era: "The clergy at that time interpreted required celibacy as an obligation not to marry, but not as an obligation to renounce living with a woman. As we know, at the end of the fifteenth century, the great majority of priests were living with concubines."[23] Renaissance scholar Erasmus, born to a priest in 1466, reported the flagrant lechery and greater illegitimacy that resulted from the requirement of priestly celibacy.[24]

That prevailing historical pattern of Roman Catholicism vis-à-vis celibacy is similar to the way some Catholics have described the current situation. Edward Henriques asks:

> Is it not significant that canon law imposes no punishment whatever upon such extra-parochial diversions as clerical fornication, adultery, sodomy, flagrant promiscuity, or any other form of sexual aberration, not even for continual and prolonged concubinage, but only for "committing" matrimony?[25]

According to Emmett McLoughlin, such illicit indulgences are not at all rare:

> No priest who has heard priests' confession and has any respect for the truth will deny that sexual affairs are extremely common among the clergy. The principal concern of the hierarchy seems to be that priests should keep such cases quiet and refrain from marriage.[26]

Thomas Doyle, who has served as a lawyer at the Vatican Embassy in Washington estimates that several thousand American priests may be inclined toward pedophilia and he calls this "the most serious problem that we in the church have faced in centuries."[27] Jesuit John Carmody is convinced that Catholicism's ban on clerical marriage has "no basis in Scripture, tradition, or theological understanding" and is therefore an "unfounded restriction of basic human rights." Moreover, this perversion of the gospel has brought an "excess of coldness, rigidity, and neurosis among today's clergy."[28]

The Protestant reformation arose in no small part over the issue of celibacy. Its leaders attempted to de-escalate the crusade against marital sexuality of those in sacred vocations. Sixteenth-century reformer John Calvin was convinced that the medieval prohibition of clerical marriage violated the wholesome biblical endorsement of marriage for religious leaders. While Calvin approved sexual abstinence for unmarried Christians in special circumstances, he observed that mandatory celibacy "not only deprived the church of good and fit pastors" but brought with it "a sink of iniquities" and cast many into an "abyss of despair." He held that the Catholic hierarchy in his European culture permitted "those to whom they forbid an honorable and modest use of the marriage bed to run unpunished into every sort of lust."[29] Regarding the vow of perpetual chastity, Calvin observed: "Experience shows how much better it would have been never to have imposed this yoke upon priests, than to shut them up in a furnace of lust, to burn with a perpetual flame."[30]

After the Protestant reformers exalted the goodness of marriage and depreciated celibacy, the Catholic church responded by making more authoritative its different viewpoint. At the Council of Trent in 1563 a policy was approved that was intended to decrease concubinage among priests. Affirmed then, and reaffirmed by popes in recent centuries, was this harshly stated decree: "If anyone says that the married state surpasses that of virginity or celibacy, and that it is not better and happier to remain in virginity or celibacy than to be united in matrimony, let him be accursed."[31]

Celibacy is an issue that has not only caused dissension within Western culture but also is among the reasons for the eleventh-century schism between Greek and Latin Catholics. In Eastern Catholicism, married men have always been permitted to become priests, and most of them have integrated marriage into their consecrated life. Because of this, Vatican Council II recognized in 1965 that celibacy is not a necessary doctrine for the priesthood and that there are "married priests of outstanding merit" in the Eastern church.[32]

In an encyclical, Pope John XXIII stated: "Human beings have the right to choose freely the state of life which they prefer, and therefore the right to set up a family, with equal rights and duties for man and woman, and also the right to follow a vocation to the priesthood or the religious life."[33] Had that liberal pontiff lived longer he might have carried out the implication of his expression of inalienable human rights and extended the priesthood to married priests and to women.

This historical sketch of priestly celibacy in Catholicism displays the emergence of sexual attitudes markedly different from those of original Christianity. After dealing with this subject, William Cole draws this severe but sound conclusion: "The church has been guilty of preserving and preaching a point of view not generic to Christian faith, an attitude which originated in Hellenistic dualism and which is not only un-biblical but also anti-biblical."[34] In particular, the dominant church of Europe has been a poor conduit for Jesus' views on marriage. Some of his major interpreters in the post-biblical period have assumed that Jesus abstained from marriage and encouraged his disciples to do likewise. That prevailing view is a fiction prompted largely by monks who lived after the second century. They wished to enhance their celibate ideal by projecting it on the founder of Christianity. Literary critic Northrop Frye shares painter-poet William Blake's revulsion to the distortions of the sexuality of Jesus and his mother. He writes: "The Bible must be shaken upside down before it will yield all its secrets. The priests have censored and clipped and mangled: they give us a celibate Jesus born of a virgin without the slightest 'stain' of sexual contact, which is blasphemous nonsense."[35]

Roman Catholicism continues to be crippled by the mandatory vow of clerical celibacy that has been imposed by the papacy, even though a large majority of North American priests and the congregations they minister do not favor the requirement. A survey of 1800 active Catholics shows that priests receive little support from their communities toward fulfilling their vow.[36] The critical shortage of priests in the United States is caused chiefly by requiring youth who might be attracted by the ministerial vocation to contemplate lifelong celibacy for themselves.[37] While the number of American Catholics is increasing, the current number of seminary students has declined by about sixty percent over the past generation. Moreover, the quality of those now entering training for the priesthood is recognized by church officials to be lower than it was earlier this century. More than one thousand American priests resign annually to marry, and the median age of the remaining priests is fifty-six and rising.[38] Inadequate discipline of priests who break their vows in various ways has resulted, in part, from an eagerness to retain as many as possible.

In *Full Pews and Empty Altars*, sociologists Richard Schoenherr and Lawrence Young accurately document from a six-year investigation that "the Roman Catholic church faces a staggering loss of diocesan priests in the United States as it moves into the twenty-first century." They forecast that there will be only one priest per 2,200 parishioners in another decade. This greatly increases the responsibility for the already overloaded active parish priests. Compounding the problem is the barring of even celibates from the priesthood who happen to be female. "To preserve the more essential elements of Roman Catholicism," Schoenherr and Young conclude, "the nonessentials, first compulsory celibacy and later male exclusivity, will need to be eliminated as defining characteristics of priesthood."[39]

The shortage of priests because of compulsory celibacy is a worldwide problem. Adrian Hastings reports that because of this constriction "the vast majority of Catholic Africans are being deprived of any sort of regular Eucharist."[40] Between 1965 and 1985 there was a fifty-five percent drop in African priests relative to the Catholic population, but the paucity of priests in South America has been even more pronounced.[41] In Brazil, for example, the world's largest Catholic nation, there is one priest for about 10,000 Catholic laypersons.

Research data confirms a wise saying of Horace, who lived before the coming of Christianity: "If you drive out nature with a pitchfork, she will still find a way back."[42] On the basis of his extensive investigation, psychotherapist Richard Sipe of Johns Hopkins University estimates that about half of all Catholic priests in the United States violate their celibacy vows. His 1990 book, *A Secret World*, claims that the majority of those who do not remain celibate indulge in heterosexual intimacies. Approximately one quarter of them are sexually active homosexuals and one-tenth are pedophiles. Sipe makes clear that his study was not strictly scientific; his percentages may be too high because half of the one thousand priests whom he consulted were undergoing therapy.

Jason Berry, a devout Catholic, has conducted a lengthy investigation of child molestation by American priests and cover-ups by their superiors. Along with some other researchers, he estimates the numbers of active homosexual priests are much higher than in society generally and that Sipe's figures are too conservative.[43] In the 1980s, litigation costs to the Catholic church due to pedophilia was about four hundred million dollars.[44] More recently, priest-sociologist Andrew Greeley has extrapolated from findings by a commission established by Cardinal Joseph Bernardin of Chicago that several thousand American priests are sexually abusing minors, involving more than 100,000 victims.[45] Moreover, in North America, the percentage of homosexually oriented men going into the priesthood is rising significantly.[46] Regarding the current malaise, Roman Catholic priest Paul Dinter writes:

> Mandatory celibacy . . . discourages openness and accountability and encourages the clergy to ignore or cover up for activity that would besmirch the priesthood. The establishment seeks to sustain its ideal of heroic celibacy behind a facade of denial.[47]

The attraction of gays to the priesthood in numbers far exceeding the proportion of the general population is ironic. Priests will be confronting a church with a strong tradition of homophobia. According to Aquinas, the most honored theologian of

Roman Catholicism, sodomy and masturbation are among the gravest of sexual sins because conception is not a possible outcome. Adultery, rape, and incest are less heinous because pregnancy may result.[48] Official Catholicism continues to reaffirm that the homosexual act is a mortal sin because it "cannot fulfill the procreative purpose of the sexual facility" and "runs contrary to a very important goal of human nature."[49] However, the Vatican continues to extol celibate conduct, which likewise lacks reproductive capabilities.

Clinical psychologist Sheila Murphy, who has worked sympathetically with "vowed celibates," prepared and administered a questionnaire to a sampling of several hundred middle-aged celibates of North American Catholicism. Sixty-two percent of the men and forty-nine percent of the women admitted engaging in sexual behavior since taking their vows. (Sexual behavior was not identified by some as genital involvement.) One third of the group believe that it is possible "to be sexually active and committed celibates at the same time." Murphy points out that her study shows that a craving for "forbidden fruit" sometimes increases when sex is repressed.[50]

Cardinal James Hickey, archbishop of the Washington archdiocese, claims that the sexual misconduct of Catholic priests is unlikely to be higher than in other segments of the population. He suggests, without supplying data, that sexual dysfunction is no more prevalent among Catholic clergy than among the clergy of faiths that sanction married clergy. Rejecting any linkage between this problem and celibacy, Hickey maintains that sexual misconduct in the priesthood will not be reduced by making celibacy optional.[51] By contrast, a group called Survivor Connections has collected more than five hundred cases of pedophilia among clergy of various faiths, but most of the cases involve Catholic priests.[52]

When accounts of priests' sexual activity with children or with adults is made public the Catholic hierarchy has launched desperate efforts at damage control. It retreats into its ivory tower and refuses to deal effectively with the departure of thousands from the priesthood to marry. What explains the Vatican's persistent defense of obligatory celibacy and its unwillingness to free the church from this vow of questionable merit? It is not because there has been a strong celibate tradition throughout the history of the church. Marriage was common for Christian leaders during the first ten centuries, beginning with Peter, the premier Bishop of Rome. Paul was de-married when he was on his missionary journeys, but he pointed out that he was atypical among the apostles.

The alleged celibacy of the founder of the church is now the main reason given by the papacy for continuing the celibate requirement for those in religious vocations. Catholic sister Margaret Maxey writes:

> Advocates of mandatory celibacy . . . presume that an unquestionable and divinely advocated celibacy of Jesus provides everyone concerned with two requisites: (1) a convincing social legitimation for a celibate priesthood; and (2) a sufficient personal motivation for choosing between personal values which, in fact, stand opposed as equally personal and equally valuable (e.g., authentically human love of others, "requiring the sacrifice" of normal human expressions of authentic love).[53]

If the Vatican remains intransigent regarding the celibacy requirement, the Catholic church in its third millenium may tragically repeat the second millenium splits over the issue. This will probably not happen because the hierarchy will accept the ordination of married men in the century ahead. Recognizing the surplus of clergy in churches without obligatory celibacy, a good case can be made that the shortage of priests would soon end if celibacy were optional.

Anthony Padovano, a theologian trained in Rome, finds the thrust of this book much in line with his interests. He is president of CORPUS, the national association for a married priesthood, as well as vice-president of the International Federation of Married Catholic Priests. He has expressed to me the hope that a new pope will accept married priests, not merely out of pragmatic necessity to fill empty altars, but out of faithfulness to the optional status of celibacy during the first millennium of the church. Padovano thinks that the acceptance of a married Jesus could provide a sound basis for reversing the error of the priestly celibacy law, which is man-made in every sense of that word. At the 1995 conference of CORPUS, Padovano charged:

> I believe that mandatory celibacy may have done as much or more evil than any other Church policy, especially when one considers all its consequences in terms of the exclusion of women and the negative reading it gives the laity on sexuality. . . . Is it not more likely that a married Jesus would more easily equate the Reign of God with weddings, with the joy of the bridegroom, with the embrace of a lost son, with an expansive role for women, a role so magnanimous that two thousand years later the Church still does not equal it?[54]

The Vatican has to choose between continuing to require vows of celibacy while dangerously diminishing the quantity and quality of priests, or to embrace early church traditions and remove the celibacy requirement. The leadership of a great number of priests who are intellectually able and emotionally healthy is needed as never before. A sign of the future elimination of the vow of priestly celibacy is displayed in Pope John Paul II's permitting dozens of married Episcopal priests to become Roman Catholic priests. When the next Vatican Council meets, some bishops may bring their wives and some may even bring their husbands!

His Birth and Ours

The literary-historical investigations of Jesus' genesis can be compared to scientific treatments of human genesis. Until the publication of Charles Darwin's *Origin of Species* and *Descent of Man*, there was a consensus in Western civilization that the birth of humankind happened a few thousand years ago by the special intervention of God in the creation of the first man and his spouse. Then came the theory of natural selection, which was first heatedly debated in England and then in America. At the famous Scopes trial, William Jennings Bryan proclaimed: "The Christian believes that man came from above. The evolutionist believes he must have come from below."[55] Such polarized thinking has been recognized to be inconsistent with the Garden of Eden story, where the paragon human is described as a combination of earth's mud and divine breath.

Out of that debate most theists have come to realize that biological evolution is compatible with the doctrine that God created the universe. Indeed, the emergence of humanity as a distinct species from some lower form was regarded by Darwin himself as a beautiful expression of the Creator's order. Darwin, whose academic training was mainly in theology, touches on this in the conclusions of his two major works. In rejecting the belief that God directly functions as a biochemical agent, he wrote: "To my mind it accords better with what we know of the laws impressed on matter by the Creator, that the production and extinction of the past and present inhabitants of the world should have been due to secondary causes." Drawing on philosophical theology, Darwin here acknowledged God as the primary cause of life but dignified secondary or scientific causation as God's way of working. Darwin found "grandeur" in the view that the Creator acts most powerfully through biological regularity rather than in the alleged abrogations of nature's order.[56]

Darwin should be appreciated for his service to religion in helping to free the opening chapters of Genesis from a literalistic interpretation. There is now less emphasis on a transcendent Omnipotence who made all present species in a week by a series of momentous acts, and correspondingly there is more emphasis on an immanent Spirit who is perennially creative through the chemical elements of nature. Now widely accepted is a dual causality:

God is understood as the ultimate cause of the universe and the distinctive human spirit, but evolutionary process is recognized as the method by which God creates all life.

In criticism of Christians who think that human creation must be discontinuous with the rest of organic life, evolutionary theologian Teilhard de Chardin writes:

> Many people suppose that the superiority of the spirit would be "jeopardized" if its first manifestation were not accompanied by some interruption of the normal advance of the world. One ought rather to say that precisely because it is spirit its appearance must take the form of a crowning achievement, or a blossoming.[57]

With regard to the birth of the "Second Adam," the reconciliation between science and religion has not progressed as far as in the discussion of the birth of the first humans. In a movement paralleling in time and place the debate over biological evolution, shock waves of the Christological argument reached the American public in the first part of the twentieth century. A rapprochement might be accomplished between the supernaturalist and the naturalist points of view if both sides could adapt to the conception of Jesus an outlook that is accepted by the majority of Americans with regard to the evolution of the universe and life within it. The dynamic Spirit of God need not circumvent the natural processes in generating the world in its totality or in generating Jesus in particular. This viewpoint, which might be designated religious naturalism, avoids an either/or conceptualization rigidity and is more in line with the thinking of ancient writers.

The apostles held that Jesus was without sin because of his godly decisions and actions throughout his ministry. Judging from the Acts of the Apostles and the letters of the New Testament, Paul and the other early missionaries never mentioned virginal conception, and accordingly it is not in the confessional statements of the earliest church. Those who insist that the alleged "virgin birth of Christ" is central to Christianity err both in evaluating it as factual history and in declaring it essential theology. Gordon Kaufman rightly views the virgin birth doctrine as a threat to the foundational Christian claim that God became human. That Mennonite theologian comments on the doctrine:

> It does not portray Jesus as either truly God or truly man: he is apparently half and half. A kind of pasted-together being, he not unreasonably is taken by many moderns to be simply a piece of fantastic and incredible mythology, rather than the one point within human history which is a genuine clue to ultimate reality, the very man who is the revelation of the very God.[58]

Other theologians, ranging from liberal to conservative, also use one doctrine of orthodoxy in criticism of another doctrine. Dietrich Bonhoeffer makes this incisive query regarding the doctrine of the virgin birth: "Does it not miss the decisive point of the incarnation by implying that Jesus has not become man wholly as we are?"[59] Paul Tillich likewise rejects the doctrine because it "takes away one of the fundamental doctrines of Chalcedon," namely that of the full humanity of Christ.[60] Emil Brunner agrees with Tillich that a being who has no human father cannot be truly human.[61]

The doctrine of virginal conception could more accurately be called the doctrine of virginal deception, for it falsifies the core of Christian belief. The earliest Christians had little difficulty in believing that Jesus was both the son of Joseph and the son of God, but later theologians, who did not appreciate the dual parenthood paradox, engaged in historical fabrications to eliminate Joseph from the God-husband-wife triangle.

To make the alleged virginal conception of Jesus more palatable to reasonable Christians, there have been furtive attempts in the course of church history to interpret the doctrine in a non-supernatural manner. Origen points out that parthenogenesis is a scientific fact for some animal species. That early Christian apologist argued that God has created vultures who can reproduce asexually, so it is not incredible for such to be done by a human.[62] In contemporary zoology there is additional evidence of eggs developing independently of fertilization. Bees, frogs, and turkeys have been stimulated to reproduce without sperm fertilization, but it is unlikely that such can be accomplished with mammals.[63] Even though parthenogenesis is a natural though rare occurrence for some animals, how is this relevant to the doctrine of Jesus' virginal conception? Do not those who advocate it want to show that Jesus' conception is unique and unlike that of any other creature?

Another problem in associating the conception of Jesus with scientific parthenogenesis is that only female clones are a genetic possibility.[64] During the first month of a human pregnancy, the embryo starts forming female genitals. Then, if the fertilizing sperm carried a Y chromosome to combine with the X chromosome of the ovum, a male development replaces the female structures. If the sperm carried a redundant X chromosome, the embryo continues to create a female.

Scientific objections to the Gospel nativity stories can be reduced if the biblical view of dual parenthood is used in their interpretation. The ancient outlook joins with modern biology in rejecting human conception without insemination and its revival would result in a fuller recognition that divine activity does not exclude human cooperation. The notion of dual parenthood illustrates a central claim of Paul, that "in all things God works for good with those who love him" (Rom. 8:28). This theology should be corrective to the supernaturalists who find the divine mainly in the events in which sense is dumb and flesh retires. Those who can find nothing spiritual in carnal intercourse need to recall that the first blessing in the Bible is on marital sexuality. The frowning disapproval of sexual passion in the history of Western civilization has in no little way been influenced by those who have wrongly given an asexual interpretation to the relationship between Mary and Joseph, and then have exalted them as models of holiness.

If Christians do not understand the way in which the Bible presumes a dual view of origins, much theological confusion can result. Consider the way in which the Bible is purported to be the "Word of God." A child might imagine occasional sound bites from heaven booming down to scare or to direct people. The collection of scriptural books might better be explained as the outcome of both human and divine action. Likewise, in the catechism I memorized as a child, "God" is the one word answer to the first question, "Who made you?" I also realized that my parents were involved in my creation, and no attempt was made by them to direct me to think otherwise. They dignified my existence by teaching me that every child was a special gift from God, but they did not suggest that new matter went into my creation. Unless children are encouraged to juxtapose the different ways of theological and biological speaking, as they grow up in a scientific culture they may think of religious statements as deceptive.

His Sexuality and Ours

More basic than the historical question of Jesus' male-female relationships is this theological and psychological question: assuming that Jesus was what the early Christians declared him to be—the "Messiah," the "Son of God," and the "Son of Man"—could such a person have had erotic urges? If Jesus was truly a human, as affirmed in the New Testament and in the Chalcedon Creed, he must have had sexual desire. Sex—expressed or repressed—is an essential of human nature.

Contemporary Christians are now beginning to relate to Jesus our understanding of human sexuality. A survey of American Catholics in 1985 disclosed that three out of four think Jesus had sexual feelings.[65] Catholic spokesperson Richard McBrien writes: "Jesus was fully a human being, with sexual desires and with an understanding of sexual struggle."[66] Protestant theologian James Nelson comments: "If we are offended at the thought that Jesus was ever inclined toward a fully sexual union, such offense might simply betray the suspicion that sex is unworthy of the Savior because it is unworthy of us. But we need not project our own alienation upon him."[67]

A semantic problem has long obscured associating anything erotic with Jesus. It has been presumed that he and his followers shunned sexual passion because the Greek New Testament never uses the word *eros*, the root of the common English adjective "erotic." In ancient Greek culture, however, *eros* was transformed by a dialogue of Plato that became highly influential. In the Symposium, two kinds of *eros* are separated as far as possible. Noble, heavenly *eros* is perfected to the extent it is removed from vulgar, earthly *eros*. The former seeks after clear knowledge; the latter is "of the body rather than of the soul" and is experienced in heterosexual relations. According to Plato, woman has no part in the creation of heavenly love.[68] Such polarization of types of love and the devaluation of sexual gratification made *eros* unfit for an incarnational theology that integrated flesh and spirit.

The main word for love in the Septuagint is *agape* (or *agapan*, verb). Scholars have generally assumed that the translators of the Hebrew Scriptures and the authors of the New Testament selected agape in order to avoid the sensual association connoted by *eros*.[69] The alleged antithetical difference between those Greek terms has been greatly influenced by Anders Nygren's *Agape and Eros*. He contended that *agape* is opposed to all kinds of natural human love. Whereas human love is egocentric and possessive, Christian love "has nothing to do with desire and longing."[70]

However, the Septuagint does not support the common assumption that *agape* should be defined in a way that stands in contrast to ordinary human love. That Greek translation has no word for sexual love that differentiates it from other kinds of love. *Agape* and its cognates are used hundreds of times in the Septuagint to express the whole spectrum of human relationships.[71] Significantly, *agape* occurs more frequently in the sensuous Song of Songs than in all the other books of the Septuagint. That translation was the principal quarry from which the vocabulary of the New Testament was mined.

Love is the central concept of Christianity as well as the most powerful of human impulses. The principal declaration of the New Testament is that "God is *agape*" (1 John 4:8); correspondingly, the central human duty according to both the Torah and the Gospels is to love God and neighbor. Jesus expanded the concept of one's neighbor to extend beyond ethnic and gender boundaries. A person who should be loved as one's self could be a stranger on the road to Jericho or an intimate companion. Although the New Testament contains no explicit comment on Jesus' sexuality, and few of his teachings focused on sexuality, his expressions of love have an abiding significance for understanding the relationship between men and women.

The quintessence of Christian ethics is expressed in these words attributed to Jesus: "Love (*agapan*) one another even as I have loved (*agapan*) you" (John 13:34). *Agape* should not be torn away from its wide range of meaning in the Greek Bible of early Christianity. Jesus followed the Jewish practice of using the human family as the model for teachings about the heavenly Father.[72] All expressions of authentic love share in the same essential quality, an attraction of one being for another that enables its possessors to move toward their full human potential.

Jesus and his apostles did not think of love as counter to the normal desire for human fulfillment in marriage or in friendship. To love and be loved, they believed, is a desire shared by God and good humans. Although love is sometimes completely unrequited, usually there is some reciprocation. The mutuality of love is displayed in the encounter of Jesus with a woman who kissed his feet profusely and massaged them with ointment. He showed his appreciation for the pleasure he had received by acknowledging that "she loved (*agapan*) much" (Luke 7:47). In accord with that usage, the New Testament counsels husbands to love (*agapan*) their wives and advocates that they mutually submit to one another.[73]

What bearing do the sexual attitudes and practices of Jesus have on Christian morality? The significance of his attitude toward the opposite sex is easily discernible. Leonard Swidler concludes: "Jesus vigorously promoted the dignity and equality of women in the midst of a very male-dominated society: Jesus was a feminist, and a very radical one. Can his followers attempt to be anything less—*De Imitatione Christi?*" Swidler adds: "It is an overwhelming tribute to man's intellectual myopia not to have discerned it effectively in two thousand years."[74]

Prominent opponents of Christianity have sometimes seen more clearly than those within the church that Jesus was woman's advocate. Emperor Julian, in an effort to restore Rome to paganism, lampooned Jesus for forgiving wayward women.[75] Friedrich Nietzsche, Christianity's most influential philosophical adversary, was disgusted with the equality theme of the New Testament because he preferred the patriarchal way of treating women as "confinable property."[76] Nietzsche was followed by H. L. Mencken, who faulted "the religion preached by Jesus" because it raised women to equality.[77]

Scorn of women has been so much a part of church history that Julian, Nietzsche, and Mencken ought to have appreciated much of institutional Christianity. In his *Short History of Women*, John Langdon-Davies has judiciously contrasted Jesus' respect for women with the contempt for women of some churchmen. "To read the early church fathers," he asserts, "is to feel sometimes that they had never heard of the Nazarene, except as a peg on which to hang their . . . furious misogyny."[78] Tertullian, the first prominent Latin church father, provides the most extreme denunciation of women. In oft-quoted words, he asks them:

> Do you not know that each of you is also an Eve? . . . You are the devil's door; you are the unsealer of that forbidden tree, you are the first deserter of the divine law, you are the one who persuaded him whom the devil was too weak to attack. How easily

you destroyed man, the image of God! Because of the death which you brought upon us, even the Son of God had to die.[79]

In world religions, menstruation has provided men a pervasive rationalization for excluding women from sharing equally in the holy community. Some have associated it with a presumed "curse" by which God punished a disobedient Eve and her daughters. We have seen that Jesus disregarded his culture's blood taboo when he accepted a hemorrhaging woman.[80] The implication of that act is displayed in this counsel by an anonymous third-century Syrian:

> Separate not from the menstruant; for she who had the flow of blood was not rejected when she touched our Savior's clothing. . . . Therefore, a woman when she is menstruating, and a man when an issue comes forth from him, and a husband and wife when they consort and rise up one from another: let them assemble without restraint, without bathing, for they are clean.[81]

Unfortunately, most Christians soon forgot the Gospel teaching and treated menstruants as defiling. Male prejudice toward a healthy process explains why the priesthood of women is rejected in Eastern Orthodoxy[82] and in Roman Catholicism.[83] The notion of "monthly impurity" has not only been a main cause for denying religious authority to women but has been even more damaging in causing many people in and out of the church to view sex as sordid and dirty.[84]

During the past century there has been a shifting away from the dominant viewpoint on women through most of church history. Wherever Jesus' spirit has deeply permeated our globe, women's true place has been acknowledged. Sociologist David Mace has rightly claimed: "Of all the world's great religious teachers, Jesus is unique in the respect he assigned to women as persons and in the extent to which he sought and enjoyed their companionship."[85] Unlike Confucius, Siddhartha, Hillel, Muhammad, and

Aquinas—to single out a few top-ranking religious geniuses of world culture—Jesus attempted to break the domestic-drudge mold in which women have commonly been cast.

Patriarchy is now being combated by a worldwide movement of Christian feminists. They have caused one of the most influential Protestant churches to withdraw its historical opposition to the ordination of women. Episcopal bishop C. L. Meyers had argued that only a male priest could symbolize God, since "the sexuality of Christ is no accident nor is his masculinity incidental."[86] But now the Anglican communion has rejected the gender ban on the priesthood. Catholic theologian Maria Bingemer of Brazil writes that "Jesus' treatment of women . . . proclaimed to them the Good News about a reign of the discipleship of equals."[87] Harold Phillips comments on the prime motivation for this movement:

> In the liberation of womanhood, political, economic, social, is there any single factor that has had as much influence as the gospel of Jesus? He who immortalized the widow's mite, the woman with the box of ointment, the cottage of Bethany with its two sisters, Mary and Martha, he who spoke some of his noblest and profoundest words to an outcast woman at a well in Samaria has done more to liberate and redeem womanhood from servility, inferiority, and injustice than any other in history.[88]

Jesus' positive attitude toward weddings and children shows that there is no basis for Christians to depreciate those who marry. To those who thought that the religious life should be focused on fasting, he compared his way of life to nuptial feasting.[89] Jesus used the wedding party as an apt symbol of the joyfulness he was promoting.[90] One of the ironies of history has been the unfounded assumption in much of church tradition that Jesus was an abstinent killjoy, and that Christians should therefore refrain from experiences that give personal pleasures. In *Sexuality and the Christian Tradition*, Catholic scholar Joseph Blenkinsopp rightly notes that "Jesus is presented as untouched by sexual desire in such a way as to make it too easy to conclude that the Christian God looks unfavorably on human sexuality and sexual activity of any kind."[91]

Regarding children, Jesus' disciples had difficulty in understanding his affection for them and his delight in their presence. Presuming that he wanted to spend his time only with adults, the disciples attempted to shelter him from children. Angered by their attitude, Jesus said: "Let the children come to me; do not stop them, for the realm of God belongs to them" (Mark 10:14). When Jesus overheard an argument among his disciples over who had the most prestige, he told them, "Whoever wants to be first must be last of all and serve all." Then he put his arms around a child and remarked, "Whoever welcomes a child like this in my name welcomes me" (Mark 9:35–37). To reinforce this teaching, Jesus directed his most outspoken criticism toward child abuse:

> If any of you puts a stumbling block before one of these little ones who has faith in me, it would be better for you to be drowned in the deep sea with a large millstone fastened around your neck. . . . Be careful not to treat with contempt a single one of these little ones. (Matt. 18:6, 10)

As long as it is recognized that Jesus was a sexual being and had a warm appreciation of marriage and children, his actual marital status is incidental to his full humanity and to his role as model of Christian morality. The imitation of Jesus should be relevant to the situation of all Christians regardless of whether they are single, married, separated, or divorced. G. W. Lampe, Professor of Divinity at Cambridge University, states what it means to follow Jesus:

> It means the imitation of his total commitment to God, his obedience to God's will, and his attitude of unswerving love for others which was the fruit of his openness to God. . . . The Chris-

tian is called, not to reproduce the externals of the life of Jesus, but to live in the spirit of Jesus. . . . We have to try to share Jesus' attitudes. It would, indeed, be a serious defect in his attitude to man if he had depreciated, or had no understanding of marriage and parenthood, or if his life and teaching had been such as to have no relevance to married and family life.[92]

After reviewing what the Gospels say about Jesus' sexuality, Rosemary Ruether judiciously concludes:

Jesus' life gives no exclusive sanctification to a particular sexual life style, whether celibate or married, hetero- or homosexual, as the normative model for Christians. On the other hand, there are aspects that are open to all of these options. None of these options is enshrined. None is ruled out as irretrievably contrary to the Gospel. Most of all, the Synoptic world is not a world obsessed with sexuality, either as the darkest sin or as the path of fulfillment.[93]

While acknowledging that the "historical probabilities favor marriage rather than celibacy" for Jesus, Charles Davis also comments:

The demand that all in the name of a healthy sexuality should conform to the Jewish cultural outlook is intolerant. . . . Not every element in human personality and not every faculty in human nature must be developed and exercised in the same way by every single individual. If he [Jesus] was married, his marriage was a particular fact about him in his cultural context: no evidence makes it an essential feature of his personal religion.[94]

Assuming that the divine incarnation could have been as fully expressed in a feminine form, it is also not basic to Christianity that its founder was male. Jesus' gender was not emphasized in early Christianity. The creeds of the early ecumenical councils at Nicea and at Chalcedon use *anthropos* (human being) several times to describe Jesus' manhood. In its Latin translation, the foundational Nicene Creed affirms that God became human (*homo* is used rather than *vir*, the word for male). In the Greek New Testament Jesus is referred to as male (*aner*, or genitive *andros*) only several times,[95] but he is frequently called *anthropos*. Paul describes Jesus as one who "appeared among us as *anthropos* and became humbly obedient to death by crucifixion" (Phil. 2:7–8). That apostle referred to Jesus only as *anthropos,* showing that he did not view him as primarily a male but as the generic man who defines for both females and males what it means to be genuinely human. Paul also designated Jesus as *Theou Sophia*, God's Wisdom, thereby designating Jesus as the personification of the Creator's feminine companion.[96] Since Jesus was devoted to overturning patriarchy as well as other kinds of oppression, his maleness had little significance.

If Jesus never married, as most Christians throughout history have thought, what significance should that have for the lifestyle of Christians? Is marriage, with its agonies and ecstasies, such a profound experience that Christians should reject Jesus as a viable pattern to be copied? This seems to have been the outlook of Daniel Callahan when he wrote: "It is almost impossible for a contemporary man to model his life on Christ's. Most of us will marry."[97]

Another approach to an alleged unmarried Jesus would be to stress that Christians should pattern their lives after only those qualities of his that are essential to full humanity. It could well be claimed that being a complete human does not depend upon experiencing either marriage or old age. Through misfortune rather than intent one or both of these experiences might be missed. Jesus did not experience the gratifications or difficulties of old age, but that fact need not make him less relevant as a pattern for the aged to imitate. Likewise, marriage is a nonessential for complete humanity, so a married or unmarried person of either sex has an equal potential for representing Jesus, the paradigm of true humanity.

A problem arises in this regard in Semitic religions, where marriage has traditionally been viewed as prerequisite to self-realization. Because of the need for many offspring in the under-populated ancient world, the Hebrews understandably regarded marriage as obligatory for all humans. Procreation was prerequisite to the biological immortality those people craved. That value is expressed in a promise of God to Abraham: "I will bless you abundantly and make your offspring as numerous as the stars in the sky and as the sand on the seashore" (Gen. 22:17). The perspective of classical Judaism is expressed in the judgments that "any man who has no wife is no proper man,"[98] or that "the Divine Presence rests only upon a married man, because an unmarried man is but half of a man."[99] Robert Gordis, a contemporary rabbi, less stringently states: "Judaism regards marriage and not celibacy as the ideal human state, because it alone offers the opportunity for giving expression to all aspects of human nature."[100]

Islam has followed its parent Semitic religion in making marriage obligatory.[101] According to the Qur'an, God's decree is simply this: "Those of you who are single shall marry."[102] Muhammad, who was frequently espoused, taught that Muslims should marry at least once. He said, "When a man marries he has fulfilled half of the religion; so let him fear God regarding the remaining half."[103]

Traditional Judaism and Islam have gone to an extreme in requiring marriage and in assuming that the humanity of an unmarried adult is necessarily diminished. Christians have also occasionally taken the same stance. For example, Michael Baigent, Richard Leigh, and Henry Lincoln write:

Could God, incarnate as Jesus, truly claim to be a man, to encompass the spectrum of human experience, without coming to know two of the most basic, most elemental facets of the human condition? . . . We do not think the Incarnation truly symbolizes what it is intended to symbolize unless Jesus was married and sired children.[104]

Protestants have often suspected clergy who remain unmarried as being immoral or abnormal. Karl Barth has rightly criticized fellow Protestants who, in reaction to Catholic priestly celibacy, have declared marriage to be an obligation for every able-bodied person.[105] Protestant William Hoyt questions the strong marriage sanctions in some professions:

Does one have to be sexually active to be sexually authentic? Rather, is it not the fully sexed person who can decide what his sexual role will be without feeling the need to prove to himself or anyone else that he is virile? . . . One may ask whether the unofficial but widely enforced rule that Protestant ministers must marry has always had wholesome results. A man can be called to be a minister without being called to be a husband and father. Indeed, is not marriage a requirement not only in the ministry but in many other segments of our society for those who wish to be promoted in the organization, or included in the social life, or become eligible for income shelters? . . . We need liberation for those who wish to live a celibate life; we must grant them the recognition that they too may be dealing authentically with their sexual nature.[106]

There are many unmarried adults who are well adjusted and skillful in interpersonal relations, as well as married folk who lack such. Celibacy can be chosen for reasons other than the fear or shame of intimacy. Personal responsibility for some significant task may cause some individuals to opt not to marry and propagate. Bishop Francis Asbury, who traveled on horseback thousands of miles annually to establish Methodist communities in early America, realized that marriage was inappropriate for circuit riders. He lamented that hundreds of his itinerant preachers had quit out of preference for a settled family life.[107] Or consider Beethoven, a lifelong bachelor who was warmly disposed toward matrimony. To maintain that he was less an expression of manhood than Bach, who married and had many children, is both uncharitable and unwise. Erasmus and Pope John XXIII are likewise superb examples of the divinely inspired human spirit, even though, as Catholic priests, they presumably were not sexually active. McBrien mentions other well-known persons to show that "there are well-integrated, courageous, forceful, responsible, and thoroughly dedicated human beings who do not marry."[108]

As we have noted, the early Roman Catholic leaders gave a contextual interpretation to "Be fruitful, multiply, and fill the earth" (Gen. 1:28), the first command of Scripture. They realized that the earth was relatively empty of humans millennia earlier and that survival was more precarious before civilization arose. In order to give priority to lifelong virginity, the church fathers claimed that God had rescinded the Genesis order to propagate profusely because the earth had become completely inhabited. We now know that human population sixteen centuries ago was about five percent of what it is today.

Failure to multiply in ancient Judaism was associated with homicide; now population multiplication on a global scale must be viewed as equivalent to homicide. Obsession with increasing the quantity of life is causing enormous overcrowding and accompanying misery in many areas of the earth. Yet, ironically, the Catholic church has stressed in this century the biblical injunction that has been overly obeyed. John Paul II has stated that a married couple "will not have recourse to contraception, which is essentially opposed to love and parenthood."[109] The Vatican bans on contraception and masturbation have been driven by the presumption that every seminal discharge should be potentially directed toward ovum fertilization. The Catholic rejection of condoms has the effect of increasing babies among those least able to afford more, even at the expense of destroying actual lives on our AIDS-ravaged globe. The prohibition of abortion by some churches at even the earliest stage of embryo development also contributes significantly to the greatest ecological problem of our future.

Now that the reproductive function of marriage ought no longer be primary, it can be seen more clearly that the life of bachelors, or those earlier stigmatized as "spinsters," need not be less than fully human. In light of the ominous overpopulation problem on our globe, a Christian might decide that he or she can best express the "mind of Christ" by choosing to remain unmarried and concentrate on maximizing the quality rather than the quantity of life. Judging by the sharp increase in the number of single adults in the past generation`in the United States, the single status option is now more appealing than in the past. However, modern medical technology has effectively isolated the procreative from other functions of marriage. Methods of birth control have given individuals the freedom to decide the question of marriage independently of the question of adding new life to a crowded planet.

The recorded words of Jesus contain nothing about the responsibility to reproduce. When sex is understood as primarily procreative, it tends to be viewed as a means, often messy and embarrassing, to a good end. Correspondingly, the joyful and communicative aspects of sexuality are given grudging consideration. But for Jesus the primary purpose of sexuality was the complementary union of two individuals.[110]

Devoted gay and lesbian couples focus on companionship rather than reproduction, and they may find in the gospel of Jesus an acceptance of their lifestyle. In his era, homosexual practice was associated with the city of Sodom, presumed to be damned by God and destroyed in early Hebrew history.[111] In the Gospels there is only one possible reference to homosexual activity. Jesus obliquely indicated that the rejection of his message in Galilean cities was more deserving of harsh judgment than the behavior of the Sodomites.[112] He wished to shift the focus of fellow Galileans from the alleged depravity of some distant group they reviled to their own need for repentance because of failure to be hospitable and loving.

When love and fidelity are mutually covenanted, whether the pair bonding is between those of the same or of the opposite sex, the church has questionable authority for attempting to impose celibacy on those who cannot obtain a marriage license or who are not publicly wed. A loving and committed couple who "cling together in one flesh" may be more "joined by God" than two who have obtained a clerical blessing or a state license. If those who have participated in formal nuptial rites are in a situation of permanent alienation, it is they who are "living in sin." Ironically, many Christians regard cohabitation to be wicked if it is not sanctioned by a public official even though neither priests nor state officers performed weddings in the biblical culture.

Undiscriminating attempts to duplicate Jesus' pattern of life without attention to the different contextual situations of his culture and one's own can do violence to the integrity of Jesus' message and lifework. If historical probability favors a married Jesus, as I think would be concluded from a judicious examination of the life and times of Jesus, this subverts the celibate Christian's claim that he or she is following Jesus' pattern more closely. But it should not cause the married Christian to engage in the similar error of narrowly assuming that the married life is necessarily holier because Jesus was married. Nor should it cause anyone to think that marriage and parenthood are so essential to an individual's full humanity that to be without one or both experiences deprives one of his or her true humanity.

Jesus lived in a specific time and place, and his actions were relative to that historical environment. To follow him does not involve having his particular gender, sharing his economic class, or living in a Nazareth-like town. Rather, Christians attempt to exemplify in their different cultures the most Christlike expression of loving attitudes, enabling relationships, and courageous deeds. One of the challenges of the Christian life is to discern what elements of Jesus' life are dated and dispensable forms and what are integral and necessary qualities for the life of God's people.

The New Testament testifies that Jesus came "to set at liberty those who are oppressed" (Luke 4:18), and it affirms that "where the spirit of the Lord is, there is freedom" (2 Cor. 3:17). Consequently, those who accept Jesus as the model of the Christian life should maximize responsible sexual freedom. Unless the imitation of Jesus is interpreted broadly, it can involve the surrender of individuality and make a travesty of Christian freedom.

Paul saw the image of God reflected in all its brilliance in the person of Jesus.[113] By his tragic and triumphant life, he brought to full flowering the potentialities of human nature. Kenneth Foreman has commented on Paul's doctrine: "Jesus is the truly normal—that is to say, standard—human being. To become like him, to belong to his family rather than to that of Adam the First, is not to become freakish and abnormal; it is to discover what being human really is."[114] According to that Pauline perspective, Jesus is on center, not ec-centric, vis-à-vis authentic human nature, and it is the purpose of the gospel to enable people to be conformed to him.[115] In a word, the more Christlike, the more human. In Pauline thought, Jesus was the standard for evaluating moral maturity.[116]

The apostle sketched the prime values intrinsic to the life of his "Lord." Jesus was posing in the studio of Paul's mind as he painted his moral masterpiece. Since Jesus is the quintessential personification of love, Paul's ode to *agape* may be read with this legitimate substitution of subject:

> Jesus is patient and kind. He is not jealous, boastful, snobbish, or rude. Jesus is not selfish, irritable, or resentful; he does not gloat when others go wrong, but is gladdened by the truth. Jesus is cautious in exposing, eager to believe the best, always hopeful, conquering through endurance. (1 Cor. 13:4–7)

Those virtues, which can be embodied by the unmarried or the married, are what count most in genuine Christian living. In the context of discussing the option of marriage, Paul advises: "Let each of you lead the life that the Lord has assigned, to which God called you" (1 Cor. 7:17). The vocation for each individual is to express love by the way appropriate to one's situation. There should be no more reason for a person to have anxieties over abstaining from marriage than for a vegetarian to feel guilty about renouncing meat. Likewise, those who indulge in marriage and those who enjoy meat should recognize that while their lifestyles are the most common, theirs are not the only healthy types. Unwholesomeness results from those who become celibates or who fast on the one hand, and from those who become married or reject dietary restrictions on the other hand, because they believe their personal choice to be morally and religiously superior to the alternative ways of life. In judging the single versus the non-single status, Paul's counsel of tolerance should be appropriated from another situation:

> Meat eaters and vegetarians should not pass judgment on one another, for God has accepted them. . . . Meat eaters have the Lord in mind, since they thank God for their food; while those who abstain have the Lord in mind no less, since they too give thanks. . . . All that I know of the Lord Jesus convinces me that nothing is intrinsically unholy. (Rom. 14:3, 6, 14)

It may be providential that there is no explicit comment in the New Testament regarding the way in which Jesus physically expressed his sexuality. If the records of earliest Christianity had called attention to his marital status, there may have been established this immutable doctrine: the sexual lifestyle required for the holier life is whatever Jesus had. As it is, each Christian is free to respond to the prodding of her or his own flesh-spirit and resolve what his or her lifestyle should be.

NOTES

ONE Introduction

1. Merton Strommen et al., *A Study of Generations* (Minneapolis: Augsburg, 1972), 367.

2. Helmut Lehman, ed., *Luther's Works*, vol. 54 (Philadelphia: Fortress, 1957), 154.

3. George Frein, ed., *Celibacy* (New York: Herder, 1968), 129.

4. William Phipps, "Did Jesus or Paul Marry?" *Journal of Ecumenical Studies* 5 (1968): 741–44.

5. I received letters endorsing my position from New Testament Professor Frederick Grant of New York's Union Theological Seminary and from President James McCord of Princeton Theological Seminary. Also, Catholic theologians Charles Davis (*London Observer*, 28 March 1971, 25) and Eugene Bianchi (*National Catholic Reporter*, 13 September 1974, 8) have supported my hypothesis in their reviews of my book.

6. Rev. 14:1–4, 19:7–9, 20:6.

7. Alexander Smyth, *The Occult Life of Jesus of Nazareth* (Chicago: Progressive Thinker Publishing House, 1899), 82.

8. Michael Baigent, Richard Leigh, and Henry Lincoln, *Holy Blood, Holy Grail* (New York: Dell, 1983), 313.

9. Margaret Starbird, *The Woman with the Alabaster Jar* (Santa Fe: Bear, 1993), 155.

10. *Christian Herald*, March 1971, 46.

11. Stephen Sapp, *Sexuality, the Bible, and Science* (Philadelphia: Fortress, 1977), 51.

12. George Gallup, ed., *Religion in America*, Report no. 70 (Princeton, N.J.: Gallup International, 1971), 32.

13. John Spong, *Born of Woman* (San Francisco: Harper, 1992), 198.

14. Francis Mugavero, "Sexuality—God's Gift" (1976), reprinted in Joan Ohanneson, *And They Felt No Shame* (Minneapolis: Winston, 1982), 332–33.

15. Donald Goergen, *The Sexual Celibate* (New York: Seabury, 1974), 26.

16. William Phipps, *Genesis and Gender* (New York: Praeger, 1989), 12–13.

17. Lactantius, *Divine Institutes* 6, 23.

18. 1 Cor. 1:23.

19. See William Phipps, *Muhammad and Jesus: A Comparison of the Prophets and Their Teachings* (New York: Paragon House, 1995).

20. Robert Funk, ed., *The Five Gospels* (New York: Macmillan, 1993), 7.

21. Joseph Blenkinsopp, *Sexuality and the Christian Tradition* (Dayton, Ohio: Pflaum, 1969), 81.

22. Tom Driver, "A Stride Toward Sanity," *Christianity and Crisis* (31 October 1977): 246.

23. John Robinson, *The Human Face of God* (Philadelphia: Westminster, 1973), 63.

24. Norman Pittenger, *Christology Reconsidered* (London: SCM, 1970), 61.

25. Diogenes Laertius, *Lives of the Philosophers* 8, 19.

26. Deut. 22:12.

27. Matt. 9:20, 14:36.

28. Hilary, *The Trinity* 35.

29. Augustine, *Incomplete Work Against Julian* 4, 57.

30. Leander Keck, *A Future for the Historical Jesus* (Nashville: Abingdon, 1971), 34.

31. Robert Gordis, "Re-Judaizing Christianity," *Center* (September 1968): 10, 13.

32. Jaroslav Pelikan, *Jesus through the Centuries* (New Haven, Conn.: Yale University Press, 1985), 1.

33. Claude Montefiore, *Jewish Quarterly Review* 6 (1894), 381.

34. *Psychology Today*, November 1989, 58.

TWO Beginnings and Maturation

1. Charles Glock and Rodney Stark, *Religion and Society in Tension* (Chicago: Rand McNally, 1965), 95.

2. Raymond Brown, *The Birth of the Messiah* (New York: Dou-

bleday, 1993); Hans von Campenhausen, *The Virgin Birth in the Theology of the Ancient Church* (Naperville, Ill.: Allenson, 1964).

3. John Otwell, *And Sarah Laughed* (Philadelphia: Westminster, 1977), 192.

4. Geza Vermes, *Jesus the Jew* (London: Collins, 1973), 217.

5. E.g., Gen. 6:3; Job 27:3.

6. E.g., Isa. 32:15, 44:3–4; Ps. 104:30.

7. Kiddushin 30b.

8. Israel Abrahams, "Marriage (Jewish)," *Encyclopaedia of Religion and Ethics* (New York: Scribner's, 1928).

9. Genesis Rabbah 8, 9.

10. George Moore, *Judaism in the First Centuries of the Christian Era*, vol. 1 (New York: Schocken, 1971), 437; J. Abelson, *The Immanence of God in Rabbinical Literature* (London, 1912), 207.

11. See William Phipps, "The Sex of God," *Journal of Ecumenical Studies* 16 (1979): 515–18.

12. Aboth 3:2; cf. Matt. 18:20.

13. Sotah 17a.

14. Leonard Swidler, *Biblical Affirmations of Woman* (Philadelphia: Westminster, 1979), 21–43.

15. James Muilenburg, in *The Interpreter's Bible*, vol. 1, ed. George Buttrick (Nashville: Abingdon, 1952), 301.

16. Ruth 3:1–6, 16–18.

17. Gen. 24.

18. Genesis Rabbah 68, 4; Israel Abrahams, "Marriages Are Made in Heaven," *Jewish Quarterly Review* 2 (1890): 173.

19. Jacquetta Hawkes, *Pharoahs of Egypt* (New York: American Heritage, 1965), 62.

20. James Pritchard, ed., *Ancient Near Eastern Texts* (Princeton, N.J.: Princeton University Press, 1955), 370.

21. Homer, *Iliad* 10, 144.

22. Cyrus Gordon, "The Double Paternity of Jesus," *Biblical Archaeology Review* 4, no. 2 (1978): 26.

23. Matt. 1:1–16; Luke 3:23–31.

24. Diogenes Laertius, *Lives of the Philosophers* 3, 2.

25. Plutarch, *Life of Alexander* 2.

26. Suetonius, *Lives of the Caesars* 2, 94.

27. Philo, *On the Decalog* 107; *On the Special Laws* 2, 2, 225.

28. Philo, *On Abraham* 254; *On the Change of Names* 131, 137.

29. Philo, *On the Cherubim* 40–47.

30. Miles Dawson, ed., *The Basic Thought of Confucius* (New York: Garden City Publishing Co., 1939), 145.

31. Alexis Kegame, *La Philosophie Bantu* (Brussels, 1956), 351.

32. Gerhard Delling, "Parthenos," in *Theological Dictionary of the New Testament*, ed. Gerhard Kittel (Grand Rapids, Mich.: Eerdmans, 1967).

33. Gen. 34:3; Joel 1:8.

34. Homer, *Iliad* 2, 514; Sophocles, *Trachiniae* 1219; Aristophanes, *Nubes* 530; James Moulton, *The Vocabulary of the Greek Testament* (London: Hodder & Stoughton, 1930); Harry Leon, *The Jews of Ancient Rome* (Philadelphia: Jewish Publication Society, 1960), 130, 232.

35. Josephine Ford, "The Meaning of 'Virgin,'" *New Testament Studies* 12 (July 1966): 298.

36. S. H. Preston, "Mortality Trends," *Annual Review of Sociology* 3 (1977): 163–78.

37. Deut. 22:20–21.

38. Deut. 22:23–24; 2 Sam. 3:14; Philo, *On the Special Laws* 3, 12; Ephraim Neufeld, *Ancient Hebrew Marriage Laws* (London: Longmans, 1944), 144.

39. Matt. 1:18–19; Kiddushin 3, 8.

40. Tobit 7:12–9:6.

41. Kethuboth 1, 5; Louis Epstein, *Sex Laws and Customs in Judaism* (New York: Ktav, 1967), 126.

42. See Jane Schaberg, *The Illegitimacy of Jesus* (San Francisco: Harper, 1987), who speculates that Mary was a rape victim. However, she admits, "we have no evidence from the late first and the second centuries C.E. to indicate that Jewish or Gentile Christians ever entertained the possibility that Jesus was illegitimately conceived" (p. 192).

43. Exod. 21:10.

44. Marcus Cohn, "Marriage," *The Universal Jewish Encyclopedia* (New York: Ktav, 1948).

45. 1 Cor. 7:2–4.

46. Charles Davis, "Tradition and Redaction in Matthew 1:18–2:23," *Journal of Biblical Literature* 90 (1971), 412–13.

47. Vermes, 214–15.

48. John Robinson, *The Human Face of God* (Philadelphia: Westminster, 1973), 46.

49. Rosemary Ruether, *Mary—the Feminine Face of the Church* (Philadelphia: Westminster, 1977), 34–35.

50. Luke 1:18, 27.

51. Luke 1:13–15; Acts 13:2, 15:28.

52. G. B. Caird, *The Gospel of St. Luke* (New York: Seabury, 1963), 31; see Niddah 31a.

53. Edward Barrett, "Can Scholars Take the Virgin Birth Seriously?" *Bible Review* 4, no. 5 (October 1988): 29.

54. Matt. 23:9.

55. Mary Baker Eddy, *Science and Health with Key to the Scriptures* (Boston: Eddy Trustees, 1934), 16.

56. Gen. 1:27.

57. Midrash Pesiqta Rabbah 139a.

58. Luke 15:8–32.

59. Luke 7:35.

60. Prov. 3:19–20, 8:22–36.

61. See C. K. Barrett, *The Gospel According to St John* (London, SPCK, 1956), 127–31.

62. Elizabeth Stanton, *The Woman's Bible* (New York: European Publication Co., 1895), 14.

63. Ibid., 113.

64. Wisdom of Solomon 7:1–6.

65. Ignatius, *Trallians* 9, 1.

66. Ignatius, *Ephesians* 18, 2.

67. Ignatius, *Ephesians* 19, 1; *Smyrnaeans* 1, 1.

68. Ignatius, *Smyrnaeans* 13, 1.

69. The Gospel of Philip 71, 73.

70. The Gospel of Philip 55.

71. Origen, *Against Celsus* 1, 57.

72. Tertullian, *Against Marcion* 4, 10.

73. Leonard Swidler, *Yeshua* (Kansas City: Sheed & Ward, 1988), 2.

74. Alfred Edersheim, *The Life and Times of Jesus the Messiah*, vol. 2 (New York: Longmans, 1891), 15. Hendrickson Publishers, which

has issued a newly typeset edition, advertises it as "one of the most important references" on Jesus' life.

75. Edersheim, vol. 1, xiii.

76. Lev. 19:18; Sifra on Deuteronomy 41.

77. Frederick Grant, *Ancient Judaism and the New Testament* (New York: Macmillan, 1959), 109.

78. James Charlesworth, ed., *Jesus' Jewishness* (New York: Crossroad, 1991).

79. George Moore, *Judaism in the First Centuries of the Christian Era,* vol. 2 (New York: Schocken, 1971), 127.

80. Kiddushin 29a.

81. See Gen. 17:25, 34:14–19; Exod. 4:26; J. P. Hyatt, "Circumcision," in *Interpreter's Dictionary of the Bible*, ed. George Buttrick (New York: Abingdon, 1962).

82. Philo, *On the Special Laws 1*, 4–7.

83. Gen. 17:9–14.

84. Genesis Rabbah 46, 4.

85. Martin Buber, *Israel and the World* (New York: Schocken, 1948), 181.

86. David Mace, *The Christian Response to the Sexual Revolution* (New York: Abingdon, 1970), 20.

87. Exod. 13:11–15; Lev. 12:2–8; Luke 2:21–24.

88. Herbert Danby, *The Mishnah* (London: Oxford Press, 1933), 793.

89. Josephus, *Against Apion 1*, 12.

90. Deut. 6:7.

91. Philo, *Embassy to Gaium 31*.

92. See Moore, *Judaism in First Centuries*, 202..

93. Berakoth 3, 3; Eighteen Benedictions 5–6.

94. E.g., Sirach 5:23.

95. Aboth 5, 21.

96. Jer. Kethuboth 32c; see Moore, *Judaism in the First Centuries*, vol. 3, 104.

97. See Sirach 5:23.

98. See Moore, *Judaism in the First Centuries*, vol. 1, 314.

99. John Meier, *A Marginal Jew* (New York: Doubleday, 1991), vol. 1, 271–278; Rainer Riesner, *Jesus als Lehrer* (Tubingen: Mohr, 1981), 227.

100. Niddah 5, 6.

101. Josephus, *Life* 2.

102. Josephus, *Against Apion* 2, 19.

103. Frederick Bruner, *Matthew*, vol. 2 (Dallas: Word, 1990), 670–71.

104. David Mace, *Hebrew Marriage* (London: Epworth, 1953) 144.

105. Kiddushin 66d.

106. Yebamoth 6, 6.

107. Israel Abrahams, *Studies in Pharisaism and the Gospels* (New York: Ktav, 1967), 78.

108. Zohar 1, 55b; see Yebamoth 62b.

109. Mark 10:6–9.

110. Robert Grant, *The Earliest Lives of Jesus* (New York: Harper, 1961), 14, 38–49.

111. Joseph Klausner, *Jesus of Nazareth* (New York: Macmillan, 1925), 409.

112. David Flusser, *Jesus* (New York: Herder, 1969), 18.

113. Tosefta Kiddushin 1, 11.

114. Aboth 2, 2.

115. Mark 6:3; Matt. 13:55.

116. Aboth 4, 5.

117. Yebamoth 62b.

118. 1 Cor. 9:5; Eusebius, *Church History* 3, 20.

119. Neufeld, 139.

120. Shulhan Aruk 4 (Eben ha-Ezer); see Benjamin Schlesinger, *The Jewish Family* (Toronto: University of Toronto Press, 1971), 8.

121. Ludwig Kohler, *Hebrew Man* (Nashville: Abingdon, 1957), 89.

122. Eccles. 7:26, 28.

123. Yebamoth 63b.

124. Kethuboth 63a; Sotah 4b.

125. Yebamoth 6, 6.

126. Claude Montefiore, *The Synoptic Gospels,* vol. 2 (New York: Ktav, 1968), 265.

127. Louis Epstein, *Sex Laws and Customs in Judaism* (New York: Ktav, 1948), 14–15.

128. Kiddushin 4, 13.

129. Luke 3:23, 4:32, 36.

130. See William Phipps, *The Wisdom and Wit of Rabbi Jesus* (Louisville: Westminster John Knox, 1993), 57–60.

131. Testament of Moses 7:9–10.

132. Psalms of Solomon 4:7.

133. See Moore, *Judaism in the First Centuries,* vol. 2, 190–93.

134. Jerusalem Berakoth 14b.

135. Matt. 23:3.

136. Matt. 5:20.

137. Luke 11:42.

138. 1 Sam. 21:1–6.

THREE   The Celibacy Debate

1. "Celibacy," in *The Anchor Bible Dictionary,* ed. David Freedman (New York: Doubleday, 1992).

2. Isa. 57:8.

3. B. Z. Goldberg, *Sex in Religion* (New York: Liveright, 1970), 345–49; Frederick Conybeare, *Russian Dissenters* (New York: Russell, 1962), 367–68.

4. Tertullian, *On Monogamy* 3.

5. Tertullian, *To His Wife* 6.

6. Jerome, *Letter* 22, 6.

7. Floyd Filson, *A Commentary on the Gospel According to St. Matthew* (New York: Harper, 1960), 207.

8. Ian Wilson, *Jesus: The Evidence* (London: Weidenfeld and Nicolson, 1984), 97.

9. Hans Küng, *On Being a Christian* (New York: Doubleday, 1976), 193.

10. Paul VI, *Sacerdotalis Caelibatus* 21 (1967).

11. *National Catholic Reporter,* 20 April 1979, 12.

12. Elaine Pagels, *Adam, Eve, and the Serpent* (New York: Random House, 1988), 14–16.

13. Phipps, *The Wisdom and Wit of Rabbi Jesus,* 91.

14. Alan McNeile, *The Gospel According to St. Matthew* (London: Macmillan, 1915), 262.

15. Lev. 21:20.

16. Lev. 22:24.

17. Josephus, *Antiquities* 4, 290.

18. Gittin 9:10; Ketuboth 7:6.

19. Josephus, *Antiquities* 18, 136.

20. Gen. 2:24.

21. Eric Fuchs, *Sexual Desire and Love* (New York: Seabury, 1983), 65.

22. Walter Wink, *Engaging the Powers* (Minneapolis: Fortress, 1992), 132.

23. Matt. 19:25.

24. Jesus' position is clearly stated by Paul in 1 Cor. 7:10–11.

25. L. William Countryman, *Dirt, Greed, and Sex* (Philadelphia: Fortress, 1988), 188.

26. Hos. 1:2, 3:1.

27. Ezek. 16.

28. Justin, *Apology* 1, 15; Clement, *Miscellanies* 3, 6, 50.

29. Quentin Quesnell, "Made Themselves Eunuchs for the Kingdom of Heaven," *Catholic Biblical Quarterly* 30 (1968): 358.

30. William Thompson, *The Jesus Debate* (New York: Paulist, 1985), 162.

31. Uta Ranke-Heinemann, *Eunuchs for the Kingdom of Heaven* (New York: Penguin, 1991), 32–33.

32. Paul Dinter, "Disabled for the Kingdom," *Commonweal* 12 (October 1990): 571–73.

33. Bruce Malina and Richard Rohrbaugh, *Social Science Commentary on the Synoptic Gospels* (Minneapolis: Fortress, 1992), 122.

34. Matt. 1:18–23.

35. Matt. 25:34–36.

36. Matt. 18:23–35.

37. Robert Funk, ed., *The Five Gospels* (New York; Macmillan, 1993), 220–21.

38. Isa. 39:7; Jer. 29:2.

39. Ben Witherington, *Women in the Ministry of Jesus* (New York: Cambridge University Press, 1984), 151.

40. John Meier, *A Marginal Jew,* vol. 1 (New York: Doubleday, 1991), 134–35; Michael Cook, *Responses to 101 Questions about Jesus* (New York: Paulist, 1993), 34.

41. John Robinson, *The Human Face of God* (Philadelphia: Westminster, 1973), 56.

42. I Cor. 9:5; Bruno Brinkman, "The Humanity of Christ," *The Way* 15 (1975): 213.

43. 2 Sam. 18:18; this conflicts with 2 Sam. 14:27, where four children are mentioned.

44. Francis Cleary, "Chapter and Verse," *Universitas* (University of St. Louis), October 1975, 4.

45. Deut. 22:5.

46. Plato, *Cratylus* 414.

47. Luke 1:13, 3:19, 8:3, 14:20, 17:32, 20:28.

48. Luke 7:39, 8:2, 11:27, 13:11–12.

49. Luke 19:3; I Sam. 9:2.

50. Mark 1:6.

51. Quoted in Clement of Alexandria, *Miscellanies* 3, 7, 59.

52. London *Observer*, 28 March 1971, 25.

53. Mark 1:30–31.

54. Jean Audet, *Structures of Christian Priesthood* (New York: Macmillan, 1968), 41.

55. I Cor. 7:10, 12, 25.

56. I Cor. 7:28.

57. Joan Timmerman, *Sexuality and Spiritual Growth* (New York: Crossroad, 1992), 29.

58. I Cor. 7:8, 11, 34; William Phipps, *Was Jesus Married?* (New York: Harper, 1970), 106–8; Eduards Areus, "Was St. Paul Married?" *Bible Today* (April 1973): 1188–91.

59. I Cor. 9:5.

60. Gen. 5.

61. Matt. 1:3–6 includes Tamar, Rahab, Ruth, and Bathsheba.

62. Vern Bullough, *The Subordinate Sex* (Baltimore: Penguin, 1964), 78.

63. See 2 Kings 4:1.

64. Isa. 7:3, 8:3, 8:18.

65. Mark 15:21; Rom. 16:13.

66. Jean Barreau, *Les Memoires de Jesus* (Paris, 1978).

67. Schalom Ben-Chorin, *Bruder Jesus* (Munich: List, 1967), 128–29.

68. George Buchanan, "Jesus and Other Monks of New Testament Times," *Religion and Life* 48 (1979): 136–41.

69. James Mays, ed., *Harper's Bible Commentary* (San Francisco: Harper, 1988), 973.

70. Geza Vermes, *Jesus the Jew* (London: Collins, 1973), 100–101.

71. Exod. 19:15.

72. Philo, *Life of Moses* 2, 68–69.

73. Edward Peters, *Catholic World*, March 1971, 322.

74. Robert Stern, "How Priests Came to Be Celibate," in *Celibacy in the Church*, ed. William Bassett and Peter Huizing (New York: Herder, 1972), 81.

75. James Charlesworth, *Jesus within Judaism* (New York: Doubleday, 1988), 58, 72–74; H. H. Rowley, *The Dead Sea Scrolls and the New Testament* (London: SPCK, 1957), 28–32.

76. Linda Elder, "The Woman Question and Female Ascetics Among Essenes," *Biblical Archaeologist* 57, no. 4 (1994): 225.

77. *Damascus Document* 4, 21; *Rule of the Congregation* 1, 6–11; *War of the Sons of Light* 7, 4–6; see Hans Huber, "Zolibat in Qumran?" *New Testament Studies* 17 (1971): 167.

78. *Damascus Document* 7, 6–9.

79. Philo, *Hypothetica* 11, 14; Josephus, *Wars* 2, 120; Pliny the Elder, *Natural History* 5, 15.

80. Lev. 21:13–15.

81. Carol Newsom and Sharon Ringe, eds., *The Women's Bible Commentary* (Louisville: Westminster John Knox, 1992), 43.

82. Num. 6.

83. Judges 11:35–37.

84. Eusebius, *Church History* 2, 4.

85. Yoma 8:1.

86. Ketuboth 5:6.

87. 1 Cor. 7:3–5.

88. Tertullian, *On Monogamy* 3; Jerome, *Against Jovinian* 1, 7; Johannes Weiss, *Earliest Christianity*, vol. 2 (New York: Harper, 1937), pl. 582; Rudolf Bultmann, *Theology of the New Testament*, vol. 1 (New York: Scribner's, 1951), pl. 202.

89. Those new translations have been informed by the contextual

consideration of William Phipps, "Is Paul's Attitude Toward Sexual Relations Contained in 1 Cor. 7:1?" *New Testament Studies* 28 (1982): 125–31.

90. Hirschel Revel, "Celibacy," *The Universal Jewish Encyclopedia* (New York: Ktav, 1969).

91. Yebamoth 62b.

92. Orson Hyde, *Journal of Discourses of Brigham Young* 4 (1857): 259.

93. A. E. Young, *Wife No. 19* (Hartford, Conn., 1876), 307.

94. John 2:3; Ogdon Kraut, *Jesus Was Married* (Salt Lake City: Kraut, 1969), 10.

95. Donavan Joyce, *The Jesus Scroll* (New York: Signet Publication, 1972), 78.

96. Max Thurian, *Marriage and Celibacy* (London: SCM Press, 1959), 49.

97. *L'Osservatore Romano*, 10 March 1971.

98. *New York Times*, 29 January 1971, 44.

99. *National Catholic Reporter*, 25 December 1970.

100. Rudolf Bultmann, *Jesus and the Word* (New York: Scribner's, 1958), 58.

101. Kiddushin 4, 13.

102. Wendell Phillips, *An Explorer's Life of Jesus* (New York: Morgan, 1975), 120.

103. Roland de Vaux, *Ancient Israel* (New York: McGraw-Hill, 1961), 29.

104. Malina and Rohrbaugh, 121.

105. *Apostolic Constitutions* 4, 11.

106. John Milton, *Paradise Lost* 4, 750–53.

107. 1 Tim. 3:2, 12; 5:14; Titus 1:6.

108. Rom. 16:5; Gal. 6:10; Philemon 2.

109. *Apostolic Constitutions* 8, 51.

110. *Didascalia Apostolorum* 4.

111. Luke 14:28.

112. Vernon McCasland, *The Pioneer of Our Faith* (New York: McGraw-Hill, 1964), 155.

113. Joseph Blenkinsopp, *Celibacy, Ministry, Church* (New York: Herder, 1968), 37.

114. Louis Cassels, *The Real Jesus* (New York: Doubleday, 1968), 77.

115. Aboth 5, 21.

116. Ephraim Neufeld, *Ancient Hebrew Marriage Laws* (London: Longmans, 1944), 143.

117. Meier, *A Marginal Jew*, vol. 1, 282.

118. Kethuboth 62b.

119. Mark 3:31–35; Luke 4:29.

120. Mark 2:1, 3:19.

121. John Crossan, *Four Other Gospels* (Minneapolis: Winston, 1985), 91–111.

122. Irenaeus, *Against Heresies* 1, 25, 3.

123. Clement, *Miscellanies* 3, 2, 10.

124. Morton Smith, *Clement of Alexandria and a Secret Gospel of Mark* (Cambridge: Harvard University Press, 1973), 447.

125. Mark 14:51–52.

126. Hugh Montefiore, *For God's Sake* (Philadelphia: Westminster, 1969), 182.

127. Robinson, *The Human Face of God*, 64.

128. John Boswell, *Christianity, Social Tolerance, and Homosexuality* (Chicago: University of Chicago Press, 1980), 115.

129. Ibid., 226.

130. Troy Perry and Charles Lucas, *The Lord Is My Shepherd and He Knows I'm Gay* (Los Angeles: Nash, 1972), 150.

131. John 13:23; Mark 14:45.

132. Tom Horner, *Jonathan Loved David* (Philadelphia: Westminster, 1978), 123–24.

133. Ibid., 122.

134. Rosemary Ruether, "The Sexuality of Jesus," *Christianity and Crisis* 38 (29 May 1978): 137.

135. Quoted in Malcolm Boyd, "The Sexuality of Jesus," *The Witness* 74 (July/August 1991): 14.

136. Ibid., 14–15.

137. *Christian Century* (27 October 1976): 934–35.

138. Gen. 29:13; Exod. 4:27; 2 Sam. 14:33, etc..

139. Crossan, *Four Other Gospels*, 118.

140. Raymond Brown, *The Death of the Messiah*, vol. 1 (New York: Doubleday, 1994), 303.

141. Plato, *Republic* 559.

142. Pseudo-Justin, *On the Resurrection* 3.

143. D. H. Lawrence, *Lady Chatterley's Lover* (New York: Cardinal, 1957), 266.

144. D. H. Lawrence, *The Escaped Cock* (Los Angeles: Black Sparrow, 1973), 57–58.

145. Samuel Terrien, *Till the Heart Sings* (Philadelphia: Fortress, 1985), 124, 160.

146. John Crossan, *Jesus* (San Francisco: Harper, 1994), v, 119, 121; Epictetus, *Discourses* 3, 22.

147. Gerd Theissen, *The First Followers of Jesus* (London: SCM, 1978), 14–15.

148. E. P. Sanders, "Jesus in Historical Context," *Theology Today* 50 (October 1993): 430–31, 448.

149. Homes Dudden, "Asceticism," in *A Dictionary of Christ and the Gospels* (Edinburgh: Clark, 1908).

150. Jean von Allmen, *A Companion to the Bible* (New York: Oxford, 1958), 256.

151. Adolf Harnack, *What Is Christianity?* (New York: Harper, 1957), 83.

152. Rainer Maria Rilke, *Visions of Christ* (Boulder: University of Colorado Press, 1967), 21, 70–73.

153. Rudolf Bultmann, *Jesus and the Word* (New York: Scribner, 1958), 99.

154. Mark 4:38; Luke 5:1–6.

155. Luke 7:24–34.

156. Mark 2:19; Matt. 22:1–10; Luke 14:7–11.

157. John 2:1–11.

158. Jeffery Cave, "Sermon at Manhattan's Church of the Epiphany," 27 June 1971.

159. F. Caballero, *Eli, la Espana treinta anos ha* (Leipzig: Brockhaus, 1881), 61.

160. William Purcell, ed., *The Resurrection* (Philadelphia: Westminster, 1966), 75.

161. Matt. 10:37–38.

162. See Matt. 13:44.

163. Edward Schillebeeckx, *Celibacy* (New York: Sheed and Ward, 1968), 24–25; cf. Vatican II's *Lumen Gentium* 5, 42.

164. Thomas Berry, *Religions of India* (New York: Bruce, 1971), 95–98, 197–201; Mircea Eliade, *Yoga* (Princeton, N.J.: Princeton University Press, 1969), 49–50.

165. Pius XII, *Sacra Virginitas* (1954) 1.

166. *Optatam Totius* 4, 10.

167. John Paul II, "The Apostolic Exhortation on the Family," *Origins* (24 December 1981): 443.

168. Ernest Renan, *Life of Jesus* (Boston: Little, Brown, 1899), 130.

169. Friedrich Nietzsche, *Genealogy of Morals* 3, 7.

170. Honolulu *Star-Bulletin*, 14 November 1970.

171. R. C. Zaehner, ed., *The Concise Encyclopedia of Living Faiths* (Boston: Beacon, 1959), 279–81.

172. Sigmund Freud, *Civilization and Its Discontents* (New York: Norton, 1961), 56.

173. Richard McBrien, *Catholicism* (San Francisco: Harper, 1994), 564.

174. Bernard Shaw, Preface to "Androcles and the Lion," in *Complete Plays*, vol. 5 (New York: Dodd, Mead, 1962), 387–92.

175. J. P. Migne, ed., *Patrologia Latina*, vol. 178 (Paris, 1844–1866), col. 5872.

176. Richard Cromie, Southminister Presbyterian Church sermon, Pittsburgh, 25 January 1976.

177. Harvey Cox, *The Seduction of the Spirit* (New York: Simon and Schuster, 1973), 230.

178. Letha Scanzoni and Nancy Hardesty, *All We're Meant to Be* (Waco, Tex.: Word Books, 1974), 150–51.

179. Lewis Smedes, *Sex for Christians* (Grand Rapids, Mich.: Eerdmans, 1976), 78.

180. *The Urantia Book* (Chicago: Urantia Foundation, 1955), 1402–3.

181. Joseph Fichter, *The Holy Family of Father Moon* (Kansas City: Leaven, 1975), 72.

182. Sun Myung Moon, *The New Future of Christianity* (Washington, D.C.: Unification Church, 1974), 124–26.

183. Zola Levitt, *The Spirit of Sun Myung Moon* (Irvine, Calif.: Harvest House, 1976), 79.

184. Hak Ja Han Moon, "True Parents and the Completed Testament Age" (New York: Unification Christianity, 1993), 7.

185. *Bacon's Essays* (London: Macmillan, 1885), 27.

186. Gerard Sloyan, *Jesus in Focus* (Mystic, Conn.: Twenty-Third Publications, 1983), 132.

187. Tim Stafford, *The Sexual Christian* (Wheaton, Ill.: Victor Books, 1989), 156–57.

188. Mark 3:21.

189. Laurence Marshall, *The Challenge of New Testament Ethics* (London: Macmillan, 1960), 177.

190. Mark 10:19.

191. Mark 7:9–13.

192. Matt. 6:24.

193. Luke 19:8–9.

194. Mark 10:29–30; Matt. 10:37, Thomas, *Logia* 55 and 101.

195. *Austin Seminary Bulletin*, November 1971, 47–48.

196. Matt. 6:24.

197. Morton and Barbara Kelsey, *Sacrament of Sexuality* (Warwick, N.Y.: Amity House, 1986), 161, 177.

198. Howard and Charlotte Clinebell, *The Intimate Marriage* (New York: Harper, 1970), 185.

199. Sigmund Freud, *Collected Papers,* vol. 2 (New York: Basic Books, 1959), 92.

200. Wilhelm Reich, *The Sexual Revolution* (New York: Simon and Schuster, 1974), 9–10.

201. Rosemary Ruether, "The Ethic of Celibacy," *Commonweal* (2 February 1973): 394.

202. 1 Cor. 7:32–33.

203. Manuel Galvez, *Holy Wednesday* (New York: Appleton-Century, 1934), 135.

204. Quoted in Joan Ohanneson, *And They Felt No Shame* (Minneapolis: Winston, 1983), 104.

205. George Frein, ed., *Celibacy* (New York: Herder, 1968), 133–34.

206. Migne, ed., *Patrologia Latina* 17, 236.

207. Jeremy Taylor, *Works*, vol. 5 (London, 1928), 253.

208. *Bacon's Essays*, 27.

209. Jerome, *Letters* 22, 7.

210. Ketuboth 63.

211. Alfred Guillaume, *The Life of Muhammad: A Translation of Ibn Ishaq's Sirat Rasul Allah* (Lahore: Oxford University Press, 1955), 106–7, 155.

212. See Phipps, *Muhammad and Jesus*, 57–70, 141.

213. John Calvin, *Opera* (Brunswick, 1871), 10a, 228.

214. Ibid., 13, 230.

215. Increase Mather, *The Life and Death of That Reverend Man of God, Mr. Richard Mather* (Cambridge, 1670), 25.

216. Clement of Alexandria, *Miscellanies* 3, 6, 49.

217. Jerome, *Against Jovinian* 1, 16.

218. Jerome, *To Eustochium* 24; cf. Song of Songs 5:4.

219. Chrysostom, *Letters to Theodore* 2, 3.

220. Schillebeeckx, *Celibacy*, 100.

221. Mark 6:34.

222. Mark 2:15–19.

223. Norman Williams, *The Ideas of the Fall and of Original Sin* (London: Longmans, 1927), 19, 224, 304, 378.

224. Jerome, *Against Jovinian* 1, 20.

225. Ibid., 1, 36.

226. Ibid., 1, 12.

227. Jerome, *Letters* 22, 20.

228. Matt. 5:28; Jerome, *Letters* 22, 5; Jerome, *Against Jovinian* 1, 49.

229. *New York Times*, 10 October 1980, 3.

230. Augustine, *Against Julian* 4, 14.

231. Augustine, *City of God* 14, 17–18.

232. See Augustine, *Against Two Letters of the Pelagians* 1, 33.

233. Emil Brunner, *Man in Revolt* (Philadelphia: Westminster, 1947), 348.

234. Augustine, *Holy Virginity* 27.

235. Thomas Aquinas, *Summa Theologica* 2-2, q. 152, 5; Pius XII, *Sacra Virginitas* 2 (1954).

236. Robert Graves, *King Jesus* (New York: Farrar, 1946), 266.

237. Ibid., 310.

238. Ibid., 308–9.

239. Reginald Trevett, *The Church and Sex* (New York: Hawthorn, 1960), 43.

240. Clifford Howard, *Sex and Religion* (London: Williams and Norgate, 1925), 153.

241. Matthew Black, ed., *Peake's Commentary on the Bible* (London: Nelson, 1962), 246.

242. Ps. 51:5; 58:3.

243. Yadaim 3:5.

244. Black, 469.

245. William Phipps, "The Plight of the Song of Songs," *Journal of the American Academy of Religion* 42 (1974): 82–84.

246. Otto Eissfeldt, *The Old Testament: An Introduction* (New York: Harper, 1965), 89.

247. *Eerdmans' Handbook to the World's Religions* (Grand Rapids, Mich.: Eerdmans, 1994), 87.

248. Shakespeare, Sonnet 129.

249. Luke 22:15.

250. Ps. 45:11, 119:20; Exod. 20:17.

251. Pesikta Rabbati 24, 2.

252. Gospel of Thomas 37.

253. Lactantius, *Divine Institutes* 6, 23.

254. Leander Keck, ed., *The New Interpreter's Bible*, vol. 8 (Nashville: Abingdon, 1995), 191.

255. David Mace, *Whom God Hath Joined* (Philadelphia: Westminster, 1953), 30–31.

256. Tom Driver, "Sexuality and Jesus," *Union Seminary Quarterly Review* 20 (1965): 243, 240.

257. McBrien, 562–63, 566.

258. George Caird, *A Commentary on the Revelation of St. John the Divine* (New York: Harper, 1966), 179.

259. Jean D'Aragon, *The Jerome Biblical Commentary*, vol. 2 (Englewood Cliffs, N.J.: Prentice-Hall, 1968), 484.

260. Hans von Campenhausen, *Tradition and Life in the Church* (Philadelphia: Fortress, 1968), 119.

261. 1 Cor. 7:8, 27, 40.

262. 1 Thess. 4:17; 1 Cor. 15:51.

263. 1 Cor. 7:26–31.

264. Tertullian, *To His Wife* 5; *On Monogamy* 16; Jerome, *Against Jovinian* 1, 12.

265. Tertullian, *An Exhortation to Chastity* 9.

266. Gen. 1:28; Tertullian, *An Exhortation to Chastity* 6.

267. Augustine, *On Marriage and Concupiscence* 1, 14–15.

268. Jerome, *Against Helvidius* 23; John Chrysostom, *On Virginity* 19.

269. Susanne Heine, *Women and Early Christianity* (Minneapolis: Augsburg, 1988), 67.

270. Meier, *A Marginal Jew*, 339.

271. *Detroit Free Press*, 27 September 1970, 15D.

272. *Minutes of the 120th General Assembly* (Atlanta: Presbyterian Materials Distribution Service, 1980), part 1, 177, 181.

273. Will Deming, *Paul on Marriage and Celibacy* (New York: Cambridge University Press, 1995), 219.

274. Marcus Borg, *Jesus in Contemporary Scholarship* (Valley Forge, Pa.: Trinity Press, 1994), 7.

275. Don Cuppit, *Crisis of Moral Authority* (Philadelphia: Westminster, 1972), 44.

276. For further support of this position, see Josephine Ford, *A Trilogy on Wisdom and Celibacy* (Notre Dame, Ind.: University of Notre Dame Press, 1967), 24–25.

277. M. D. Goldman, "Was Jeremiah Married?" *Australian Biblical Review* 2 (1952): 43–47.

278. Jer. 32:6–15.

279. Jer. 29:5–6.

280. Vernon McCasland, *Religions of the World* (New York: Random House, 1969), 129.

281. Tertullian, *Against Marcion* 4, 38.

282. Cyprian, *On the Dress of Virgins* 22.

283. Pius XII, *Sacra Virginitas* 2 (1954).

284. Pius XI, *Sacerdotii Fastigium* 20, 12 (1935).

285. Jerome, *Letters* 108, 23.

286. Jerome, *Against Jovinian* 1, 36.

287. Jerome, *Letters* 108, 23.

288. Mark 4:8.

289. Jerome, *Letters* 48, 2; 123, 9.

290. Otto Bochert, *The Original Jesus* (New York, 1933), 319.

291. Lucien Legrand, *The Biblical Doctrine of Virginity* (New York: Sheed, 1963), 43.

292. Jacques Maritain, *Moral Philosophy* (New York: Scribner's, 1964), 454.

293. Kent Nerburn, *Letters to My Son* (San Rafael, Calif.: New World Library, 1993), 160.

294. In his witty manner, Voltaire gives expression to this outlook. When the angel of annunciation appeared to Mary, she invited him to take a seat. Gabriel replied, "Je n'ais pas de quoi." Possessing neither bottom nor body, Gabriel was incapable of having sex in spite of his masculine name.

295. Clement, *Miscellanies* 3, 12, 87.

296. Ibid., 3, 6, 48.

297. D. H. Lawrence, *A Propos of Lady Chatterley's Lover* (London, 1931), 65.

298. Maurice Wiles, "Studies in Texts: Luke 20:34–36," *Theology* 60 (1957): 501–2.

299. Ronald Goetz, "God of the Living," *Christian Century* (19 February 1975): 157.

300. Philip Schaff, *History of the Christian Church*, vol. 2 (New York: Scribner's, 1914), 397.

301. Eric Krell, *Created in Our Image* (Milwaukee: Bible-Truths Expositors, 1970), 20–33.

302. Los Angeles *Herald Examiner*, 21 November 1970.

303. Honolulu *Star-Bulletin*, 14 November 1970.

304. Paul Jewett, *Man as Male and Female* (Grand Rapids, Mich.: Eerdmans, 1975), 110–11.

305. London *Observer*, 28 March 1971, reprinted in *The Critic*, March 1972, 57.

306. Wolfhart Pannenberg, *Jesus: God and Man* (Philadelphia: Westminster, 1968), 342.

307. Frank Somerville, Religious News Service, Baltimore, 24 February 1981, 3.

308. Joseph Jeffers, *Yahweh Yesterday, Today, and Tomorrow* (Orange, Calif., 1969), 44.

309. Heb. 5:8.

310. Oscar Cullmann, *The Christology of the New Testament* (Philadelphia: Westminster, 1959), 95.

311. Richard Langsdale, *The Sixth Jar* (New York: Vantage Press, 1973), 101, 115.

312. See Elisabeth Moltmann-Wendel, *The Women around Jesus* (New York: Crossroad, 1982), 88.

313. Langsdale, *The Sixth Jar*, 141.

314. William Shakespeare, *Romeo and Juliet* 2, 2, 133–35.

315. Anthony Burgess, *Man of Nazareth* (New York: McGraw Hill, 1979), 97–104.

316. John Erskine, *The Human Life of Jesus* (New York: McClelland, 1945), 27–28.

FOUR   Women and Magdalene

1. Sir. 25:24, 42:13–14.

2. Aboth 2:7.

3. Josephus, *Against Apion* 200.

4. Joachim Jeremias, *Jerusalem in the Time of Jesus* (Philadelphia: Fortress, 1969), 376; see also Rudolf Bultmann, *Jesus and the Word* (New York: Scribner's, 1958), 61.

5. 1 Cor. 9:5, 16:19; Rom. 16:3, 7; Acts 18:2, 18–19.

6. Acts 18:26.

7. Clement of Alexandria, *Miscellanies* 3, 6, 53.

8. Luke 8:3, 22:27.

9. Mark 1:31.

10. See Gen. 26:14; Job 1:3.

11. Luke 12:37; 17:8.

12. John 13:5.

13. 1 Sam. 25:41.

14. Luke 10:38–42; cf. Acts 22:3.

15. Luke 11:31.

16. Rosemary Ruether, *New Woman/New Earth* (New York: Crossroad, 1975), 66.

17. Mark 1:41, 6:34, 8:2; Matt. 20:34; Luke 10:33, 15:20.

18. Mark 9:36–37.

19. John 16:21.

20. Aristotle, *Politics* 1, 254b–260a.

21. Mark 1:16–20.

22. Mark 4:37–38.

23. Matt. 8:20.

24. Mark 8:27, 9:2.

25. Mark 11:15–18.

26. Elisabeth Moltmann-Wendel and Jürgen Moltmann, *Humanity of God* (New York: The Pilgrim Press, 1983), 38.

27. Lev. 20:10; Deut. 22:23–24.

28. John 8:2–11.

29. Otto Baab, "Adultery," in *The Interpreter's Dictionary of the Bible*, ed. George Buttrick (Nashville: Abingdon, 1962).

30. Aulus Gellius, *Attic Nights* 10, 23, 5.

31. Matt. 21:23, 31.

32. Mark 2:17.

33. Matt. 25:1–3; Luke 13:21; 18:1–5.

34. Luke 15:8–10.

35. Harlan Musser, *Sex: Our Myth-Theology?* (Ardmore, Pa.: Dorrance, 1981), 84.

36. Bruce Barton, *The Man and the Book Nobody Knows* (New York: Bobbs-Merrill, 1924), 43.

37. Claude Montefiore, *The Synoptic Gospels*, vol. 1 (New York: Ktav, 1968), 389.

38. Lev. 15:27.

39. Niddah 7:1.

40. Mark 5:25–34.

41. Lev. 19:2.

42. Lev. 20:13.

43. Jacob Neusner, *A Rabbi Looks at Jesus* (New York: Doubleday, 1993), 84, 111.

44. E.g., Isa. 49:15; Jer. 31:20.

45. Lev. 21:11.

46. Luke 10:30–35.

47. Walter Wink, *Engaging the Powers* (Minneapolis: Fortress, 1992), 116.

48. Mark 8:31–32, 9:31–32, 10:32–37.

49. 1 Sam. 10:1; 2 Kings 9:6.

50. John Crossan, *Jesus* (San Francisco: Harper, 1994), 192.

51. Aristotle, *Nicomachean Ethics* 1124b.

52. Joseph Haroutunian, *God With Us* (Philadelphia: Westminster, 1965), 207–12.

53. Gail O'Day, quoted in Carol Newsom and Sharon Ringe, eds., *The Women's Bible Commentary* (Louisville: Westminster John Knox, 1992), 294.

54. Walter Burghardt, ed., *Woman: New Dimensions* (New York: Paulist, 1977), 123.

55. Leonard Swidler, *Catholic World*, January 1971, 182.

56. Ben Witherington, *Women and the Genesis of Christianity* (Cambridge: Cambridge University Press, 1990), 237–38.

57. Wink, *Engaging the Powers*, 129.

58. Mark 8:10; Matt. 15:39.

59. Elisabeth Moltmann-Wendel, *The Women around Jesus* (New York: Crossroad, 1982), 68.

60. Mark 15:40–41; Matt. 27:56; Luke 8:2, 24:10.

61. Edgar Hennecke and Wilhelm Schneemelcher, eds., *New Testament Apocrypha*, vol. 1 (Philadelphia: Westminster, 1963), 246, 256.

62. Matt. 27:56; Mark 15:40; Luke 23:56, 24:10; John 18:25.

63. Matt. 26:56.

64. Eaton Barrett, *Woman*, part 1.

65. C. H. Dodd, *The Interpretation of the Fourth Gospel* (Cambridge: Cambridge University Press, 1958), 441.

66. Newsom and Ringe, eds., *The Women's Bible Commentary*, 301.

67. 1 Cor. 15:3–8.

68. E.g., Matt. 17:3, 9; Acts 16:9; 26:16.

69. 1 Cor. 15:20; Phil. 3:21.

70. Acts 26:12–19.

71. Mark 16:6; Matt. 28:5; Luke 24:5; John 20:15.

72. Extracted from Origen, *Against Celsus* 2, 55, in Celsus, *On the True Doctrine* (New York: Oxford, 1987), 67–68.

73. Celsus, *On the True Doctrine*, 86, 121.

74. Elaine Pagels, *Origins of Satan: The New Testament Origins of Christianity's Demonization of Jews, Pagans, and Heretics* (New York: Random House, 1995), xv.

75. Colin Parkes, *Bereavement* (New York: International Universities Press, 1972), 48, 59, 103, 164.

76. J. William Worden, *Grief Counseling and Grief Therapy* (New York: Springer, 1982), 24.

77. Ernest Renan, *The Life of Jesus* (London: Dent, 1927), 102, 230–31.

78. Ernest Renan, *Les Apotres* (Paris: Levy, 1866), 11–13, 44.

79. Ibid., 70.

80. Josephus, *Antiquities* 18, 64.

81. Nikos Kazantzakis, *Report to Greco* (New York: Simon and Schuster, 1965), 239–42.

82. Joseph Klausner, *From Jesus to Paul* (Boston: Beacon, 1961), 255–58.

83. Jack Lundbom, *Interpretation*, vol. 49 (April 1995), 172; William Phipps, *Genesis and Gender* (New York: Praeger, 1989), 87–102.

84. John 20:6, 14, 16.

85. John 10:3, 14.

86. John 17:10.

87. William Thompson, *The Jesus Debate* (New York: Paulist, 1985), 228, 234.

88. The Latin text is quoted in Susan Haskins, *Mary Magdalen* (New York: Harcourt Brace, 1994), 219.

89. Ana-Maria Rizzuto, *The Birth of the Living God* (Chicago: University of Chicago Press, 1979), 209.

90. Robert Cole, *Spiritual Life of Children* (Boston: Houghton Mifflin, 1990), 97.

91. Gordon Kaufman, *Systematic Theology* (New York: Scribner, 1968), 425–31.

92. E.g., Mark 5:28; 1 Cor. 7:1.

93. John Marsh, *The Gospel of St. John* (Baltimore: Penguin, 1968), 637.

94. John 20:17.

95. Luke 24:11.

96. The Mishnah, Shabuot 4, 1.

97. Josephus, *Antiquities* 4, 219.

98. Haskins, *Mary Magdalen*, 84.

99. Rom. 16:7.

100. 1 Cor. 15:5, 7.

101. Chrysostom, *Homilies of Romans* 31.

102. Hippolytus, *De Cantico* 24–26, in *Corpus Scriptorum Ecclesiasticorum Latinorum*.

103. J. P. Migne, ed., *Patrologia Latina* (Paris, 1844–1866), vol. 112, col. 1474b; vol. 183, col. 1148.

104. Ibid., vol. 178, col. 486.

105. Acts 1:21–22.

106. Gal. 1.

107. John Calvin, *Commentary on a Harmony of the Evangelists*, vol. 3 (Grand Rapids, Mich.: Eerdmans, 1949), 338–39.

108. Gospel of Mary 10, 17–18 in *The Nag Hammadi Library*, ed. James Robinson (New York: Harper, 1977), 472–73.

109. Moltmann-Wendel and Moltmann, *Humanity of God*, 6.

110. Paul VI, "On the Question of the Admission of Women to the Ministerial Priesthood" (15 October 1976); *Newsweek*, 7 February 1977, 77.

111. John Paul II, Papal Letter (10 July 1995).

112. John Paul II, "On Reserving Priestly Ordination to Men Alone" (30 May 1994).

113. Gerald O'Collins and Daniel Kendall, "Mary Magdalene as Major Witness to Jesus' Resurrection," *Theological Studies* 48 (1987), 631–46.

114. Gospel of Philip 59 and 63.

115. Ibid., 73 and 81.

116. Barbara Thiering, *Jesus and the Riddle of the Dead Sea Scrolls* (San Francisco: Harper, 1992), 87–88.

117. John 20:15.

118. John 20:13; Gen. 18:12; 1 Peter 3:6.

119. Robert Funk, ed., *The Five Gospels* (New York: Macmillan, 1993), 220–21.

120. Marina Warner, *Alone of All Her Sex* (New York: Knopf, 1976), 230–32.

121. Ruether, *New Woman/New Earth*, 47.

122. Rosemary Ruether, *Mary—the Feminine Face of the Church* (Philadelphia: Westminster, 1977), 40–41.

123. John Spong, *Born of Woman* (San Francisco: Harper, 1992), 197.

124. James Baker, "The Red-Haired Saint," *Christian Century* (6 April 1977): 329–32.

125. Matt. 21:31.

126. Luke 7:37–50.

127. Migne, ed., *Patrologia Latina,* vol. 172, cols. 979–81.

128. Gregory the Great, *Homilies* 33.

129. Haskins, *Mary Magdalen,* 137, 148.

130. Reay Tannahill, *Sex in History* (New York: Stein & Day, 1980), 279.

131. Haskins, *Mary Magdalen,* 333.

132. William Blake, *The Everlasting Gospel* 1.

133. Kahlil Gibran, *Jesus, the Son of Man* (New York: Knopf, 1928), 13–15.

134. Jane Schaberg, "How Mary Magdalene Became a Whore," *Bible Review* 8 (October 1992): 37.

135. Haskins, *Mary Magdalen,* 392–93.

136. C. S. Lewis, *God in the Dock* (Grand Rapids, Mich.: Eerdmans, 1970), 236–37.

137. Haskins, *Mary Magdalen,* 336–340.

138. E. P. Sanders, *The Historical Figure of Jesus* (New York: Penguin, 1993), 124–25.

FIVE   Sexual Renunciation in Western History

1. Plato, *Cratylus* 399.

2. Plato, *Cratylus* 400.

3. Diogenes Laertius, *Lives of Eminent Philosophers* 8, 9, 42.

4. Hippolytus, *Refutation of All Heresies* 7, 17.

5. E. R. Dodds, *The Greeks and the Irrational* (Berkeley: University of California Press, 1951), 155.

6. Strobaeus, *Anthology* 3, 18, 4, 24.

7. Plato, *Republic* 402–5, 485, 559; *Phaedo* 66–67.

8. B. A. G. Fuller, *History of Greek Philosophy* (New York: Holt, 1931), 446.

9. Epicurus, *Symposium* 8, in Whitney Oates, *The Stoic and Epicurean Philosophers* (New York: Modern Library, 1957), 45.

10. Lucretius, *The Nature of the Universe* 4, 1115–1118.

11. H. W. Smyth, ed., *Harvard Essays on Classical Subjects* (Cambridge: Harvard University Press, 1912), 120.

12. Epictetus, *Discourses* 3, 12, 24.

13. Diogenes Laertius, *Lives* 7, 117.

14. Philo, *On the Contemplative Life* 2–8.

15. Porphyry, *On Abstinence* 4, 6–9.

16. Philostratus, *Apollonius of Tyana* 1, 13.

17. K. S. Guthrie, *Numenius of Apamea* (Keansburg, N.J.: Platonist Press, 1917), 97, 133.

18. Plutarch, *On the Control of Anger* 464b.

19. Henry Chadwick, *The Sentences of Sextus* (Cambridge: Cambridge University Press, 1959), 138.

20. Jerome, *Against Jovinian* 1, 49.

21. E. R. Dodds, *Pagan and Christian in an Age of Anxiety* (New York: Norton, 1970), 35; see Smyth, ed., *Harvard Essays on Classical Subjects*, 136.

22. Plotinus, *Enneads* 3, 5, 2.

23. Porphyry, *On Abstinence* 4, 20.

24. Morton Enslin, *The Ethics of Paul* (New York: Harper, 1930), 180.

25. Tertullian, *On Monogamy* 17.

26. Tertullian, *An Exhortation to Chastity* 13.

27. Joseph Swain, *The Hellenic Origins of Christian Asceticism* (New York: Columbia University, 1916), 9.

28. Cicero, *De Domo Sua* 53, 136.

29. Tertullian, *On Prescription Against Heretics* 40.

30. Athanasius, *Life of Anthony* 45.

31. Athanasius, *Life of Anthony* 5.

32. Dodds, *Pagan and Christian in an Age of Anxiety*, 31.

33. Philip Schaff, *History of the Christian Church*, vol. 2 (New York: Scribner, 1910), 390–91.

34. Herbert Workman, *The Evolution of the Monastic Ideal* (London: Epworth, 1913), 37.

35. Palladius, *Lausaic History* 8, 4; 48, 3.

36. Eusebius, *Church History* 2, 17.

37. Immanuel Kant, *Lectures on Ethics* (New York: Harper, 1963), 164.

38. Arthur Schopenhauer, *The World as Will and Idea* (London: Routledge and Kegan Paul, 1883), vol. 1, 491, 524; vol. 3, 448.

39. Friedrich Nietzsche, *The Genealogy of Morals* 3, 7.

40. Clement of Alexandria, *Miscellanies* 3, 60.

41. W. Flinders Petrie, *Egypt and Israel* (London: SPCK, 1923), 134.

42. Philostratus, *Apollonius of Tyana* 1, 2; 6, 10; 8, 7.

43. Clement of Alexandria, *Miscellanies* 1, 71.

44. Augustine, *On the Morals of the Manichaeans* 10.

45. Arthur Voobus, *History of Asceticism in the Syrian Orient*, vol. 1 (Louvain: Corpus Scriptorum Christianorum Orientalium, 1958), 114, 168.

46. William Phipps, "Did Ancient Indian Celibacy Influence Christianity?" *Studies in Religion* 4 (1974): 45–50.

47. Geoffrey Parrinder, *Upanishads, Gita, and Bible* (New York: Harper, 1972).

48. Swami Bhaktipada, *Joy of No Sex* (Moundsville, W.V.: Palace Publishing, 1988), 11–14, 116.

49. Marina Warner, *Alone of All Her Sex* (New York: Knopf, 1976), 24.

50. Justin, *Dialogue with Trypho* 2; *Apology* 2, 13.

51. Justin, *Dialogue with Trypho* 100.

52. Susan Haskins, *Mary Magdalen* (New York: Harcourt Brace, 1994), 140–41.

53. Justin, *Dialogue with Trypho* 48.

54. Justin, *Dialogue with Trypho* 54.

55. Justin, *Dialogue with Trypho* 66–67; *Apology* 1, 33.

56. Justin, *Dialogue with Trypho* 67.

57. Justin, *Apology* 1, 21.

58. Tertullian, *Apology* 21, 9–14.

59. Plutarch, *Life of Alexander* 2.

60. Tertullian, *On the Flesh of Christ* 20.

61. Origen, *Genesis Homilies* 17.

62. Exod. 15:20.

63. Gregory of Nyssa, *On Virginity* 19.

64. Athanasius, *The Incarnation of the Word of God* 8, 5.

65. Karl Barth, *Church Dogmatics*, vol. 1/2 (Edinburgh: Clark, 1956), 192–94.

66. Matt. 1:25.

67. The Protevangelium of James 9:2; 19–20.

68. Lalitavistara 6; see Alfred Foucher, *A Life of Buddha According to the Ancient Texts* (Middletown, Conn.: Wesleyan University Press, 1963), 23–30.

69. Jerome, *Against Jovinian* 1, 42.

70. Jerome, *Against Helvidius* 8.

71. Luke 2:7; 7:12; 8:42.

72. Jerome, *Letters* 48, 21.

73. Jerome, *Against the Pelagians* 2, 4; John 20:19, 26.

74. Jerome, *Against Helvidius* 21.

75. Jerome, *Against Helvidius* 14 and 17.

76. 1 Cor. 9:5; Jerome, *Against Jovinian* 1, 39.

77. Gen. 2:24; Jerome, *Against Jovinian* 1, 16.

78. William Phipps, *Influential Theologians on Wo/Man* (Washington, D.C.: University Press of America, 1980), 37–55.

79. Jerome, *Against Jovinian* 1, 16.

80. Raymond Brown et al., *The Jerome Biblical Commentary* (Englewood Cliffs, N.J.: Prentice-Hall, 1968), xx.

81. John Kelly, *Jerome* (New York: Harper, 1975), 335.

82. See Walter Abbott, ed., *The Documents of Vatican II* (New York: Association Press, 1966), 94–95.

83. Gordon Laing, *Survivals of Roman Religion* (New York: Longmans, 1931), 92–93.

84. Catullus, *Poem* 63, 5–17.

85. Ovid, *Fasti* 4, 240.

86. John Ferguson, *The Religion of the Roman Empire* (Ithaca, N.Y.: Cornell University Press, 1970), 29; Franz Cumont, *The Oriental Religions in Roman Paganism* (Chicago: Open Court, 1911), 56–57.

87. Hoffman Hayes, *The Dangerous Sex* (New York: Putnam, 1964), 107.

88. Augustine, *On the Annunciation of the Lord* 3.

89. Aquinas, *Summa Theologica* 3, q. 28, 2.

90. Aquinas, *Summa Theologica* 3, q. 28, 3.

91. Aquinas, *Summa Theologica* 3, q. 28, 1; Aristotle, *On the Generation of Animals* 729a.

92. Aeschylus, *Eumenides* 11, 661–663.

93. See Marina Warner, *Alone of All Her Sex* (New York: Knopf, 1976), 236–38.

94. Mary was "wholly conceived in original sin" according to Aquinas, *Summa Theologica* 3, q. 31, 7.

95. Henry Morris, *The Battle for Creation* (San Diego: Creation-Life, 1976), 308.

96. Mary Baker Eddy, *Science and Health* (Boston, 1975), 29–30, 64–69.

97. Mary Baker Eddy, *Miscellaneous Writings* (Boston, 1896), 181.

98. Jane Schaberg, *The Illegitimacy of Jesus* (San Francisco: Harper, 1987), 12–13.

99. Martin Elze, *Tatian und Seine Theologie* (Gottingen: Vandenhoeck, 1960), 61–68.

100. Origen, *On Prayer* 24, 5; Eusebius, *Church History* 4, 29; Irenaeus, *Against Heresies* 1, 28, 1.

101. Epiphanius, *Against Heresies* 45, 2.

102. Clement, *Miscellanies* 3, 12, 80–81.

103. Clement, *Miscellanies* 3, 6, 49.

104. Theodoret, *Treatise on Heresies* 3, 12, 81.

105. Arthur Voobus, *Celibacy, a Requirement for Admission to Baptism in the Early Syrian Church* (Stockholm: Estonian Society, 1951), 17–19.

106. Tertullian, *Against Marcion* 4, 7.

107. Mark 3:35; Tertullian, *Against Marcion* 4, 19.

108. Tertullian, *Against Marcion* 4, 24.

109. Plato, *Republic* 329.

110. Clement of Alexandria, *Miscellanies* 3, 3, 18 and 21.

111. Irenaeus, *Against Heresies* 3, 21, 10; *Proof of the Apostolic Preaching* 32.

112. Irenaeus, *Against Heresies* 5, 19, 1.

113. Irenaeus, *Against Heresies* 3, 22, 4.

114. Origen, *Matthew Homilies* 10, 17.

115. Origen, *Sermons on Romans* 9.

116. Eusebius, *Church History* 6, 8.

117. Origen, *Sermons on Matthew* 15, 1–3.

118. Dodds, *Pagan and Christian in an Age of Anxiety*, 32–33.

119. Theodoret, *Church History* 2, 19; Socrates, *Church History* 2, 26.

120. Uta Ranke-Heinemann, *Eunuchs for the Kingdom of Heaven* (New York: Penguin, 1990), 134–35.

121. 1 Cor. 9:5; Matt. 16:18.

122. Ranke-Heinemann, *Eunuchs for the Kingdom of Heaven*, 47–48.

123. Emil Brunner, *The Divine Imperative* (Philadelphia: Westminster, 1947), 364.

124. Methodius, *Symposium* 7, 3.

125. Ambrose, *Duties of the Clergy* 1, 258.

126. Peter Brown, *The Body and Society* (New York: Columbia University Press, 1988), 351.

127. Augustine, *Confessions* 6, 23; 8, 29.

128. Augustine, *On Marriage and Concupiscence* 2, 14.

129. Augustine, *On the Birth of the Lord*, sermon 121.

130. Augustine, *On the Merits and Forgiveness of Sins* 2, 11, 16; *Unfinished Work Against Julian* 6, 22.

131. Augustine, *Sermons* 151, 5; Peter Brown, *Augustine of Hippo* (Berkeley: University of California Press, 1969), 388–96.

132. Augustine, *Against Julian* 5, 8, 15.

133. Augustine, *On Christian Doctrine* 3, 8.

134. Augustine, *The Good of Marriage* 10.

135. Christian Cochini, *Apostolic Origins of Priestly Celibacy* (San Francisco: Ignatius, 1990), 92, 112.

136. Vern Bullough, *Sexual Practices and the Medieval Church* (Buffalo: Prometheus, 1982), xi.

137. Robert Keable, *The Great Galilean* (Boston: Little, Brown, 1929), 91.

138. Martin Marty, ed., *New Theology*, no. 9 (New York: Macmillan, 1972), 211.

139. Philip Schaff, ed., *A Select Library of Nicene and Post-Nicene Fathers*, vol. 14 (Grand Rapids, Mich.: Eerdmans, 1956), 322.

140. William of St. Thierry, *Life of Bernard* 1, 3. This treatment provided no cure, for he reveled in the Song of Songs and composed dozens of sermons on those lusty poems. See William Phipps, "The Plight of the Song of Songs," *Journal of the American Academy of Religion* 42 (March 1974): 90–92.

141. Augustine, *On Forgiveness of Sin* 2, 36.

142. Augustine, *City of God* 14, 17.

143. Mark 15:24; John 19:2.

144. Leo Steinberg, *The Sexuality of Christ in Renaissance Art and in Modern Oblivion* (New York: Random House, 1983), 87–91.

145. Aquinas, *Summa Theologica* 2-2, q. 152, 1.

146. Aquinas, *Summa Theologica* 2-2, q. 151, 3; Augustine, Soliloquies 1, 10.

147. Jacob Burckhardt, *On History and Historians* (New York: Harper, 1965), 37–38.

148. Ronald Smith, ed., *Søren Kierkegaard* (New York, 1965), 77–79, 171.

149. Peter Rohde, *Søren Kierkegaard* (New York: Humanities Press, 1963), 69–70.

150. Smith, ed., *Søren Kierkegaard*, 266–67.

151. Ibid., 119.

152. Søren Kierkegaard, *Attack Upon Christendom* (Boston: Beacon, 1956), 213.

153. James Gibbons, *The Faith of Our Fathers* (Baltimore, 1895), 456.

154. J. W. Rehage, "Celibacy, Canon Law of," in *New Catholic Encyclopedia* (New York: McGraw-Hill, 1966).

155. Paul VI, *Sacerdotalis Caelibatus* 21 (1967).

156. Anthony Padovano, "Joseph's Son," *Corpus Reports* (July 1995): 11.

157. Nikos Kazantzakis, *The Last Temptation of Christ* (New York: Simon & Schuster, 1960), 496; for a fuller treatment, see William Phipps, *The Sexuality of Jesus* (New York: Harper, 1973), 121–31.

158. Joan Ohanneson, *And They Felt No Shame* (Minneapolis: Winston, 1982), 70, 78.

159. James Atkinson, ed., *Luther's Works*, vol. 44 (Philadelphia: Fortress, 1966), 178.

160. *D. Martin Luthers Werke*, vol. 12 (Weimar, 1891), 94.

161. See Richard Friedenthal, *Luther* (New York: Harcourt, 1970), 432–33.

162. Helmut Lehman, ed., *Luther's Works*, vol. 54 (Philadelphia: Fortress, 1957), Table-talk n. 1472.

163. John Calvin, *The First Epistle of Paul the Apostle to the Corinthians* (Grand Rapids, Mich.: Eerdmans, 1960), 12.

164. Charles Hodge, *Systematic Theology,* vol. 3 (New York: Scribner's 1895), 369–71.

SIX   Significance of the Topic

1. See William Phipps, *Genesis and Gender* (New York: Praeger, 1989), 9–14, 51–66.
2. See William Phipps, *Assertive Biblical Women* (New York: Greenwood, 1992), 139–44.
3. Ketubot 62b.
4. See William Phipps, *Recovering Biblical Sensuousness* (Philadelphia: Westminster, 1975).
5. Mark 10:2–9.
6. 1 Cor. 7:25.
7. 1 Cor. 9:5.
8. 1 Tim. 3:2, 12; Titus 1:6.
9. Luke 7:33–34.
10. 2 John 7.
11. Peter Brown, *The Body and Society* (New York: Columbia University Press, 1988), 61.
12. Ambrose, *On Educating Virgins* 5, 36.
13. Augustine, *Of Holy Virginity* 35.
14. Edward Schillebeeckx, *Ministry* (New York: Crossroad, 1981), 85.
15. Socrates, *Church History* 5, 22.
16. Damasus, *Decretal to the Bishops of Gaul* 2, 5.
17. "Celibacy, History of," *New Catholic Encyclopedia* (New York: McGraw-Hill, 1966).
18. Henry Lea, *History of Sacerdotal Celibacy in the Christian Church,* vol. 1 (New York: Macmillan, 1907), 43, 385, 388.
19. James Cleugh, *Love Locked Out* (New York: Crown, 1964), 298.
20. John Boswell, *Christianity, Social Tolerance, and Homosexuality* (Chicago: University of Chicago Press, 1980), 216–66.
21. Ibid., 227.
22. Gordon Taylor, *Sex in History* (London: Harper, 1953), 69.
23. Eric Fuchs, *Sexual Desire and Love* (New York: Seabury, 1983), 135.

24. Roland Bainton, *Erasmus of Christendom* (New York: Scribner, 1969), 181.

25. James Colaianni, ed., *Married Priests and Married Nuns* (New York: McGraw, 1968), 86.

26. Emmett McLoughlin, *People's Padre* (Boston: Beacon, 1954), 93–94.

27. *New York Times*, 4 May 1986, 26.

28. John Carmody, "Celibacy and the Religious Experience of Roman Catholicism," *Religion in Life* 40 (spring 1971): 17, 23.

29. John Calvin, *Institutes of the Christian Religion* 4, 12, 23, and 28.

30. John Calvin, *Theological Treatises* (Philadelphia: Westminster, 1954), 212.

31. "Doctrine on the Sacrament of Matrimony," canon 10.

32. Presbyterorum Ordinis 16, in *Documents of Vatican II*, ed. Walter Abbott (New York, Guild, 1966), 565.

33. John XXIII, *Pacem in Terris*, 4/10/63, part 1.

34. William Cole, *Sex in Christianity and Psychoanalysis* (New York: Oxford, 1955), 285.

35. Northrop Frye, *Fearful Symmetry* (Boston: Beacon, 1962), 120.

36. *America*, 18 June 1994, 22.

37. Dean Hoge, *The Future of Catholic Leadership* (Kansas City: Sheed and Ward, 1987), 132.

38. *Wall Street Journal*, 13 November 1990, A1; *Washington Post*, 15 November 1992, C5; *Washington Post*, 8 August 1993, C3.

39. Richard Schoenherr and Lawrence Young, *Full Pews and Empty Altars* (Madison: University of Wisconsin Press, 1993), xvii, 354.

40. William Basset and Peter Huizing, eds., *Celibacy in the Church* (New York: Herder and Herder, 1972), 154.

41. Schoenherr and Young, *Full Pews and Empty Altars*, 12.

42. Horace, *Letters* 10, 24.

43. Jason Berry, *Lead Us Not into Temptation: Catholic Priests and the Sexual Abuse of Children* (New York: Doubleday, 1992), 184, 188.

44. Ibid., 372–73.

45. *America*, 20 March 1993, 7.

46. *America* 18 June 1994, 23.

47. *New York Times* 6 May 1993, A27.

48. Aquinas, *Summa Theologica* 2-2, q. 154, 12.

49. J. F. Harvey, "Homosexuality," *New Catholic Encyclopedia.*

50. Sheila Murphy, *A Delicate Dance* (New York: Crossroad, 1992), 107, 133, 136.

51. *Washington Post*, 15 August 1993, C7.

52. *Newsweek*, 16 August 1993, 44.

53. Margaret Maxey, in *New Theology* No. 9, ed. Martin Marty (New York: Macmillan, 1972), 219–20.

54. Anthony Padovano, "Joseph's Son," *Corpus Reports* (July 1995): 16.

55. Quoted in John Scopes, "The Trial That Rocked the Nation," *Reader's Digest* 78, March 1961, 141.

56. *Great Books of the Western World*, vol. 49, ed. Robert Hutchins (Chicago: Encyclopaedia Britannica, 1952), 243, 593; cf. William Phipps, "Darwin and Cambridge Natural Theology," *Bios* 54 (1983): 218–27.

57. Pierre Teilhard de Chardin, *Hymn of the Universe* (New York: Harper, 1965), 100.

58. Gordon Kaufman, *Systematic Theology* (New York: Scribner, 1968), 203.

59. Dietrich Bonhoeffer, *Christ the Center* (New York: Harper, 1966), 104.

60. Paul Tillich, *Theology of Culture* (New York: Oxford, 1959), 66.

61. Emil Brunner, *The Christian Doctrine of Creation and Redemption* (Philadelphia: Westminster, 1952), 354.

62. Origen, *Against Celsus* 1, 37.

63. Julie Miller, "Mammals Need Moms and Dads," *BioScience* 37 (1987): 379–82.

64. Walter Bodmer, *Genetics, Evolution, and Man* (San Francisco: Freeman, 1976), 637.

65. *U.S. Catholic*, October 1985, 12.

66. Richard McBrien, *Catholicism* (San Francisco: Harper, 1994), 563.

67. James Nelson, *Embodiment* (Minneapolis: Augsburg, 1978), 76.

68. Plato, *Symposium* 180–181.

69. Phipps, *Recovering Biblical Sensuousness*, 99.

70. Anders Nygren, *Agape and Eros* (Philadelphia: Westminster, 1953), 210, 236.

242 + NOTES TO PAGES 192-198

71. Phipps, *Recovering Biblical Sensuousness*, 100–102.

72. E.g., Ps. 103:13; Isa. 49:15; Luke 11:11–13.

73. Eph. 5:21–33.

74. Leonard Swidler, "Jesus Was a Feminist," *Catholic World* (January 1971): 179, 183.

75. Julian, *Convivium* 336.

76. Friedrich Nietzsche, *Antichrist* 43; *Beyond Good and Evil* 7, 238.

77. H. L. Mencken, *In Defense of Women* (New York: Time, Inc., 1963), 134, 142.

78. John Langdon-Davies, *A Short History of Women* (New York: Literary Guild of America, 1927), 202.

79. Tertullian, *On the Apparel of Women* 1, 1.

80. Mark 5:24–34.

81. *Didascalia Apostolorum* 26.

82. Nicolae Chitescu, *Concerning the Ordination of Women* (Geneva: World Council of Churches, 1964), 58.

83. Haye Van der Meer, *Women Priests in the Catholic Church?* (Philadelphia: Temple University Press, 1973), 128.

84. William Phipps, "The Menstrual Taboo in the Judeo-Christian Tradition," *Journal of Religion and Health* 19 (1980): 298–302.

85. David Mace, *The Christian Response to the Sexual Revolution* (Nashville: Abingdon, 1970), 78.

86. San Francisco *Chronicle*, 25 October 1971.

87. Ursula King, *Feminist Theology from the Third World* (Maryknoll, N.Y.: Orbis, 1994), 312.

88. George Buttrick, ed., *The Interpreter's Bible*, vol. 6 (Nashville: Abingdon, 1951), 612.

89. Mark 2:18–19.

90. Matt. 22:2; Luke 12:36; 14:8.

91. Joseph Blenkinsopp, *Sexuality and the Christian Tradition* (Dayton, Ohio: Pflaum, 1969), 84.

92. William Purcell, ed., *The Resurrection* (Philadelphia: Westminster, 1966), 93–95.

93. Rosemary Ruether, "The Sexuality of Jesus," *Christianity and Crisis* 38 (29 May 1978): 135.

94. London *Observer*, 28 March 1971, 25.

95. Luke 24:19; John 1:30; Acts 2:22.

96. 1 Cor. 1:24; see Prov. 8:1–31.

97. Daniel Callahan, "Self-Identity in an Urban Society," *Theology Today* 24 (April 1967): 38.

98. Genesis Rabbah 17, 2.

99. Zohar Hadash 4, 50b.

100. Robert Gordis, "Re-Judaizing Christianity," *Center* (September 1968): 15.

101. Alfred Guillaume, "The Influence of Judaism on Islam," in *The Legacy of Israel*, ed. E. Bevan (Oxford: Oxford University Press, 1927), 165.

102. Qur'an 24:32.

103. Mishkat 13, 1.

104. Michael Baigent, Richard Leigh, and Henry Lincoln, *Holy Blood, Holy Grail* (New York: Dell, 1983), 409.

105. Karl Barth, *Church Dogmatics*, vol. 3/4 (Edinburgh: Clark, 1961), 141.

106. William Hoyt, *Christian Century* (14 July 1971): 862.

107. Elmer Clark et al., eds., *The Journals and Letters of Francis Asbury*, vol. 2 (Nashville: Abingdon, 1958), 474.

108. McBrien, *Catholicism*, 563.

109. John Paul II, *Fruitful and Responsible Love* (New York: Seabury, 1979), 26.

110. Mark 10:7–9.

111. Gen. 19; Jude 7; 2 Pet. 2:6–10; Philo, *De Abrahamo* 26; Jubilees 16:5–6; Testament of Naphtali 4:1.

112. Luke 10:5–15.

113. 2 Cor. 4:6.

114. Kenneth Foreman, *Romans, 1 Corinthians, 2 Corinthians* (Richmond: John Knox, 1961), 37.

115. Rom. 8:29.

116. Eph. 4:13.

SELECTED BIBLIOGRAPHY

Ben-Chorin, Schalom. *Bruder Jesus*. Munich: List, 1967.

Charlesworth, James, ed. *The Old Testament Pseudepigrapha*. 2 vols. Garden City, N.Y.: Doubleday, 1985.

Dodds, E. R. *Pagan and Christian in an Age of Anxiety*. New York: Norton, 1970.

Driver, Tom. "Sexuality and Jesus." *Union Seminary Quarterly Review* 20 (1965): 235–46.

Funk, Robert, ed. *The Five Gospels*. New York: Macmillan, 1993.

Gaster, Theodor, ed. *The Dead Sea Scriptures*. Garden City, N.Y.: Doubleday, 1953.

Haskins, Susan. *Mary Magdalen*. New York: Harcourt, 1994.

Hennecke, Edgar, and Wilhem Schneemelcher, eds. *New Testament Apocrypha*. 2 vols. Philadelphia: Westminster, 1963.

Lea, Henry. *History of Sacerdotal Celibacy in the Christian Church*. New York: Macmillan, 1907.

Meier, John. *A Marginal Jew*. 2 vols. New York: Doubleday, 1991, 1994.

Migne, Jacque, ed. *Patrologia Graeca*. Paris: n.p., 1844–1864.

———. *Patrologia Latina*. Paris: n.p., 1844–1866.

Moltmann-Wendel, Elisabeth, and Jürgen Moltmann. *Humanity of God*. New York: Pilgrim Press, 1983.

Moore, George. *Judaism in the First Centuries of the Christian Era*. 2 vols. New York: Schocken, 1971.

Neusner, Jacob, trans. *The Mishnah*. New Haven, Conn.: Yale University Press, 1988.

Ohanneson, Joan. *And They Felt No Shame*. Minneapolis: Winston, 1982.

Phipps, William. *Genesis and Gender*. New York: Praeger, 1989.

———. *Recovering Biblical Sensuousness*. Philadelphia: Westminster, 1975.

———. *The Wisdom and Wit of Rabbi Jesus*. Louisville: Westminster John Knox, 1993.

Ranke-Heinemann, Uta. *Eunuchs for the Kingdom of Heaven*. New York: Penguin, 1990.

Robinson, James, ed. *The Nag Hammadi Library*. San Francisco: Harper, 1977.

Robinson, John. *The Human Face of God*. Philadelphia: Westminster, 1973.

Ruether, Rosemary. *Mary—the Feminine Face of the Church*. Philadelphia: Westminster, 1977.

Sapp, Stephen. *Sexuality, the Bible, and Science*. Philadelphia: Fortress, 1977.

Spong, John. *Born of Woman*. San Francisco: Harper, 1992.

Thackeray, H., trans. *Josephus*. 9 vols. Cambridge: Harvard University Press, 1976.

Warner, Marina. *Alone of All Her Sex*. New York: Knopf, 1976.

GENERAL INDEX

BIBLICAL INDEX